The O'Leary Series

Microsoft® Excel 2002

Brief Edition

Timothy J. O'Leary

Arizona State University

Linda I. O'Leary

Information Technology

McGraw-Hill Irwin

Boston Burr Ridge, IL Dubuque, IA Madison, WI New York
San Francisco St. Louis Bangkok Bogotá Caracas Kuala Lumpur
Lisbon London Madrid Mexico City Milan Montreal New Delhi
Santiago Seoul Singapore Sydney Taipei Toronto

McGraw-Hill Higher Education

A Division of The McGraw-Hill Companies

MICROSOFT® Excel 2002, BRIEF EDITION
Published by McGraw-Hill/Irwin, an imprint of the McGraw-Hill Companies, Inc. 1221 Avenue of the Americas, New York, NY, 10020. Copyright © 2002 by the McGraw-Hill Companies, Inc. All rights reserved. No part of this publication may be reproduced or distributed in any form or by any means, or stored in a database or retrieval system, without the prior written consent of The McGraw-Hill Companies, Inc., including, but not limited to, in any network or other electronic storage or transmission, or broadcast for distance learning.

Some ancillaries, including electronic and print components, may not be available to customers outside the United States.

This book is printed on acid-free paper.

domestic   4 5 6 7 8 9 0 QPD/QPD 0 9 8 7 6 5 4 3
international   1 2 3 4 5 6 7 8 9 0 QPD/QPD 0 9 8 7 6 5 4 3 2 1

ISBN 0-07-247235-9

Publisher: *George Werthman*
Developmental editor: *Alexandra Arnold*
Senior marketing manager: *Jeffrey Paar*
Senior project manager: *Jean Hamilton*
Manager, new book production: *Melonie Salvati*
Media producer: *David Barrick*
Freelance design coordinator: *Gino Cieslik*
Lead supplement coordinator: *Marc Mattson*
Photo research coordinator: *David A. Tietz*
Cover & interior design: *Maureen McCutcheon*
Cover image: *Digitalvision*
Typeface: *10.5/13 New Aster*
Compositor: *Rogondino & Associates*
Printer: *Quebecor World Dubuque Inc.*

Library of Congress Control Number 2001092433

INTERNATIONAL EDITION ISBN 0-07-112356-3

Copyright © 2002, Exclusive rights by The McGraw-Hill Companies, Inc. for manufacture and export.

This book cannot be re-exported from the country to which it is sold by McGraw-Hill.

The International Edition is not available in North America.

www.mhhe.com

InformationTechnology

Information Technology at McGraw-Hill/Irwin

At McGraw-Hill Higher Education, we publish instructional materials targeted at the higher education market. In an effort to expand the tools of higher learning, we publish texts, lab manuals, study guides, testing materials, software, and multimedia products.

At McGraw-Hill/Irwin (a division of McGraw-Hill Higher Education), we realize that technology has created and will continue to create new mediums for professors and students to use in managing resources and communicating information to one another. We strive to provide the most flexible and complete teaching and learning tools available as well as offer solutions to the changing world of teaching and learning.

McGraw-Hill/Irwin is dedicated to providing the tools for today's instructors and students to successfully navigate the world of Information Technology.

- **Seminar Series** McGraw-Hill/Irwin's Technology Connection seminar series offered across the country every year demonstrates the latest technology products and encourages collaboration among teaching professionals.

- **McGraw-Hill/Osborne** This division of The McGraw-Hill Companies is known for its best-selling Internet titles, *Internet & Web Yellow Pages* and the *Internet Complete Reference*. For more information, visit Osborne at **www.osborne.com**.

- **Digital Solutions** McGraw-Hill/Irwin is committed to publishing digital solutions. Taking your course online doesn't have to be a solitary adventure, nor does it have to be a difficult one. We offer several solutions that will allow you to enjoy all the benefits of having your course material online.

- **Packaging Options** For more information about our discount options, contact your McGraw-Hill/Irwin Sales representative at 1-800-338-3987 or visit our web site at **www.mhhe.com/it**.

Brief Contents

Detailed Contents

Acknowledgments

The new edition of The O'Leary Series has been made possible only through the enthusiasm and dedication of a great team of people. Because the team spans the country, literally from coast to coast, we have utilized every means of working together including conference calls, FAX, e-mail, and document collaboration. We have truly tested the team approach and it works!

Leading the team from McGraw-Hill/Irwin are George Werthman, Publisher and Alexandra Arnold, Developmental Editor. Their renewed commitment, direction, and support have infused the team with the excitement of a new project.

The production staff is headed by Jean Hamilton, Project Manager, whose planning and attention to detail has made it possible for us to successfully meet a very challenging schedule. Members of the production team include: Gino Cieslik, Designer; Pat Rogondino, Compositor; Susan Defosset, Copy Editor; Melonie Salvati, Production Supervisor; Marc Mattson, Supplement Coordinator; and David Barrick, Media Producer. We would particularly like to thank Pat and Susan—team members for many past editions whom we can always depend on to do a great job.

Finally, we are particularly grateful to a small but very dedicated group of people who helped us develop the manuscript. Colleen Hayes, Susan Demar, and Kathy Duggan have helped on the last several editions and continue to provide excellent developmental and technical support. To Steve Willis and Carol Cooper who provide technical expertise, youthful perspective, and enthusiasm, my thanks for helping get the manuscripts out the door and meeting the deadlines.

Preface

Introduction

The 20th century not only brought the dawn of the Information Age, but also rapid changes in information technology. There is no indication that this rapid rate of change will be slowing— it may even be increasing. As we begin the 21st century, computer literacy will undoubtedly become prerequisite for whatever career a student chooses. The goal of the O'Leary Series is to assist students in attaining the necessary skills to efficiently use these applications. Equally important is the goal to provide a foundation for students to readily and easily learn to use future versions of this software. This series does this by providing detailed step-by step instructions combined with careful selection and presentation of essential concepts.

About the Authors

Tim and Linda O'Leary live in the American Southwest and spend much of their time engaging instructors and students in conversation about learning. In fact, they have been talking about learning for more than 25 years. Something in those early conversations convinced them to write a book, to bring their interest in the learning process to the printed page. Today, they are as concerned as ever about learning, about technology, and about the challenges of presenting material in new ways, both in terms of content and the method of delivery.

A powerful and creative team, Tim combines his years of classroom teaching experience with Linda's background as a consultant and corporate trainer. Tim has taught courses at Stark Technical College in Canton, Ohio, Rochester Institute of Technology in upper New York state, and is currently a professor at Arizona State University in Tempe, Arizona. Tim and Linda have talked to and taught students from ages 8 to 80, all of them with a desire to learn something about computers and the applications that make their lives easier, more interesting, and more productive.

About the Book

Times are changing, technology is changing, and this text is changing, too. Do you think the students of today are different from yesterday? There is no doubt about it—they are. On the positive side, it is amazing how much effort students will put toward things they are convinced are relevant to them. Their effort directed at learning application programs and exploring the Web seems at times limitless. On the other hand, students can often be shortsighted, thinking that learning the skills to use the application is the only objective. The mission of the series is to build upon and extend this interest by not only teaching the specific application skills but by introducing the concepts that are common to all applications, providing students with the confidence, knowledge, and ability to easily learn the next generation of applications.

What's New in This Edition?

- **Introduction to Computer Essentials**—A brief introduction to the basics of computer hardware and software (Appears in Office XP, Volume I only).

- **Introduction to Windows 2000**—Two hands-on labs devoted to Windows 2000 basics (Appears in Office XP, Volume I only).

- **Introduction to the WWW: Internet Explorer and E-mail**—Hands-on introductions for using Internet Explorer to browse the WWW and using e-mail (Appears in Office XP, Volume I only).

- **Topic Reorganization**—The text has been reorganized to include main and subtopic heads by grouping related tasks. For example, tasks such as changing fonts and applying character effects appear under the "Formatting" topic head. This results in a slightly more reference-like approach, making it easier for students to refer back to the text to review. This has been done without losing the logical and realistic development of the case.

- **Clarified Marginal Notes**—Marginal notes have been enhanced by more clearly identifying the note content with box heads and the use of different colors.

  Additional Information—Brief asides with expanded discussion of features.

  Having Trouble?—Procedural tips advising students of possible problems and how to overcome.

  Another Method—Alternative methods of performing a procedure.

- **Larger Screen Figures**—Make it easier to identify elements and read screen content.

- All **Numbered Steps** and bullets appear in left margin space making it easy not to miss a step.

- A **MOUS (*Microsoft Office User Specialist*) Skills** table, appearing at the end of each lab, contains page references to MOUS skills learned in the lab.

- **Two new References** are included at the end of each text.

  Data File List—Helps organize all data and solution files.

  MOUS (*Microsoft Office User Specialist*) Skills—Links all MOUS objectives to text content and end-of-chapter exercises.

Same Great Features as the Office 2000 Series

- **Relevant Cases**—Four separate running cases demonstrate the features in each application. Topics are of interest to students—At Arizona State University, over 600 students were surveyed to find out what topics are of interest to them.

- **Focus on Concepts**—Each chapter focuses on the concepts behind the application. Students learn the essentials, so they can succeed regardless of the software package they might be using.

- **Steps**—Numbered procedural steps clearly identify each hands-on task needed to complete the step.

- **Screens**—Plentiful screen illustrations illustrate the completion of each numbered step to help students stay on track.

- **Callouts**—Meaningful screen callouts identify the results of the steps as well as reinforce the associated concept.

- **End-of-Chapter Material**

  Terminology—Questions and exercises test recall of the basic information and terminology in the lab.

  - Screen Identification
  - Matching
  - Multiple Choice

  Concepts—Questions and exercises review students' understanding of concepts and ability to integrate ideas presented in different parts of the lab.

  - Fill-In
  - Discussion Questions

  Hands-On Practice Exercises—Students apply the skills and concepts they learned to solve case-based exercises. Many cases in the practice exercises tie to a running case used in another application lab. This helps to demonstrate the use of the four applications across a common case setting. For example, the Adventure Travel Tours case used in the Word labs is continued in practice exercises in Excel, Access, and PowerPoint.

  - Step-by-Step
  - On Your Own
  - On The Web

- **Rating System**—The 3-star rating system identifies the difficulty level of each practice exercise in the end-of-chapter materials.

- **Working Together Labs**—At the completion of the brief and introductory texts, a final lab demonstrates the integration of the MS Office applications and the WWW.

Instructor's Guide

We understand that, in today's teaching environment, offering a textbook alone is not sufficient to meet the needs of the many instructors who use our books. To teach effectively, instructors must have a full complement of supplemental resources to assist them in every facet of teaching from preparing for class, to conducting a lecture, to assessing students' comprehension. *The O'Leary Series* offers a fully-integrated supplements package and Web site, as described below.

Instructor's Resource Kit

The **Instructor's Resource Kit** contains a computerized Test Bank, an Instructor's Manual, and PowerPoint Presentation Slides. Features of the Instructor's Resource Kit are described below.

- **Instructor's Manual**   The Instructor's Manual contains lab objectives, concepts, outlines, lecture notes, and command summaries. Also included are answers to all end-of chapter material, tips for covering difficult materials, additional exercises, and a schedule showing how much time is required to cover text material.

- **Computerized Test Bank**   The test bank contains over 1,300 multiple choice, true/false, and discussion questions. Each question will be accompanied by the correct answer, the level of learning difficulty, and corresponding page references. Our flexible Diploma software allows you to easily generate custom exams.

- **PowerPoint Presentation Slides**   The presentation slides will include lab objectives, concepts, outlines, text figures, and speaker's notes. Also included are bullets to illustrate key terms and FAQs.

Online Learning Center/Web Site

Found at **www.mhhe.com/oleary**, this site provides additional learning and instructional tools to enhance the comprehension of the text. The OLC/Web Site is divided into these three areas:

- **Information Center**   Contains core information about the text, supplements, and the authors.

- **Instructor Center**   Offers instructional materials, downloads, additional exercises, and other relevant links for professors.

- **Student Center**   Contains data files, chapter competencies, chapter concepts, self-quizzes, flashcards, projects, animations, additional Web links, and more.

Skills Assessment

SimNet (Simulated Network Assessment Product) provides a way for you to test students' software skills in a simulated environment. SimNet is available for Microsoft Office 97, Microsoft Office 2000, and Microsoft Office XP. SimNet provides flexibility for you in your course by offering:

- Pre-testing options
- Post-testing options
- Course placement testing
- Diagnostic capabilities to reinforce skills
- Proficiency testing to measure skills
- Web or LAN delivery of tests.
- Computer-based training tutorials (new for Office XP)
- MOUS preparation exams

For more information on skills assessment software, please contact your local sales representative, or visit us at **www.mhhe.com/it**.

Digital Solutions to Help You Manage Your Course

PageOut is our Course Web Site Development Center that offers a syllabus page, URL, McGraw-Hill Online Learning Center content, online exercises and quizzes, gradebook, discussion board, and an area for student Web pages.

Available free with any McGraw-Hill/Irwin product, PageOut requires no prior knowledge of HTML, no long hours of coding, and a way for course coordinators and professors to provide a full-course web site. PageOut offers a series of templates—simply fill them with your course information and click on one of 16 designs. The process takes under an hour and leaves you with a professionally designed Web site. We'll even get you started with sample web sites, or enter your syllabus for you! PageOut is so straightforward and intuitive, it's little wonder why over 12,000 college professors are using it. For more information, visit the PageOut Web site at **www.pageout.net**.

Online courses are also available. Online Learning Centers (OLCs) are your perfect solutions for Internet-based content. Simply put, these Centers are "digital cartridges" that contain a book's pedagogy and supplements. As students read the book, they can go online and take self-grading quizzes or work through interactive exercises. These also provide students appropriate access to lecture materials and other key supplements.

Online Learning Centers can be delivered through any of these platforms:

McGraw-Hill Learning Architecture (TopClass)

Blackboard.com

Ecollege.com (formerly Real Education)

WebCT (a product of Universal Learning Technology)

McGraw-Hill has partnerships with WebCT and Blackboard to make it even easier to take your course online. Now you can have McGraw-Hill content delivered through the leading Internet-based learning tool for higher education. At McGraw-Hill, we have the following service agreements with WebCT and Blackboard:

Instructor Advantage   Instructor Advantage is a special level of service McGraw-Hill offers in conjuction with WebCT designed to help you get up and running with your new course. A team of specialists will be immediately available to ensure everything runs smoothly through the life of your adoption.

Instructor Advantage Plus   Qualified McGraw-Hill adopters will be eligible for an even higher level of service. A certified WebCT or Blackboard specialist will provide a full day of on-site training for you and your staff. You will then have unlimited e-mail and phone support through the life of your adoption. Please contact your local McGraw-Hill representative for more details.

Technology Connection Seminar Series

McGraw-Hill/Irwin's Technology Connection seminar series offered across the country every year demonstrates the latest technology products and encourages collaboration among teaching professionals.

Computing Essentials

Available alone, or packaged with the O'Leary Series, *Computing Essentials* offers a unique, visual orientation that gives students a basic understanding of computing concepts. *Computing Essentials* is one of the few books on the market that is written by a professor who still teaches the course every semester and loves it! While combining current topics and technology into a highly illustrated design geared to catch students' interest and motivate them in their learning, this text provides an accurate snapshot of computing today. When bundled with software application lab manuals, students are given a complete representation of the fundamental issues surrounding the personal computing environment.

The text includes the following features:

- **A "Learn By Doing" approach** encourages students to engage in activity that is more interactive than the traditional learning pattern students typically follow in a concepts course. The exercises, explorations, visual orientation, inclusion of screen shots and numbered steps, and integrated internet references combine several methods to achieve an interactive learning environment for optimum reinforcement.

- **Making IT Work For You** sections visually demonstrate how technology is used in everyday life. Topics covered include how find a job online and how to protect a computer against viruses. These"gallery" style boxes combine text and art to take students step-by-step through technological processes that are both interesting and useful. As an added bonus, the *CE 2001-2002 Making IT Work Video Series* has been created to compliment the topics presented throughout the text.

- **On the Web Explorations** appear throughout the margins of the text and encourage students to go to the Web to visit several informative and established sites in order to learn more about the chapter's featured topic.

- **On the Web Exercises** present thought-provoking questions that allow students to construct articles and summaries for additional practice on topics relevant to that chapter while utilizing Web resources for further research. These exercises serve as additional reinforcement of the chapter's pertinent material while also allowing students to gain more familiarity with the Web.

- **A Look to the Future** sections provide insightful information about the future impact of technology and forecasts of how upcoming enhancements in the world of computing will play an important and powerful role in society.

- **Colorful Visual Summaries**, appearing at the end of every chapter, provide dynamic, graphical reviews of the important lessons featured in each chapter for additional reinforcement.

- **End-of-Chapter Review** material follows a three-level format and includes exercises that encourage students to review terms, concepts, and applications of concepts. Through matching, true/false, multiple choice, short answer completion, concept matching, and critical thinking questions, students have multiple review opportunities.

PowerWeb

PowerWeb is an exciting new online product available from McGraw-Hill. A nominally priced token grants students access through our web site to a wealth of resources—all corresponding to computer literacy. Features include an interactive glossary; current events with quizzing, assessment, and measurement options; Web survey; links to related text content; and WWW searching capability via Northern Lights, an academic search engine. Visit the PowerWeb site at **www.dushkin.com/powerweb**.

Interactive Companion CD-ROM

This free student CD-ROM, designed for use in class, in the lab, or at home by students and professors alike, includes a collection of interactive tutorial labs on some of the most popular and difficult topics in information technology. By combining video, interactive exercises, animation, additional content, and actual "lab" tutorials, we expand the reach and scope of the textbook. The lab titles are listed below.

- Binary Numbers
- Basic Programming
- Computer Anatomy
- Disk Fragmentation
- E-mail Essentials
- Multimedia Tools
- Workplace Issues (ergonomics/privacy/security)
- Introduction to Databases
- Programming II
- Network Communications
- Purchasing Decisions
- User Interfaces
- File Organization
- Word Processing and Spreadsheets
- Internet Overview
- Photo Editing
- Presentation Techniques
- Computer Troubleshooting
- Programming Overview
- SQL Queries

Student's Guide

As you begin each lab, take a few moments to read the *Case Study* and the *Concept Overview*. The case study introduces a real-life setting that is interwoven throughout the entire lab, providing the basis for understanding the use of the application. Also, notice the *Additional Information*, *Having Trouble?*, and *Another Method* boxes scattered throughout the book. These tips provide more information about related topics, help to get you out of trouble if you are having problems and offer suggestions on other ways to perform the same task. Finally, read the text between the steps. You will find the few minutes more it takes you is well worth the time when you are completing the practice exercises.

Many learning aids are built into the text to ensure your success with the material and to make the process of learning rewarding. The pages that follow call your attention to the key features in the text.

Creating and Editing a Document

LAB 1

Objectives appear at the beginning of the lab and identify the main features you will be learning.

objectives

After completing this lab, you will know how to:

1.	Develop a document as well as
2.	Insert and delete text and blank
3.	Display formatting marks.
4.	Use AutoCorrect, AutoText, and Auto
5.	Use automatic spelling and gramma
6.	Save, close, and open files.
7.	Select text.
8.	Undo and redo changes.
9.	Change fonts and type sizes.
10.	Bold and color text.
11.	Change alignment.
12.	Insert, size, and move pictures.
13.	Preview and print a document.

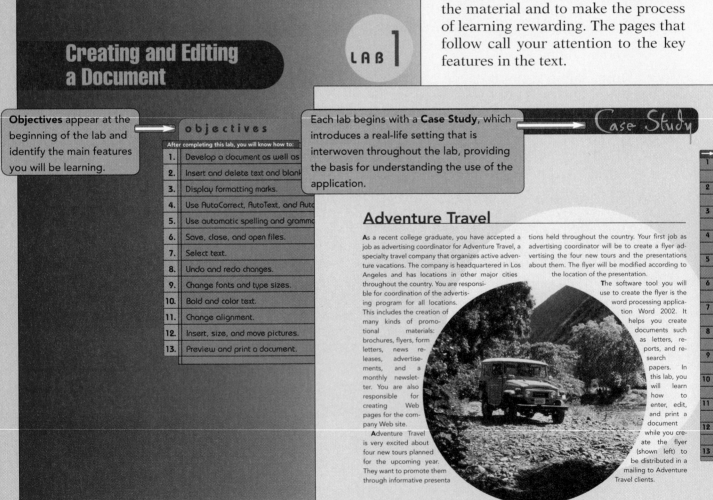

Each lab begins with a **Case Study**, which introduces a real-life setting that is interwoven throughout the lab, providing the basis for understanding the use of the application.

Case Study

Adventure Travel

As a recent college graduate, you have accepted a job as advertising coordinator for Adventure Travel, a specialty travel company that organizes active adventure vacations. The company is headquartered in Los Angeles and has locations in other major cities throughout the country. You are responsible for coordination of the advertising program for all locations. This includes the creation of many kinds of promotional materials: brochures, flyers, form letters, news releases, advertisements, and a monthly newsletter. You are also responsible for creating Web pages for the company Web site.

Adventure Travel is very excited about four new tours planned for the upcoming year. They want to promote them through informative presenta

tions held throughout the country. Your first job as advertising coordinator will be to create a flyer advertising the four new tours and the presentations about them. The flyer will be modified according to the location of the presentation.

The software tool you will use to create the flyer is the word processing application Word 2002. It helps you create documents such as letters, reports, and research papers. In this lab, you will learn how to enter, edit, and print a document while you create the flyer (shown left) to be distributed in a mailing to Adventure Travel clients.

Using Word Wrap

Now you will continue entering more of the paragraph. As you type, when the text gets close to the right margin, do not press ←Enter to move to the next line. Word will automatically wrap words to the next line as needed.

The **Concepts** that are common to all applications are emphasized— providing you with the confidence, knowledge, and ability to easily learn the next generation of applications.

1 ▸ Press →.

▸ **Type:** about some of the earth's greatest unspoiled habitats and to find out how you can experience the adventure of a lifetime.

Your screen should be similar to Figure 1.22

HAVING TROUBLE?
Do not worry about typing errors as you enter this text. You will correct them shortly.

Having Trouble? notes help resolve potential problems as you work through each lab.

The program has wrapped the text that would overlap the beginning of the next line. You will continue the paragraph a second sentence.

1 ▸ Click ⊠ Close Window in the menu bar.

Another Method
The menu equivalent is File/Close and the keyboard shortcut is Ctrl + F4.

Your screen should be similar to Figure 1.28

Another Method notes offer additional ways to perform a procedure.

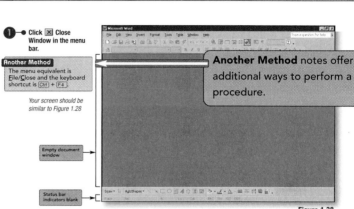

Figure 1.28

Because you did not make any changes to the document since saving it, the document window is closed immediately. If you had made additional changes, Word would ask if you wanted to save the file before closing it. This prevents the accidental closing of a file that has not been saved first. Now the Word window displays an empty document window, and the status bar indicators are blank because there are no open documents.

Opening a File

You asked your assistant to enter the remaining information in the flyer for you while you attended the meeting. Upon your return, you find a note from your assistant on your desk. The note explains that he had a little trouble entering the information and tells you that he saved the revised file as Flyer2. You want to open the file and continue working on the flyer.

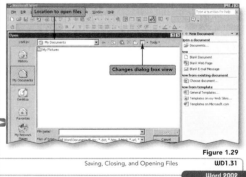

Figure 1.29

1 ▸ Move to Z (second line of paragraph below tour list).

▸ **Drag to the right until all the text including the space before the word "locations" is highlighted.**

HAVING TROUBLE?
Hold down the left mouse button while moving the mouse to drag.

Additional Information
When you start dragging over a word, the entire word including the space after it is automatically selected.

Your screen should be similar to Figure 1.41

Clear **Step-by-Step Instructions** detail how to complete a task, or series of tasks.

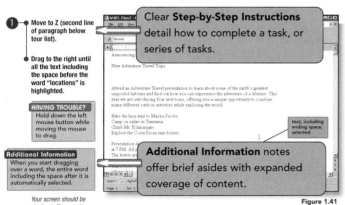

Additional Information notes offer brief asides with expanded coverage of content.

Figure 1.41

Screen captures and **callouts** to features show how your screen should look at the completion of a step.

2 ▸ Press Delete.

You also decide to delete the entire last sentence of the paragraph. You can quickly select a standard block of text. Standard blocks include a sentence, paragraph, page, tabular column, rectangular portion of text, or the entire document. The following table summarizes the techniques used to select standard blocks.

To Select	Procedure
Word	Double-click in the word.
Sentence	Press Ctrl and click within the sentence.
Line	Click to the left of a line when the mouse pointer is ⟋.
Multiple lines	Drag up or down to the left of a line when the mouse pointer is ⟋.
Paragraph	Triple-click on the paragraph or double-click to the left of the paragraph when the mouse pointer is a ⟋.
Multiple paragraphs	Drag to the left of the paragraphs when the mouse pointer is ⟋.
Document	Triple-click or press Ctrl and click to the left of the text when the mouse pointer is ⟋.
	Use Edit/Select All or the keyboard shortcut Ctrl + Alt.

Tables provide quick summaries of toolbar buttons, key terms, and procedures for specific tasks.

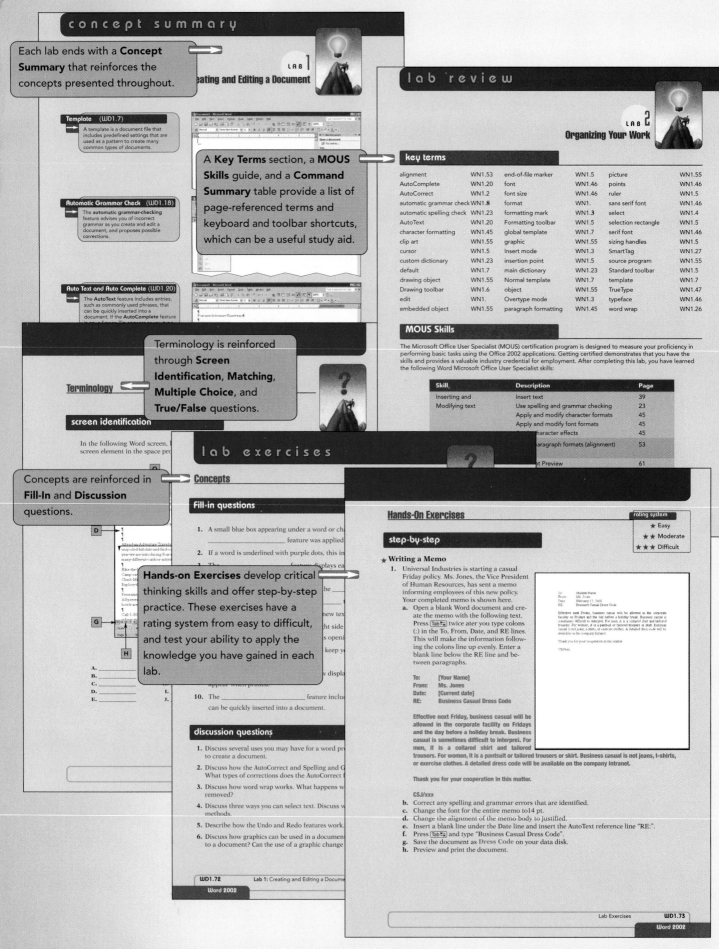

Each lab ends with a **Concept Summary** that reinforces the concepts presented throughout.

A **Key Terms** section, a **MOUS Skills** guide, and a **Command Summary** table provide a list of page-referenced terms and keyboard and toolbar shortcuts, which can be a useful study aid.

Terminology is reinforced through **Screen Identification, Matching, Multiple Choice,** and **True/False** questions.

Concepts are reinforced in **Fill-In** and **Discussion** questions.

Hands-on Exercises develop critical thinking skills and offer step-by-step practice. These exercises have a rating system from easy to difficult, and test your ability to apply the knowledge you have gained in each lab.

Introduction to Microsoft Office XP

What is Office XP?

Microsoft Office XP is a suite of applications that can be used individually and that are designed to work together seamlessly. The applications include tools used to create, discuss, communicate, and manage projects. If you share a lot of documents with other people, these features facilitate access to common documents. This version has expanded and refined the communication and collaboration features and integration with the World Wide Web. In addition, several new interface features are designed to make it easier to perform tasks and help users take advantage of all the features in the applications.

The Office XP suite is packaged in different combinations of components. The major components and a brief description are provided in the following table.

Component	Description
Word 2002	Word processor
Excel 2002	Spreadsheet
Access 2002	Database manager
PowerPoint 2002	Presentation graphics
Outlook 2002	Desktop information manager
FrontPage 2002	Web page authoring
Publisher	Desktop publishing
SharePoint	Team Web sites

The four main components of Office XP—Word, Excel, Access, and PowerPoint—are described in more detail in the following sections.

Word 2002

Word 2002 is a word processing software application whose purpose is to help you create text-based documents. Word processors are one of the most flexible and widely used application software programs. A word processor can be used to manipulate text data to produce a letter, a report, a memo, an e-mail, message or any other type of correspondence. Two documents you will produce in the first two Word labs, a letter and flyer, are shown here.

February 18, 2001

Dear Adventure Traveler,

Imagine hiking and paddling your way through the rain forests of Costa Rica, under the stars in Africa, or following in the footsteps of the ancient Inca as you backpack the Inca trail to Machu Picchu. Turn these dreams of adventure into memories you will forever by joining Adventure Travel Tours on one of our four new adventure tours.

To tell you more about these exciting new adventures, we are offering presentations in your area. These presentations will focus on the features and culture region. We will also show you pictures of the places you will visit and activities participate in, as well as a detailed agenda and package costs. Plan on attending of following presentations:

Date	Time	Location	Room
January 5 ----- 7:00 PM ----------- Town Center Hotel ------- Room 284B
February 3 ---- 7:30 PM ----------- Airport Manor ------------- Conference Room A
March 8 ------- 7:00 PM ----------- Country Inn ---------------- Mountainside Room

In appreciation of your past patronage, we are pleased to offer you a 10% discount price of any of the new tour packages. You must book the trip at least 60 days pr departure date. Please turn in this letter to qualify for the discount.

Our vacation tours are professionally developed solely for your enjoyment. W almost everything in the price of your tour while giving you the best possible value dollar. All tours include:

- Professional tour manager and local guides
- All accommodations and meals
- All entrance fees, excursions, transfers and tips

We hope you will join us this year on another special Adventure Travel Tour Your memories of fascinating places and challenging physical adventures should li long, long time. For reservations, please see your travel agent, or contact Adventure Tr at 1-800-777-0004. You can also visit our new Web site at www.AdventureTravelTours

Best regards,

Student Name

A letter containing a tabbed table, indented paragraphs, and text enhancements is quickly created using basic Word features.

Announcing
New Adventure Travel Tours

This year we are introducing four new tours, offering you a unique opportunity to combine many different outdoor activities while exploring the world.

Hike the Inca trail to Machu Picchu
Camp on safari in Tanzania
Climb Mt. Kilimanjaro
Explore the Costa Rican rain forests

Attend an Adventure Travel presentation to learn about some of the earth's greatest unspoiled habitats and find out how you can experience the adventure of a lifetime.

Presentation dates and times are January 5 at 7 PM, February 3 at 7:30 PM, and March 8 at 7 PM. All presentations are held at convenient hotel locations located in downtown Los Angeles, Santa Clara and at the airport.

Call us at 1-800-777-0004 for presentation locations, a full color brochure, and itinerary information, costs, and tour dates.

Visit Our
Web site at
AdventureTravelTours.com

A flyer incorporating many visual enhancements such as colored text, varied text styles, and graphic elements is both eye-catching and informative.

The beauty of a word processor is that you can make changes or corrections as you are typing. Want to change a report from single spacing to double spacing? Alter the width of the margins? Delete some paragraphs and add others from yet another document? A word processor allows you to do all these things with ease.

Word 2002 includes many group collaboration features to help streamline how documents are developed and changed by group members. You can also create and send e-mail messages directly from within Word using all its features to create and edit the message. You can also send an entire document as your e-mail message, allowing the recipient to edit the document directly without having to open or save an attachment.

Word 2002 is also closely integrated with the World Wide Web, detecting when you type a Web address and automatically converting it to a hyperlink. You can also create your own hyperlinks to locations within documents, or to other documents, including those at external locations such as a Web site or file server. Its many Web-editing features, including a Web Page Wizard that guides you step by step, help you quickly create a Web page. You will see how easy it is when you create the Web page shown below in the Working Together tutorial.

A Web page created in Word and displayed in the Internet Explorer browser.

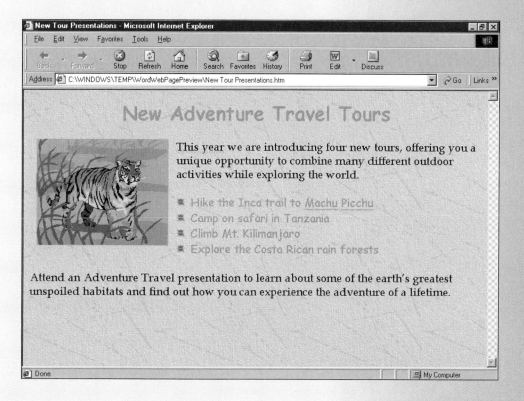

Excel 2002

Excel 2002 is an electronic worksheet that is used to organize, manipulate, and graph numeric data. Once used almost exclusively by accountants, worksheets are now widely used by nearly every profession. Marketing professionals record and evaluate sales trends. Teachers record grades and calculate final grades. Personal trainers record the progress of their clients. Excel includes many features that not only help you create a well-designed worksheet, but one that produces accurate results. Formatting features include visual enhancements such as varied text styles, colors, and graphics. Other features help you enter complex formulas and identify and correct formula errors. You can also produce a visual display of data in the form of graphs or charts. As the values in the worksheet change, charts referencing those values automatically adjust to reflect the changes.

Excel also includes many advanced features and tools that help you perform what-if analysis and create different scenarios. And like all Office XP applications, it is easy to incorporate data created in one application into another. Two worksheets you will produce in Labs 2 and 3 of Excel are shown here.

A worksheet showing the quarterly sales forecast containing a graphic, text enhancements, and a chart of the data is quickly created using basic Excel features.

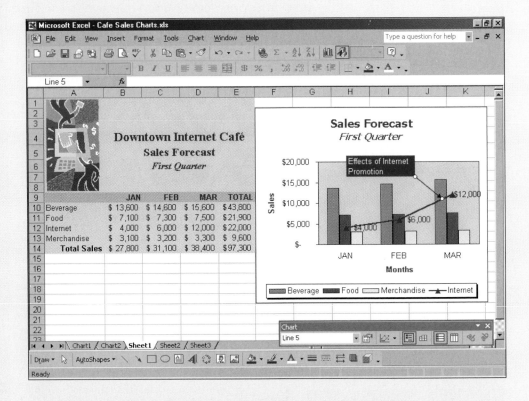

A large worksheet incorporating more complex formulas, visual enhancements such as colored text, varied text styles, and graphic elements is both informative and attractive.

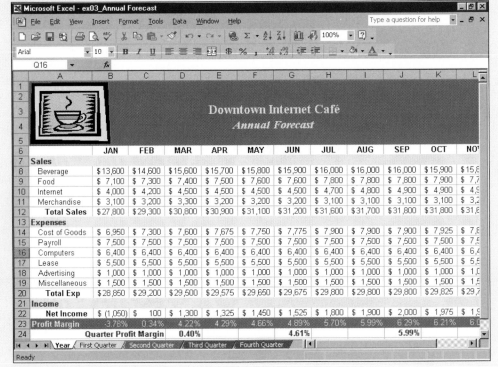

You will see how easy it is to analyze data and make projections using what-if analysis and what-if graphing in Lab 3 and to incorporate Excel data in a Word document as shown in the figures below.

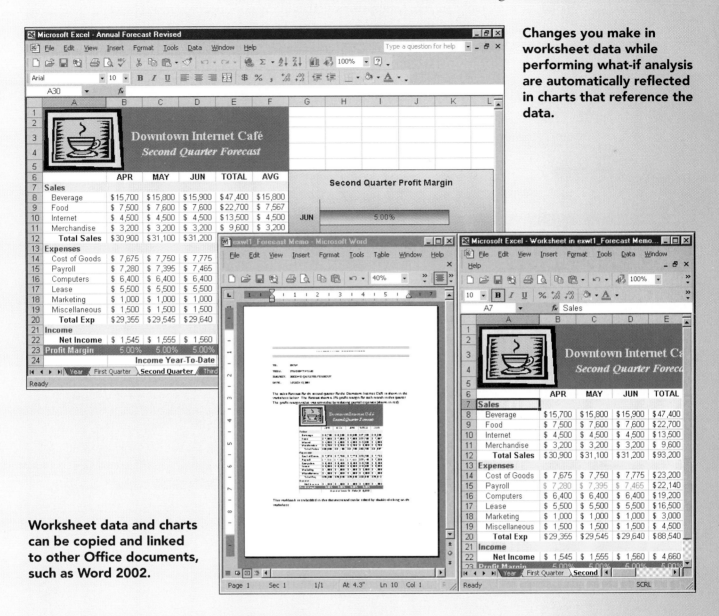

Changes you make in worksheet data while performing what-if analysis are automatically reflected in charts that reference the data.

Worksheet data and charts can be copied and linked to other Office documents, such as Word 2002.

Access 2002

Access 2002 is a relational database management application that is used to create and analyze a database. A database is a collection of related data. In a relational database, the most widely used database structure, data is organized in linked tables. Tables consist of columns (called fields) and rows (called records). The tables are related or linked to one another by a common field. Relational databases allow you to create smaller and more manageable database tables, since you can combine and extract data between tables.

The program provides tools to enter, edit, and retrieve data from the database as well as to analyze the database and produce reports of the output. One of the main advantages of a computerized database is the ability to quickly add, delete, and locate specific records. Records can also be easily rearranged or sorted according to different fields of data, resulting in multiple table arrangements that provide more meaningful information for different purposes. Creation of forms makes it easier to enter and edit data as well. In the Access labs you will create and organize the database table shown below.

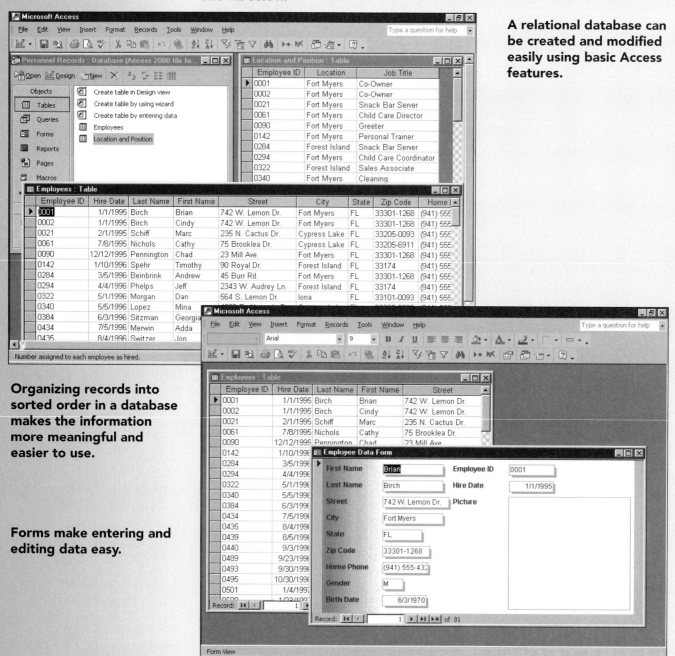

A relational database can be created and modified easily using basic Access features.

Organizing records into sorted order in a database makes the information more meaningful and easier to use.

Forms make entering and editing data easy.

Another feature is the ability to analyze the data in a table and perform calculations on different fields of data. Additionally, you can ask questions or query the table to find only certain records that meet specific conditions to be used in the analysis. Information that was once costly and time-consuming to get is now quickly and readily available. This information can then be quickly printed out in the form of reports ranging from simple listings to complex, professional-looking reports in different layout styles, or with titles, headings, subtotals, or totals.

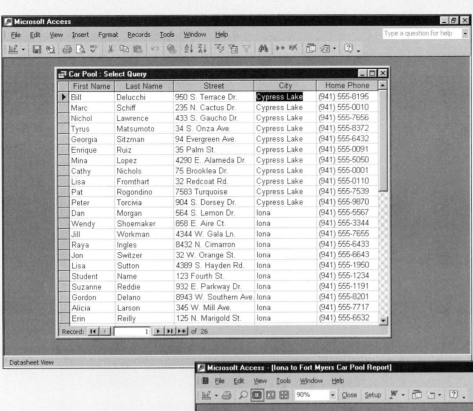

A professional-looking report can be quickly generated from information contained in a database.

PowerPoint 2002

PowerPoint 2002 is a graphics presentation program designed to help you produce a high-quality presentation that is both interesting to the audience and effective in its ability to convey your message. A presentation can be as simple as overhead transparencies or as sophisticated as an on-screen electronic display. In the first two PowerPoint labs you will create and organize the presentation shown on the next page.

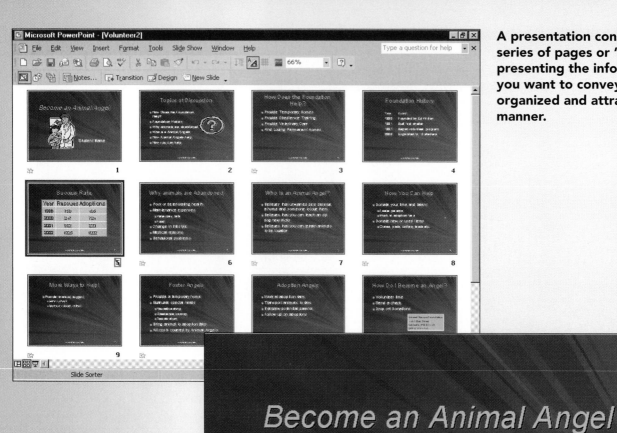

A presentation consists of a series of pages or "slides" presenting the information you want to convey in an organized and attractive manner.

When running an onscreen presentation, each slide of the presentation is displayed full-screen on your computer monitor or projected onto a screen.

Common Office XP Features

Now that you know a little about each of the applications in Microsoft Office XP, we will take a look at some of the features that are common to all Office applications. This is a hands-on section that will introduce you to the features and allow you to get a feel for how Office XP works. Although Word 2002 will be used to demonstrate how the features work, only common features will be addressed. These features include using menus, the Office Assistant and Office Help, task panes, toolbars, and starting and exiting an application. The features that are specific to each application will be introduced individually in each lab.

Additional Information

Please read the Before You Begin and Instructional Conventions sections in the Overview to Word 2002 (WDO.4) before starting this section.

Starting an Office Application

There are several ways to start an Office application. One is to use the New Office Document command on the Start menu and select the type of document you want to create. Another is to use the Documents command on the Start menu and select the document name from the list of recently used documents. This starts the associated application and opens the selected document at the same time. The two most common ways to start an Office XP application are by choosing the application name from the Start menu or by clicking a desktop shortcut for the program if it is available.

① ● Click [Start] to display the Start menu.

● Select Programs.

● Choose [W] Microsoft Word.

or

① ● Double-click the [W] Microsoft Word shortcut on the desktop.

② ● If necessary, click [□] in the title bar to maximize the window.

Your screen should be similar to Figure 1

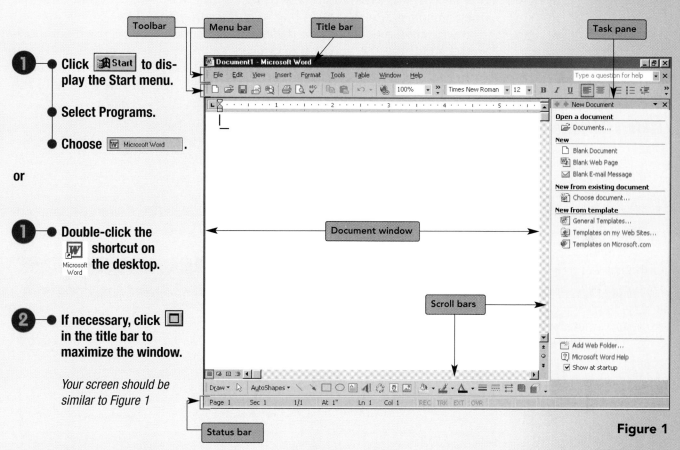

Figure 1

Additional Information

Application windows can be sized, moved, and otherwise manipulated like any other windows on the desktop. Refer to your text or, if available, to the *Introduction to Windows 2000* labs for information about working with windows.

The Word program is started and displayed in a window on the desktop. The left end of the application window title bar displays the file name followed by the program name, Microsoft Word. The right end of the title bar displays the [_] Minimize, [□] Restore, and [X] Close buttons. They perform the same functions and operate in the same way as in Windows 98 and 2000.

The **menu bar** below the title bar displays the application's program menu. The right end displays the document window's [X] Close button. As you use the Office applications, you will see that the menu bar contains many of the same menus, such as File, Edit, and Help. You will also see several menus that are specific to each application.

The **toolbars** located below the menu bar contain buttons that are mouse shortcuts for many of the menu items. Commonly, the Office applications will display two toolbars when the application is first opened: Standard and Formatting. They may appear together on one row (as in Figure 1), or on separate rows.

The large center area of the program window is the **document window** where open application files are displayed. Currently, there is a blank Word document open. The **task pane** is displayed on the right side of the document window. Task panes provide quick access to features as you are using the application. As you perform certain actions, different task panes automatically open. In this case, since you just started an application, the New Document task pane is automatically displayed, providing different ways to create a new document or open an existing document.

The **status bar** at the bottom of the window displays location information and the status of different settings as they are used. Different information is displayed in the status bar for different applications.

On the right and bottom of the document window, are vertical and horizontal scroll bars. A **scroll bar** is used with a mouse to bring additional lines of information into view in a window. The vertical scroll bar is used to move up or down, and the horizontal scroll bar moves side to side in the window.

As you can see, many of the features in the Word window are the same as in other Windows applications. The common user interface makes learning and using new applications much easier.

Using Menus

A **menu** is one of many methods you can use to accomplish a task in a program. When opened, a menu displays a list of commands.

1 ● **Click File to open the File menu.**

Your screen should be similar to Figure 2

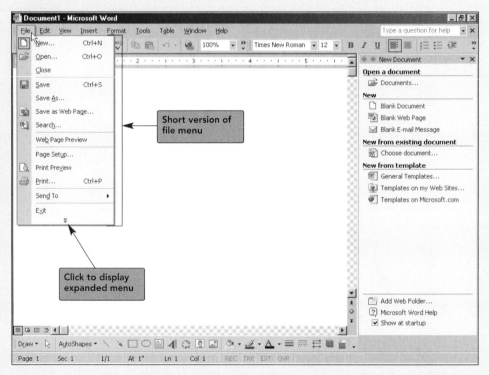

Figure 2

When an Office program menu is first opened, it may display a short version of commands. The short menu is a personalized version of the menu that displays basic and frequently used commands and hides those used less often. An expanded version will display automatically after the menu is open for a few seconds (see Figure 3).

Your screen should be similar to Figure 3

Expanded File menu

Previously hidden commands are displayed

Shortcut key

Indicates a dialog box will be displayed

Indicates a submenu will be displayed

Additional Information
Use Tools/Customize/Options and check or clear the "Always show full menus" option to change how your menus operate.

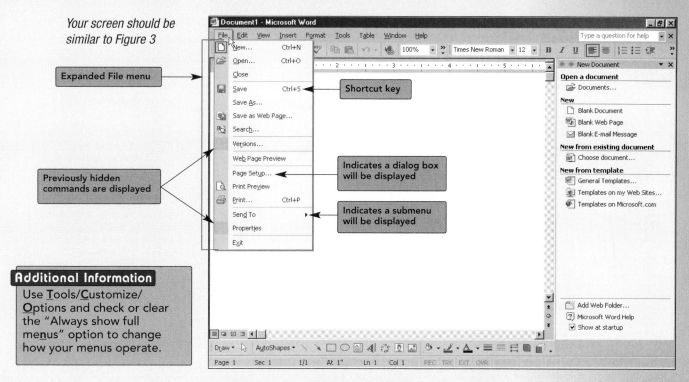

Figure 3

When the menu is expanded the hidden commands are displayed. Once one menu is expanded, others are expanded automatically until you choose a command or perform another action.

2 ● Point to each menu in the menu bar to see the full menu for each.

● Point to the File menu again.

Many commands have images next to them so you can quickly associate the command with the image. The same image appears on the toolbar button for that feature. Menus may include the following features (not all menus include all features):

Feature	Meaning
Ellipsis (...)	Indicates a dialog box will be displayed
▶	Indicates a submenu will be displayed
Dimmed	Indicates the command is not available for selection until certain other conditions are met
Shortcut key	A key or key combination that can be used to execute a command without using the menu
Checkmark	Indicates a toggle type of command. Selecting it turns the feature on or off. A checkmark indicates the feature is on.

Once a menu is open, you can select a command from the menu by pointing to it. A colored highlight bar, called the **selection cursor**, appears over the selected command.

3 ● **Point to the Send To command to select it and display the sub-menu.**

Your screen should be similar to Figure 4

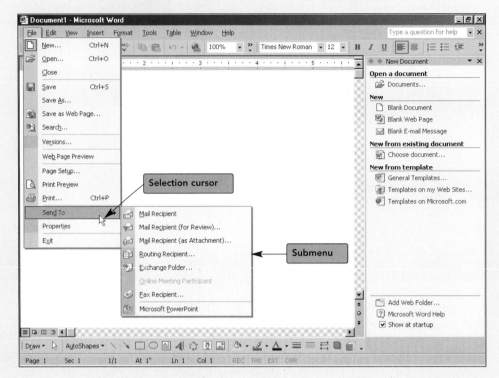

Figure 4

Then to choose a command, you click on it. When the command is chosen, the associated action is performed. You will use a command in the Help menu to access the Microsoft Office Assistant and Help features.

Note: If your screen displays the Office Assistant character as shown in Figure 5, skip step 4.

4 ● **Point to Help.**

● **Click Show the Office Assistant to choose the command.**

Your screen should be similar to Figure 5

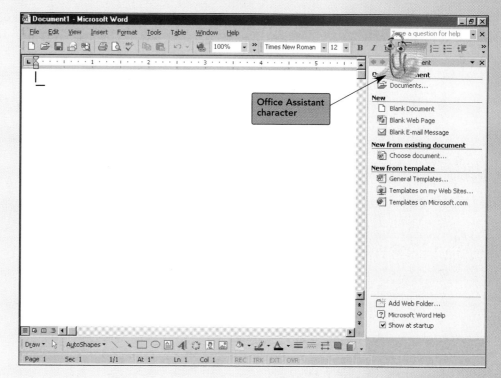

Office Assistant character

Figure 5

HAVING TROUBLE?
If the Assistant does not appear, this feature has been disabled. If this is the case, choose <u>H</u>elp/Microsoft Word <u>H</u>elp or press F1 and skip to the section "Using Help."

The command to display the Office Assistant has been executed, and the Office Assistant character is displayed. The default Assistant character is Clippit shown in Figure 5. Because there are eight different characters from which you can select, your screen may display a different Assistant character.

Using the Office Assistant

When the Office Assistant is on, it automatically suggests help topics as you work. It anticipates what you are going to do and then makes suggestions on how to perform a task. In addition, you can activate the Assistant at any time to get help on features in the Office application you are using. Clicking on the Assistant character activates it and displays a balloon in which you can type the topic you want help on. You will ask the Office Assistant to provide information on the different ways you can get help while using the program.

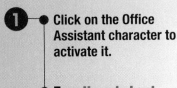

1 ● **Click on the Office Assistant character to activate it.**

● **Type How do I get help? in the text box.**

● **Click Search .**

Another Method
You could also press ⟵Enter to begin the search.

Your screen should be similar to Figure 6

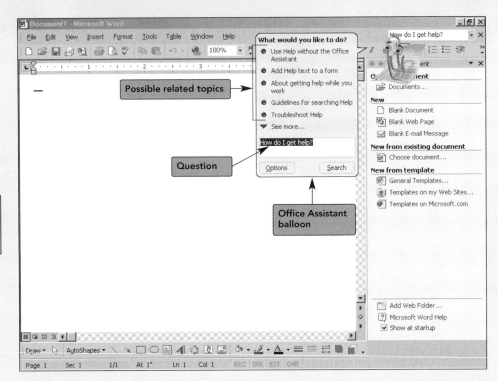

Figure 6

The balloon displays a list of related topics from which you can select.

2 ● **Select "About getting help while you work."**

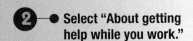

Additional Information
Clicking See more... displays additional topics.

Your screen should be similar to Figure 7

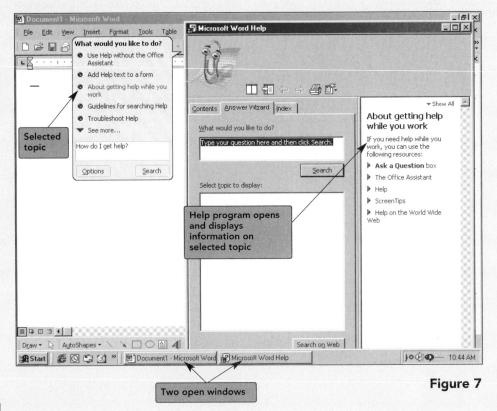

Figure 7

Another Method
You can also choose Help/Microsoft Word Help, or click ? or press F1 to start Help.

The Help program opens and displays the selected topic. Because Word Help is a separate program within Office, it appears in its own window. The Help window overlaps the Word window so that it is easy to read the information in Help while referring to the application window. The taskbar displays a button for both open windows.

Now that Help is open, you no longer need to see the Assistant. To access commands to control the Office Assistant, you will display the object's shortcut menu by right-clicking on the Assistant character. **Shortcut menus** display the most common menu options related to the selected item only.

3 ● **Right-click the Assistant to display the shortcut menu.**

● **Choose Options.**

● **Click Use the Office Assistant to clear the option.**

● **Click OK .**

● **Click □ to maximize the Help window.**

● **If necessary, click ◁▤ to display the Tabs frame.**

Your screen should be similar to Figure 8

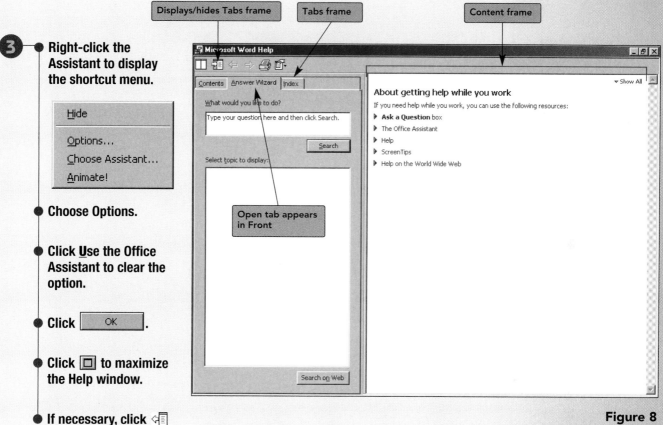

Figure 8

Using Help

In the Help window, the toolbar buttons help you use different Help features and navigate in Help.

The Help window is divided into two vertical frames. **Frames** divide a window into separate, scrollable areas that can display different information. The left frame in the Help window is the Tabs frame. It contains three folder-like tabs, Contents, Answer Wizard, and Search, that provide three different means of getting Help information. The open tab appears in front of the other tabs and displays the available options for the feature. The right frame is the content frame where the content for the selected topic is displayed.

Additional Information

You can drag the frame divider line to adjust the width of the frames. When the Tab frame is too narrow ◄ and ► appear to scroll the tabs into view.

1 ─● **Click the Contents tab to open it.**

HAVING TROUBLE?

If you cannot see the Contents tab, click the ◄ tab scroll button to bring it into view.

Your screen should be similar to Figure 9

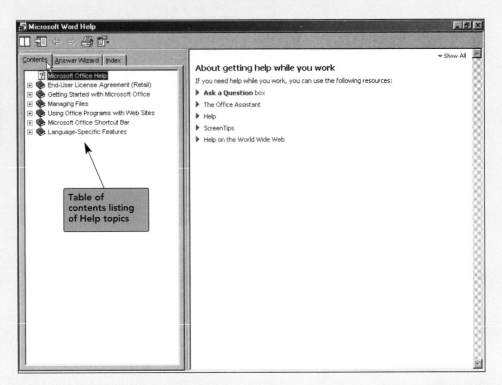

Table of contents listing of Help topics

Figure 9

Using the Contents Tab

The Contents tab displays a table of contents listing of topics in Help. Clicking on an item preceded with a ⊞ opens a "chapter," which expands to display additional chapters or specific Help topics.

1 ● **Click ⊞ next to Getting Started with Microsoft Office.**

● **Click ⊞ next to Getting Help.**

● **Click About getting help while you work.**

Your screen should be similar to Figure 10

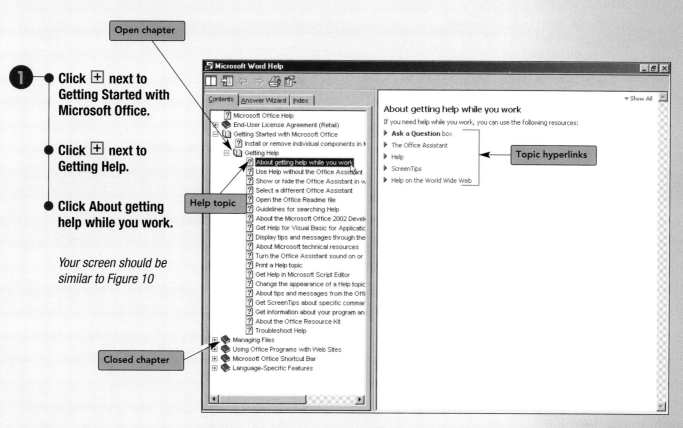

Figure 10

You have opened two chapters and selected a Help topic. Open chapters are preceded with a 📖 icon and topics with a ? icon.

Using a Hyperlink

The Help topic tells you about five resources you can use to get help. Each resource is a **hyperlink** or connection to additional information in the current document, in online Help, or on the Microsoft Office Web site. It commonly appears as colored or underlined text. Clicking the hyperlink accesses and displays the information associated with the hyperlink. A hyperlink preceded with a ▶ indicates clicking the link will display additional information about the topic.

1 ● Click the "Ask a Question box" hyperlink.

● Click the "The Office Assistant" hyperlink.

Your screen should be similar to Figure 11

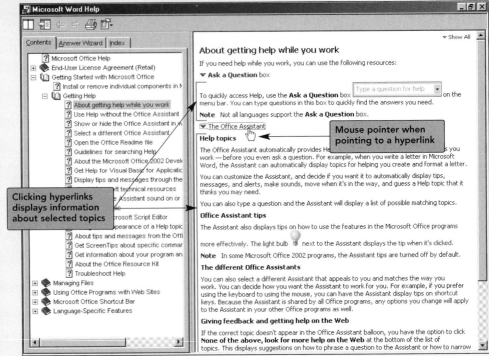

Figure 11

Additional Information
Clicking the scroll arrows scrolls the text in the frame line by line, and dragging the scroll box up or down the scroll bar moves to a general location within the frame area.

The content frame displays additional information about the two selected topics. Now, because there is more information in the content frame than can be displayed at one time, you will need to use the vertical scroll bar to scroll the additional information into the frame as you read the Help information. Also, as you are reading help, you may see text that appears as a hyperlink. Clicking on the text will display a definition of a term.

2 ● Using the scroll bar, scroll the content frame to read the information on this topic.

● Click the "shortcut keys" hyperlink.

Your screen should be similar to Figure 12

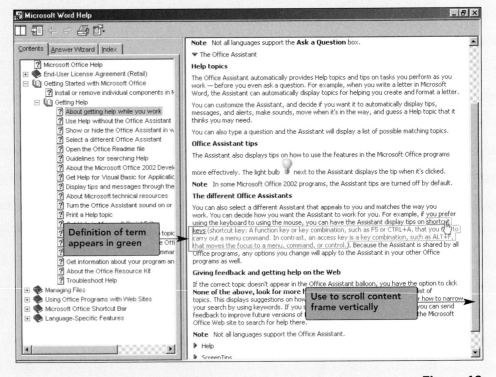

Figure 12

Scrolling the frame displays the information at the bottom of the frame while the information at the top of the frame is no longer visible. The end of the Help information is displayed in the frame. A definition of the term "shortcut keys" is displayed in green text.

3 ● **Click on the definition to clear it.**

● **Click on the Use Help without the Office Assistant topic in the Contents tab.**

Pointing to a topic in the content frame that is not fully visible displays the full topic in a ScreenTip box.

Your screen should be similar to Figure 13

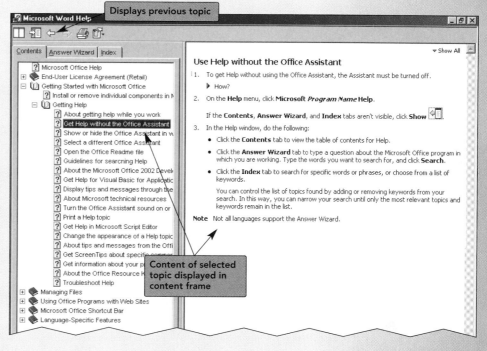

Figure 13

The content frame now displays the Help information about the selected topic. To quickly return to the previous topic,

4 ● **Click ⇦ Back.**

Your screen should be similar to Figure 14

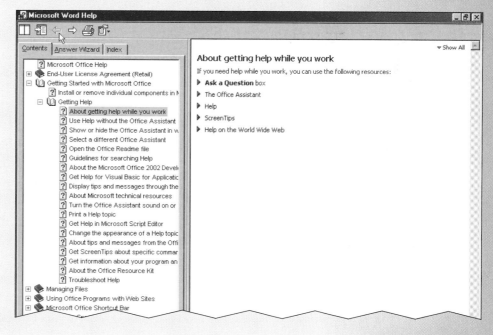

Figure 14

The topic is redisplayed as it originally appeared, without the topic selections expanded.

Using the Index Tab

To search for Help information by entering a word or phrase for a topic, you can use the Index tab.

①──● Open the Index tab.

HAVING TROUBLE?
If the Index tab is not visible in the frame, click the ▶ scroll button to display it.

Your screen should be similar to Figure 15

Enter word or phrase to locate

Alphabetical list of keywords

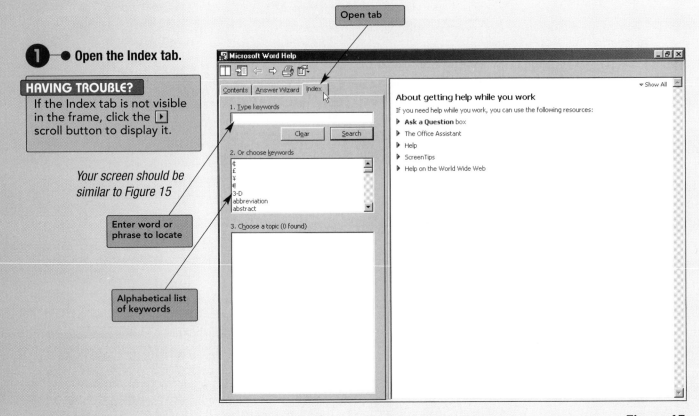

Figure 15

The Index tab consists of a text box where you can type a word or phrase that best describes the topic you want to locate. Below it is a list box displaying a complete list of Help keywords in alphabetical order. You want to find information about using the Index tab.

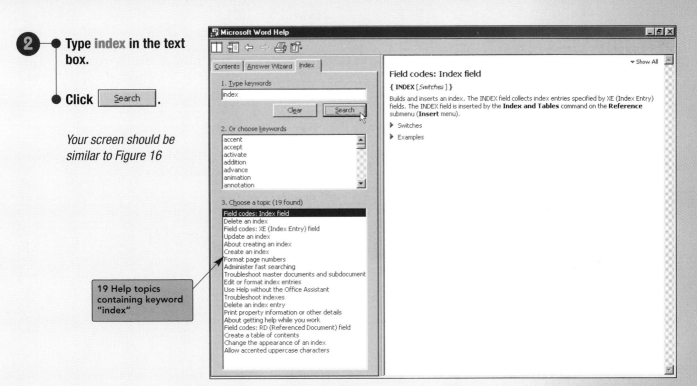

2 ● Type **index** in the text box.

● Click [Search].

Your screen should be similar to Figure 16

19 Help topics containing keyword "index"

Figure 16

The topic list displays 19 Help topics containing this word, and the content frame, displays the information on the first topic. However, many of the located topics are not about the Help Index feature. To narrow the search more, you can add another word to the keyword text box.

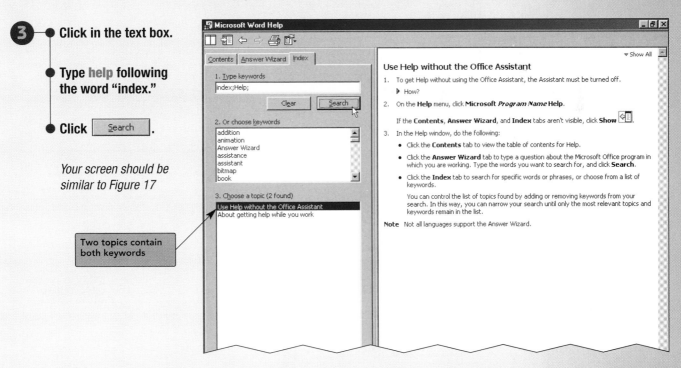

3 ● Click in the text box.

● Type **help** following the word "index."

● Click [Search].

Your screen should be similar to Figure 17

Two topics contain both keywords

Figure 17

Now only two topics were located that contain both keywords. The first topic in the list is selected and displayed in the content frame.

Using the Answer Wizard

Another way to locate Help topics is to use the Answer Wizard tab. This feature works just like the Office Assistant and the Answer box to locate topics. You will use this method to locate information on toolbars.

1 ● **Open the Answer Wizard tab.**

● **Type How do I use toolbars? in the text box.**

● **Click** Search **.**

Your screen should be similar to Figure 18

Topics related to your search

Additional Information

The search term does not need to be worded as a question. It can also be a word or phrase.

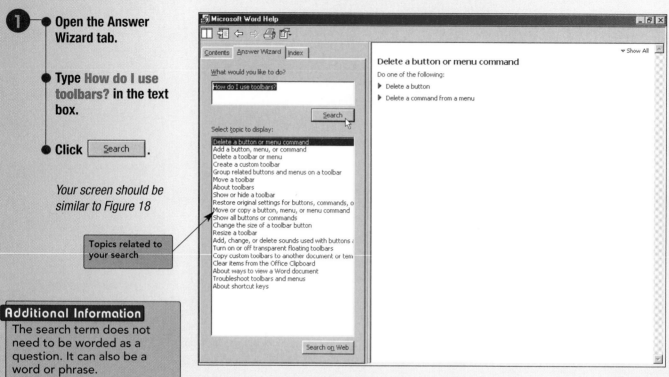

Figure 18

The topic list box displays all topics that the Answer Wizard considers may be related to the question you entered.

2 ● **Select "About toolbars" from the topic list.**

● **Click Show All.**

Your screen should be similar to Figure 19

Selected topic

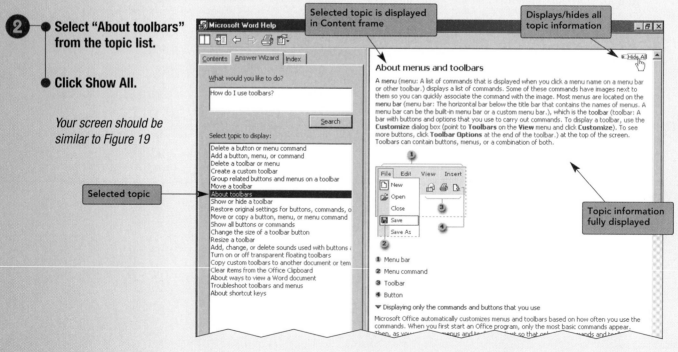

Figure 19

All topics are expanded and definitions displayed.

3 ● **Read the information about this topic.**

● **Click ☒ to close Help.**

Your screen should be similar to Figure 20

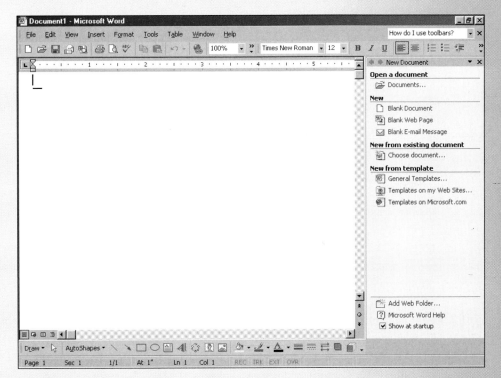

Figure 20

The Help window is closed, and the Word window is displayed again.

Getting Help on the Web

A final source of Help information is the Microsoft Office Web site. If a Help topic begins with "Web," clicking it takes you to the Web site and displays the topic in your Help window. You can also connect directly to this site from any Office application using the Help menu.

1 • Choose **H**elp/Office on the **W**eb.

• If necessary, enter your user information and make the appropriate selections to connect to the Internet.

• If necessary, click United States.

Your screen should be similar to Figure 21

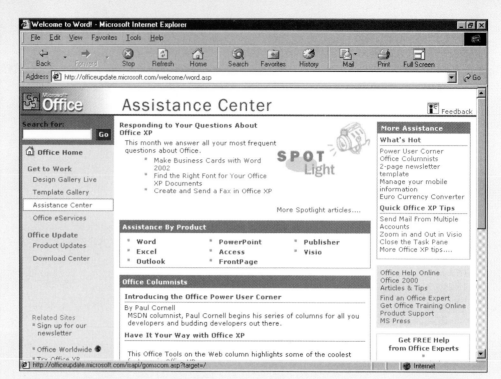

Figure 21

The browser application on your system is started and displays the Microsoft Office Web site. Now you could select any of the hyperlinks to further explore the site.

2 • Read the information on this page.

• Click ⊠ Close to close the browser.

• If necessary, disconnect from the Internet.

The Word application window is displayed again.

Using Toolbars

While using Office XP, you will see that many toolbars open automatically as different tasks are performed. Toolbars initially display the basic buttons. Like menus, they are personalized automatically, displaying those buttons you use frequently and hiding others. The More Buttons ⬇ button located at the end of a toolbar displays a drop-down button list of those buttons that are not displayed. When you use a button from this list, it then is moved to the toolbar, and a button that has not been used recently is moved to the More Buttons list.

Initially, Word displays two toolbars, Standard and Formatting, on one row below the menu bar (see Figure 22). The Standard toolbar contains buttons that are used to complete the most frequently used menu commands. The Formatting toolbar contains buttons that are used to change the appearance or format of the document.

HAVING TROUBLE?
Your screen may display different toolbars in different locations. This is because the program displays the settings that were in effect when it was last exited.

1 ● **Right-click on any toolbar to display the shortcut menu.**

Your screen should be similar to Figure 22

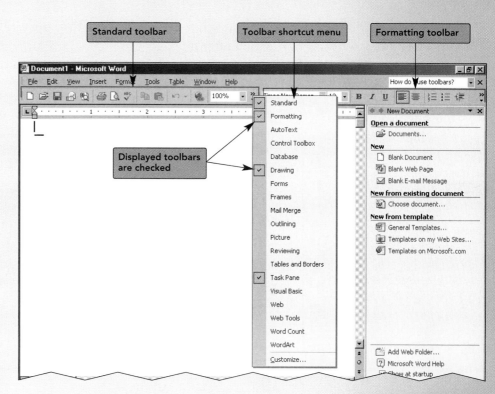

Figure 22

Additional Information
The Customize option can be used to change features of toolbars and menus.

The toolbar shortcut menu displays a list of toolbar names. The Formatting, Standard, and Task Pane options should be checked, indicating they are displayed. Clicking on a toolbar from the list will display it on-screen. Clicking on a checked toolbar will hide the toolbar.

2 ● **Click Task Pane to clear the checkmark.**

Your screen should be similar to Figure 23

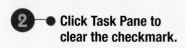

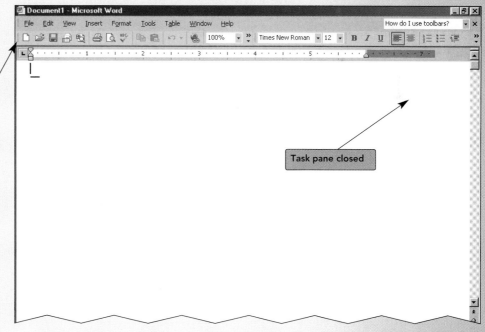

Figure 23

The task pane is closed. When a toolbar is open, it may appear docked or floating. A docked toolbar is fixed to an edge of the window and displays a vertical bar ▌ called the move handle, on the left edge of the toolbar. Dragging this bar up or down allows you to move the toolbar. If multiple toolbars share the same row, dragging the bar left or right adjusts the size of the toolbar. If docked, a toolbar can occupy a row by itself, or several can be on a row together. A floating toolbar appears in a separate window.

3 ● Drag the move handle of the Standard toolbar into the document window.

Another Method
You can also double-click the top or bottom edge of a docked toolbar to change it to a floating toolbar.

Your screen should be similar to Figure 24

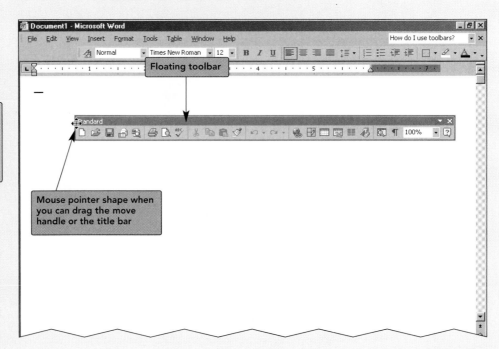

Figure 24

The Standard toolbar is now floating and can be moved to any location in the window by dragging the title bar. If you move it to the edge of the window, it will attach to that location and become a docked toolbar. A floating toolbar can also be sized by dragging the edge of toolbar.

4 ● Drag the title bar of the floating toolbar to move it to the row below the Formatting toolbar.

● Move the Formatting toolbar below the Standard toolbar.

Your screen should be similar to Figure 25

Additional Information
You can permanently display the toolbars on two rows using Tools/Customize/ Options or by choosing Customize/Options from the toolbar shortcut menu and selecting "Show Standard and Formatting toolbars on two rows."

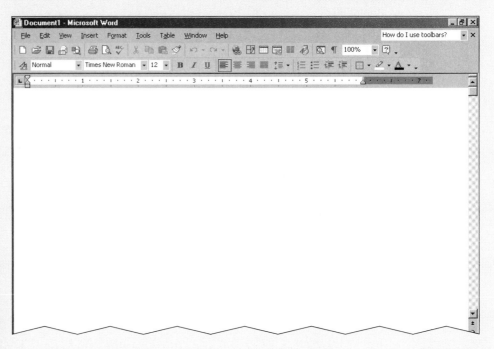

Figure 25

The two toolbars now occupy two rows. To quickly identify the toolbar buttons, you can display the button name by pointing to the button.

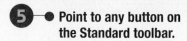

Point to any button on the Standard toolbar.

Your screen should be similar to Figure 26

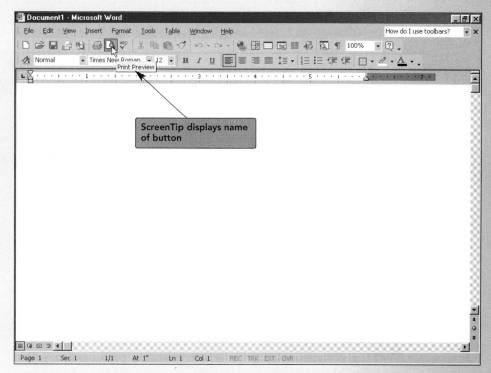

ScreenTip displays name of button

Figure 26

A ScreenTip containing the button name appears next to the mouse pointer.

Exiting an Office Application

The Exit command on the File menu can be used to quit most Windows programs. Alternatively, you can click the ⊠ Close button in the program window title bar.

Click ⊠ Close.

The program window is closed and the desktop is visible again.

lab review

Starting an Office Application

key terms

document window   I.10
frame   I.16
hyperlink   I.17
menu   I.10
menu bar   I.9
scroll bar   I.10
selection cursor   I.12
shortcut menu   I.15
status bar   I.10
task pane   I.10
toolbar   I.9

command summary

Command	Shortcut	Button	Action
Start /Programs			Opens program menu
File/E**x**it	Alt + F4		Exits Office program
View/**T**oolbars			Hides or displays toolbars
View/**Task** Pane			Hides or displays task pane
Tools/**C**ustomize/**O**ptions			Changes settings associated with toolbars and menus
Help/Microsoft Word **H**elp	F1	[?]	Opens Help window
Help/Show the **O**ffice Assistant			Displays Office Assistant

Overview to Excel 2002

What Is an Electronic Spreadsheet?

The electronic spreadsheet, or worksheet, is an automated version of the accountant's ledger. Like the accountant's ledger, it consists of rows and columns of numerical data. Unlike the accountant's ledger, which is created on paper using a pencil and a calculator, the electronic spreadsheet is created by a computer system running spreadsheet application software.

In contrast to word processing, which manipulates text, spreadsheet programs manipulate numerical data. The first spreadsheet program, VisiCalc, was introduced in 1979. Since then spreadsheets have evolved into a powerful business tool that has revolutionized the business world.

The electronic spreadsheet eliminates the paper, pencil, and eraser. With a few keystrokes, the user can quickly change, correct, and update the data. Even more impressive is the spreadsheet's ability to perform calculations from very simple sums to the most complex financial and mathematical formulas. The calculator is replaced by the electronic spreadsheet. Analysis

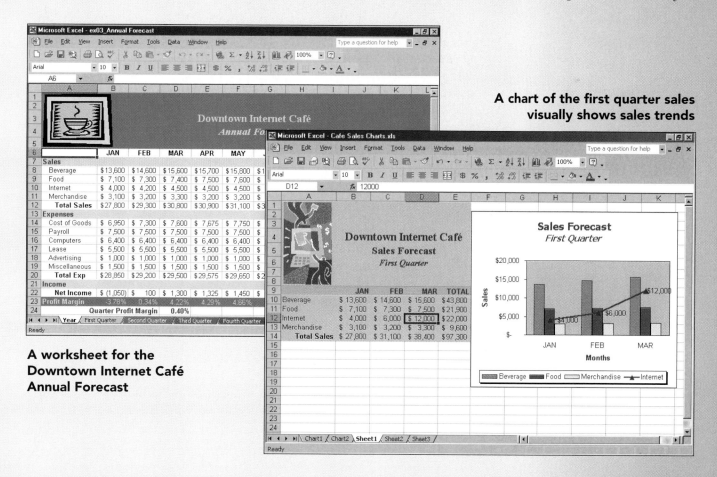

A chart of the first quarter sales visually shows sales trends

A worksheet for the Downtown Internet Café Annual Forecast

of data in the spreadsheet has become a routine business procedure. Once requiring hours of labor and/or costly accountants' fees, data analysis is now available almost instantly using electronic spreadsheets.

Nearly any job that uses rows and columns of numbers can be performed using an electronic spreadsheet. Typical uses include the creation of budgets and financial planning for both business and personal situations.

Excel 2002 Features

Spreadsheet applications help you create well-designed spreadsheets that produce accurate results. These programs not only make it faster to create spreadsheets, they also produce professional-appearing results. Their advantages include the ability to quickly edit and format data, perform calculations, create charts, and print the spreadsheet.

The Microsoft Excel 2002 spreadsheet program uses a workbook file that contains one or more worksheets. Each worksheet can be used to organize different types of related information. Numeric or text data is entered into the worksheet in a location called a cell. These entries can then be erased, moved, copied, or edited. Formulas can be entered that perform calculations using data contained in specified cells. The results of the calculations are displayed in the cell containing the formula.

The design and appearance of the worksheet can be enhanced in many ways. There are several commands that control the format or display of a cell. For instance, numeric entries can be displayed with dollar signs or with a set number of decimal places. Text or label entries can be displayed centered or left- or right-aligned to improve the spreadsheet's appearance. You can further enhance the appearance of the worksheet by changing the type style and size and by adding special effects such as bold, italic, borders, boxes, drop shadows, and shading to selected cells. Columns and rows can be inserted and deleted. The cell width can be changed to accommodate entries of varying lengths.

You can change the values in selected cells and observe their effect on related cells in the worksheet. This is called what-if or sensitivity analysis. Questions that once were too expensive to ask or took too long to answer can now be answered almost instantly and with little cost. Planning that was once partially based on instinct has been replaced to a great extent with facts. However, any financial planning resulting from the data in a worksheet is only as accurate as that data and the logic behind the calculations.

You can also produce a visual display of data in the form of graphs or charts. As the values in the worksheet change, charts referencing those values automatically adjust to reflect the changes. You can also enhance the appearance of a graph by using different type styles and sizes, adding three-dimensional effects, and including text and objects such as lines and arrows.

Case Study for Excel 2002 Labs

The Downtown Internet Café is a new concept in coffeehouses, combining the delicious aromas of a genuine coffeehouse with the fun of using the Internet. You are the new manager for the coffeehouse and are working with the owner, Evan, to develop a financial plan for the next year.

Lab 1: Your first project is to develop a forecast for the Café for the first quarter. You will learn to enter numbers, perform calculations, copy data, label rows and columns, and format entries in a spreadsheet using Excel 2002.

Lab 2: After creating the first quarter forecast for the Downtown Internet Café, you have decided to chart the sales data to make it easier to see the trends and growth patterns. You also want to see what effect a strong advertising promotion of the new Café features will have on the forecasted sales data.

Lab 3: You have been asked to revise the workbook to include forecasts for the second, third, and fourth quarters. Additionally, the owner wants you to create a composite worksheet that shows the entire year's forecast and to change the data to achieve a 5 percent profit margin in the second quarter.

Working Together: Your analysis of sales data for the first quarter has shown a steady increase in total sales. Evan, the Café owner, has asked you for a copy of the forecast that shows the growth in Internet sales if a strong sales promotion is mounted. You will include the worksheet and chart data in a memo to the owner.

Before You Begin

To the Student

The following assumptions have been made:

- Microsoft Excel 2002 has been properly installed on your computer system.

- You have the data files needed to complete the series of Excel 2002 Labs and practice exercises. These files are supplied by your instructor.

- You have completed the McGraw-Hill Windows 98 or 2000 Labs or you are already familiar with how to use Windows and a mouse.

To the Instructor

A complete installation of Office XP is required in which all components are installed and are available to students while completing the labs.

Please be aware that the following settings are assumed to be in effect for the Excel 2002 program. These assumptions are necessary so that the screens and directions in the labs are accurate.

- The New Workbook Task Pane is displayed when Excel is started (Use Tools/Options/View).

- The ScreenTips feature is active (Use Tools/Customize/Options/Show ScreenTips on toolbar).

- The Status bar is displayed (Use Tools/Options/View).

- The horizontal and vertical scroll bars are displayed (Use Tools/Options/View).

- The Paste Options and Show Insert Options buttons are displayed (Use Tools/Options/Edit).

- The Standard and Formatting toolbars are displayed on separate rows (Tools/Customize/Options).

- Full menus are always displayed (Tools/Customize/Options).

- The Normal view is on; Zoom is 100 percent (Use View/Normal; View/Zoom/100%).

- The Office Clipboard is displayed automatically. (Click Options on the Office Clipboard task pane and select Show Office Clipboard Automatically.)

- The Office Assistant feature is not on (Right-click on the Assistant character, choose Options and clear the Use the Office Assistant option.)

- All default settings for a new workbook are in effect.

In addition, all figures in the labs reflect the use of a standard VGA display monitor set at 800 by 600. If another monitor setting is used, there may be more or fewer rows and columns displayed in the window than in the figures. The 800 by 600 setting displays rows 1 through 27 and columns A through L. This setting can be changed using Windows setup.

Microsoft Office XP Shortcut Bar

The Microsoft Office XP Shortcut bar (shown below) may be displayed automatically on the Windows desktop. Commonly, it appears in the right side of the desktop; however, it may appear in other locations, depending upon your setup. The Shortcut bar on your screen may also display different buttons. This is because the Shortcut bar can be customized to display other toolbar buttons.

The Office Shortcut bar makes it easy to open existing documents or to create new documents using one of the Microsoft Office XP applications. It can also be used to send e-mail, add a task to a to-do list, schedule appointments, or access Office Help.

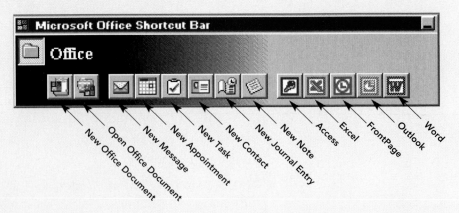

Instructional Conventions

Hands-on instructions you are to perform appear as a sequence of numbered black steps. Within each step, a series of bullets identifies the specific actions that must be performed. Step numbering begins over within each main topic heading throughout the lab.

Command sequences you are to issue appear following the word "Choose." Each menu command selection is separated by a /. If the menu command can be selected by typing a letter of the command, the letter will appear underlined and bold. Items that need to be selected will follow the word "Select" and will appear in black text. You can select items with the mouse or directional keys. (See Example A).

Example A

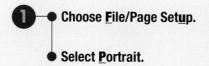

1 ● Choose **F**ile/Page Set**u**p.

● Select **P**ortrait.

Commands that can be initiated using a button and the mouse appear following the word "Click." The icon (and the icon name if the icon does not include text) is displayed following Click. The menu equivalent and keyboard shortcut appear in a margin note when the action is first introduced. (See Example B).

Example B

1 ● Click 📂 Open.

> **Another Method**
> The menu equivalent is
> **F**ile/**O**pen and the keyboard
> shortcut is Ctrl + O.

Information you are asked to type appears in blue and bold. (See Example C). File names appear in blue.

Example C

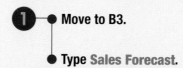

1 ● Move to B3.

● Type Sales Forecast.

2 ● Choose **F**ile/**O**pen.

● Select Forecast.

Creating and Editing a Worksheet

objectives

After completing this lab, you will know how to:

1.	Enter, edit, and clear cell entries.
2.	Save, close, and open workbooks.
3.	Specify ranges.
4.	Copy and move cell entries.
5.	Enter formulas and functions.
6.	Adjust column widths.
7.	Change cell alignment.
8.	Format cells.
9.	Insert rows.
10.	Insert and size a ClipArt graphic.
11.	Enter and format a date.
12.	Preview and print a worksheet.

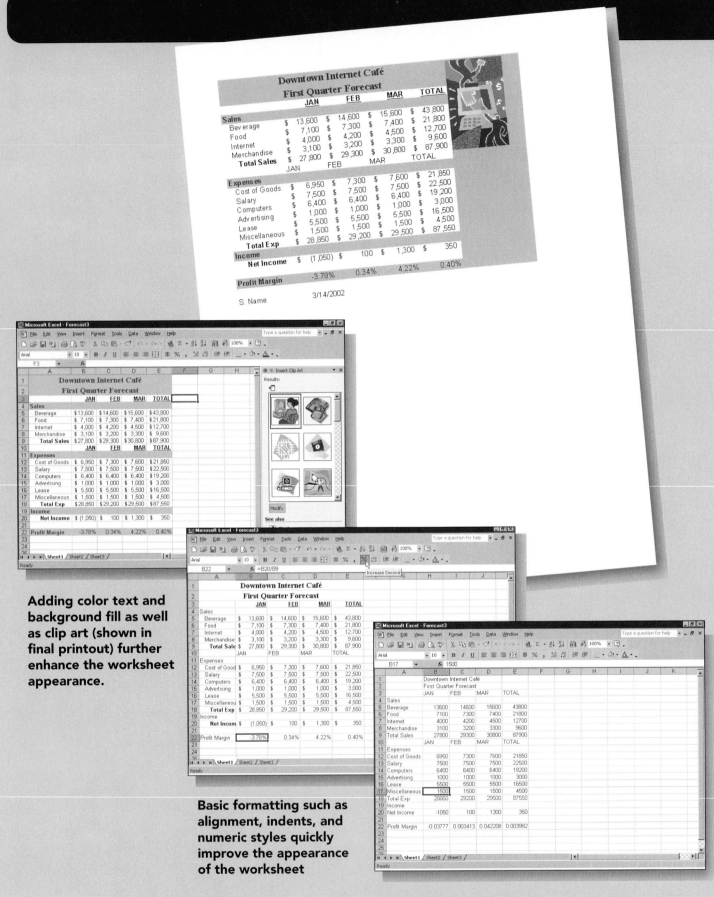

Adding color text and background fill as well as clip art (shown in final printout) further enhance the worksheet appearance.

Basic formatting such as alignment, indents, and numeric styles quickly improve the appearance of the worksheet

Enter labels, numbers, and formulas to create the basic structure of a worksheet.

Downtown Internet Café

You are excited about your new position as manager and financial planner for a local coffeehouse. Evan, the owner, has hired you as part of a larger effort to increase business at the former Downtown Café. Evan began this effort by completely renovating his coffeehouse, installing Internet hookups and outlets for laptops, and changing its name to the Downtown Internet Café. You and Evan expect to increase sales by attracting Internet-savvy café-goers, who, you hope, will use the Downtown Internet Café as a place to meet, study, or just relax.

Evan wants to create a forecast estimating sales and expenses for the first quarter. As part of a good business plan, you and Evan need a realistic set of financial estimates and goals.

In this lab, you will help with the first quarter forecast by using Microsoft Excel 2002, a spreadsheet application that can store, manipulate, and display numeric data. You will learn to enter numbers, perform calculations, copy data, and label rows and columns as you create the basic structure of a worksheet for the Downtown Internet Café. You will then learn how to enhance the worksheet using formatting features and by inserting a ClipArt graphic as shown here.

The following concepts will be introduced in this lab:

1	**Template** A template is a workbook file that includes predefined settings that can be used as a pattern to create many common types of workbooks.
2	**Text and Numeric Entries** The information or data you enter in a cell can be text, numbers, or formulas.
3	**AutoCorrect** The AutoCorrect feature makes some basic assumptions about the text you are typing and, based on these assumptions, automatically corrects the entry.
4	**Column Width** The size or width of a column controls how much information can be displayed in a cell.
5	**Copy and Move** The contents of worksheet cells can be duplicated (copied) or moved to other locations in the worksheet or between worksheets, saving you time by not having to recreate the same information.
6	**Range** A selection consisting of two or more cells on a worksheet is a range.
7	**Formulas** A formula is an equation that performs a calculation on data contained in a worksheet.
8	**Relative Reference** A relative reference is a cell or range reference in a formula whose location is interpreted in relation to the position of the cell that contains the formula.
9	**Functions** Functions are prewritten formulas that perform certain types of calculations automatically.
10	**Recalculation** Whenever a number in a referenced cell in a formula changes, Excel automatically recalculates all formulas that are dependent on the changed value.
11	**Alignment** Alignment settings allow you to change the horizontal and vertical placement and the orientation of an entry in a cell.
12	**Fonts** Fonts consist of typefaces, point sizes, and styles that can be applied to characters to improve their appearance.
13	**Number Formats** Number formats affect how numbers look onscreen and when printed.
14	**Styles** A style consists of a combination of formats that have been named and that can be quickly applied to a selection.
15	**Graphics** A graphic is a non-text element or object, such as a drawing or picture that can be added to a document.

Exploring Excel 2002

As part of the renovation of the Downtown Internet Café, new computers and the most current versions of software programs were installed, including the latest version of the Microsoft Office suite of applications, Office XP. You are very excited to see how this new and powerful application can help you create professional budgets and financial forecasts.

Starting Excel 2002

You will use the spreadsheet application Excel 2002 included in the Office suite to create the first quarter forecast for the Café.

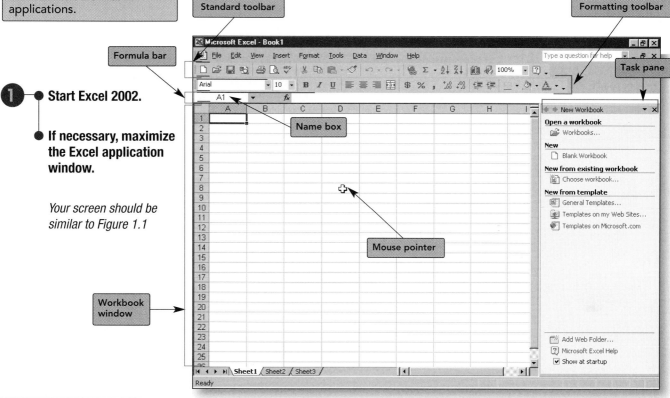

Figure 1.1

1 ● **Start Excel 2002.**

● **If necessary, maximize the Excel application window.**

Your screen should be similar to Figure 1.1

After a few moments, the Excel application window is displayed.

Exploring the Excel Window

The Excel window title bar displays the program name, Microsoft Excel, followed by Book1, the name of the open file. The menu bar below the title bar displays the Excel program menu. It consists of nine menus that provide access to the commands and features you will use to create and modify a worksheet.

The toolbars, normally located below the menu bar, contain buttons that are mouse shortcuts for many of the menu items. The **Standard toolbar** contains buttons that are used to complete the most frequently used menu commands. The **Formatting toolbar** contains buttons that are used to change the appearance or format of the document. Excel includes 23 different toolbars. Many of the toolbars appear automatically as you use different features. Your screen may display other toolbars if they were on when the program was last exited.

Below the toolbars is the formula bar. The **formula bar** displays entries as they are made and edited in the workbook window. The **Name box**, located at the left end of the formula bar, provides information about the selected item. The Edit Formula button is used to create or edit a formula.

The **task pane** is displayed on the right side of the window. There are eight different task panes that display depending on the task being performed. Since you just started Excel, the New Workbook task pane is automatically displayed providing different ways to create a new workbook or open an existing workbook.

The large area to the left of the task pane is the **workbook window**. A **workbook** is an Excel file that stores the information you enter using the program in worksheets. You will learn about the different parts of the workbook window and worksheets shortly.

The mouse pointer can appear as many different shapes. The mouse pointer changes shape depending upon the task you are performing or where the pointer is located on the window. Most commonly it appears as a ⇖ or ⊹. When it appears as a ⊹, it is used to move to different locations in the workbook window and when it appears as a ⇖, it is used to select items.

① ● **Move the mouse pointer into the center of the workbook window to see it appear as ⊹.**

● **Move the mouse pointer to the menu bar to see it appear as ⇖.**

Workbook window

Your screen should be similar to Figure 1.2

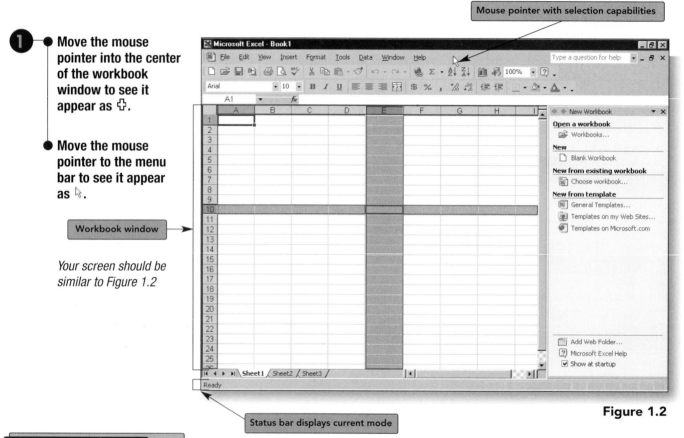

Mouse pointer with selection capabilities

Status bar displays current mode

Figure 1.2

The status bar at the bottom of the Excel window displays information about various Excel settings. The left side of the status bar displays the current mode or state of operation of the program, in this case, Ready. When Ready is displayed, you can move around the workbook, enter data, use the function keys, or choose a command. As you use the program, the status bar displays the current mode. The modes will be discussed as they appear throughout the labs.

Finally, your screen may display the Office Assistant. This feature provides quick access to online Help.

Exploring the Workbook Window

The workbook window displays a new blank workbook file containing three blank sheets. A sheet is used to display different types of information, such as financial data or charts. Whenever you open a new workbook, it displays a worksheet.

A **worksheet**, also commonly referred to as a **spreadsheet**, is a rectangular grid of **rows** and **columns** used to enter data. It is always part of a workbook and is the primary type of sheet you will use in Excel. The worksheet is much larger than the part you are viewing in the window. The worksheet actually extends 256 columns to the right and 65,536 rows down.

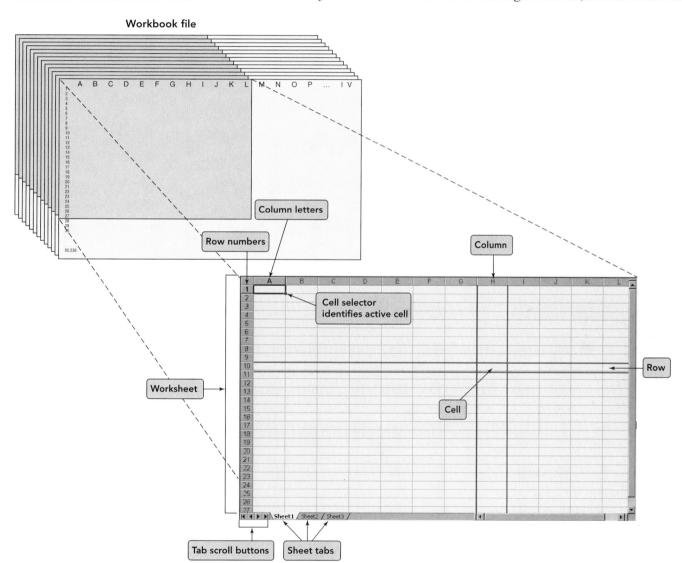

The **row numbers** along the left side and the **column letters** across the top of the workbook window identify each worksheet row and column. The intersection of a row and column creates a **cell**. Notice the heavy border, called the **cell selector**, surrounding the cell located at the intersection of column A and row 1. The cell selector identifies the **active cell**, which is the cell your next entry or procedure affects. Additionally, the Name box in the

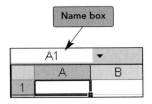
Name box

A1

A | B
1

formula bar displays the **reference**, consisting of the column letter and row number of the active cell. The reference of the active cell is A1.

Each sheet in a workbook is named. The default names are Sheet1, Sheet2, and so on, displayed on **sheet tabs** at the bottom of the workbook window. The name of the **active sheet**, which is the sheet you can work in, appears bold. The currently displayed worksheet in the workbook window, Sheet1, is the active sheet.

1 ● **Click the Sheet2 tab.**

Another Method

You can also press Ctrl + Page Down to move to the next sheet and Ctrl + Page Up to move to the previous sheet.

Your screen should be similar to Figure 1.3

Blank worksheet in Sheet 2

Active sheet

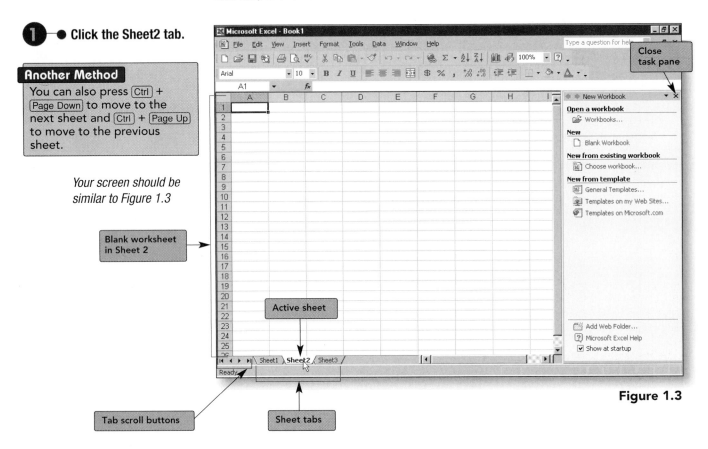

Figure 1.3

Tab scroll buttons

Sheet tabs

An identical blank worksheet is displayed in the window. The Sheet2 tab letters are bold, the background is highlighted, and it appears in front of the other sheet tabs to show it is the active sheet.

The sheet tab area also contains **tab scroll buttons**, which are used to scroll tabs right or left when there are more worksheet tabs than there is available space. You will learn about these features throughout the labs.

2 ● Click the Sheet1 tab to make it the active sheet again.

● Click ☒ in the task pane title bar to close the task pane.

Another Method
The <u>V</u>iew/Tas<u>k</u> Pane command can also be used to hide the task pane.

Your screen should be similar to Figure 1.4

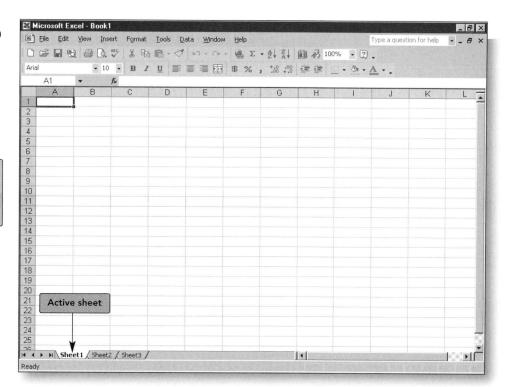

Figure 1.4

With the task pane closed, the workbook window is now the full width of the application window space, allowing much more of the worksheet to be displayed.

Moving around the Worksheet

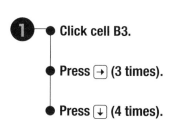

Another Method
You can use the directional keys in the numeric keypad (with NumLock off) or, if you have an extended keyboard, you can use the separate directional keypad area.

Either the mouse or the keyboard can be used to move the cell selector from one cell to another in the worksheet. To move using a mouse, simply point to the cell you want to move to and click the mouse button. Depending upon what you are doing, using the mouse to move may not be as convenient as using the keyboard, in which case the directional keys can be used. You will use the mouse, then the keyboard to move the cell selector.

1 ● Click cell B3.

● Press → (3 times).

● Press ↓ (4 times).

Your screen should be similar to Figure 1.5

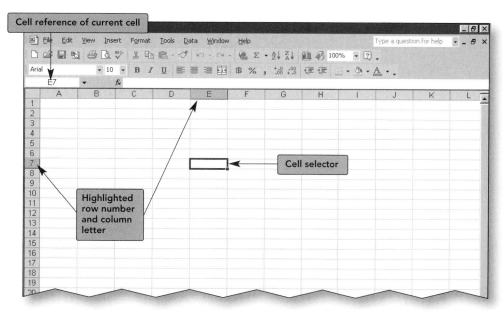

Figure 1.5

The cell selector is now in cell E7, making this cell the active cell. The Name box displays the cell reference. In addition, the row number and column letter appear highlighted to further identify the location of the active cell.

As you have learned, the worksheet is much larger than the part you are viewing in the window. To see an area of the worksheet that is not currently in view, you need to scroll the window. Either the keyboard or the mouse can be used to quickly scroll a worksheet. Again, both methods are useful depending upon what you are doing. The key and mouse procedures shown in the tables that follow can be used to move around the worksheet.

Keys	Action
Page Down	Moves cell selector down one full window
Page Up	Moves cell selector up one full window
Alt + Page Down	Moves cell selector right one full window
Alt + Page Up	Moves cell selector left one full window
Ctrl + Home	Moves cell selector to upper-left corner cell of worksheet
Home	Moves cell selector to beginning of row
End →	Moves cell selector to last-used cell in row
End ↓	Moves cell selector to last-used cell in column

Mouse	Action
Click scroll arrow	Scrolls worksheet one row/column in direction of arrow
Click above/below scroll box	Scrolls worksheet one full window up/down
Click right/left of scroll box	Scrolls worksheet one full window right/left
Drag scroll box	Scrolls worksheet multiple windows up/down or right/left

In addition, if you hold down the arrow keys, the Alt + Page Up or Alt + Page Down keys, or the Page Up or Page Down keys, you can quickly scroll through the worksheet. When you use the scroll bar, however, the cell selector does not move until you click on a cell that is visible in the window.

You will scroll the worksheet to see the rows below row 25 and the columns to the right of column L.

2 • Press Page Down
(3 times).

• Press Alt +
Page Down (3 times).

*Your screen should be
similar to Figure 1.6*

HAVING TROUBLE?
Your screen may display
more or fewer rows and
columns depending on your
screen and system settings.

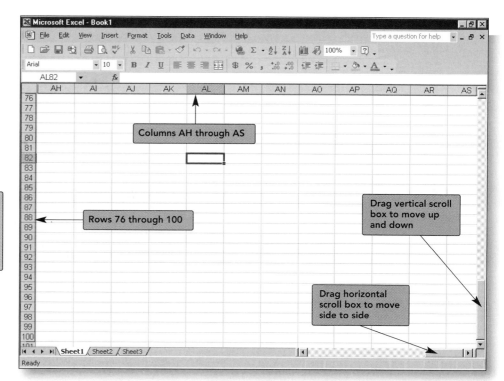

Figure 1.6

The worksheet scrolled downward and left three full windows and the window displays rows 76 through 100 and columns AH through AS of the worksheet. The cell selector is in cell AL82. As you scroll the worksheet using the keyboard, the cell selector also moves.

It is even more efficient to use the scroll bar to move long distances.

3 • Slowly drag the vertical scroll box up the scroll bar until row 1 is displayed.

• Slowly drag the horizontal scroll box left along the scroll bar until column A is displayed.

Additional Information
The position of the scroll box
indicates the relative location
of the area you are viewing
within the worksheet and the
size of the scroll box
indicates the proportional
amount of the used area.

*Your screen should be
similar to Figure 1.7*

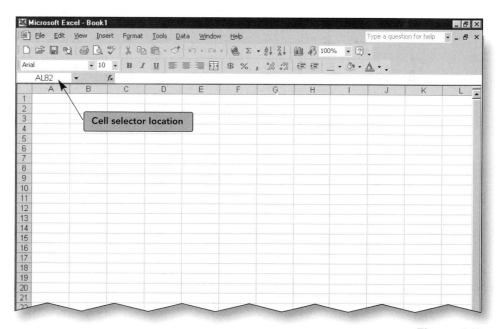

Figure 1.7

Notice that the Name box displays the cell selector location as AL82. When you use the scroll bar to scroll the worksheet, the cell selector does not move.

4 ● Practice moving the cell selector around the worksheet using each of the keys presented in the table on page EX1.10.

● Press `Ctrl` + `Home` to move to cell A1.

Another Method

You can also type a cell address in the Name box to move to that location.

Your screen should be similar to Figure 1.8

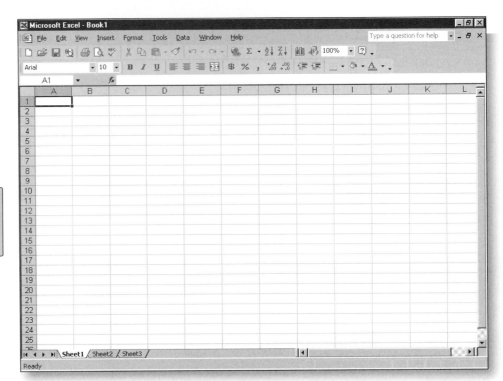

Figure 1.8

You can use the mouse or the keyboard with most of the exercises in these labs. As you use both the mouse and the keyboard, you will find that it is more efficient to use one or the other in specific situations.

Creating New Workbooks

Now that you are familiar with the parts of the workbook and how to move around, you are ready to create a worksheet showing the forecast for the first three months of operation for the Downtown Internet Café.

Using the Default Workbook Template

When you first start Excel, a new blank Excel workbook is opened. It is like a blank piece of paper that already has many predefined settings. These settings, called **default** settings, are generally the most commonly used settings and are stored as a workbook template.

concept 1

Templates

1 A workbook **template** is a file that includes predefined settings that can be used as a pattern to create many common types of workbooks. Every Excel workbook is based on a template. The default settings for a basic blank workbook are stored in the Book.xlt template file. Whenever you create a new workbook using this template, the same default settings are used.

Many other templates are available within Excel and on the Microsoft Internet site that are designed to help you create professional-looking workbooks. They include templates that create different styles of balance sheets, expense statements, loan amortizations, sales invoices, and timecards. You can also design and save your own workbook templates.

You will use the default workbook template to create the worksheet for the Café. As you create a new workbook, the development progresses through several stages.

Developing a Workbook

Workbook development consists of four steps; planning, entering and editing, testing, and formatting. The objective is to create well-designed worksheets that produce accurate results and are clearly understood, adaptable, and efficient.

Step	Description
1. Plan	Specify the purpose of the workbook and how it should be organized. This means clearly identifying the data that will be input, the calculations that are needed to achieve the results, and the output that is desired. As part of the planning step, it is helpful to sketch out a design of the worksheet to organize the worksheet's structure. The design should include the worksheet title and row and column headings that identify the input and output. Additionally, sample data can be used to help determine the formulas needed to produce the output.
2. Enter and edit	Create the structure of the worksheet using Excel by entering the worksheet labels, data, and formulas. As you enter information, you are bound to make errors that need to be corrected or edited, or you will need to revise the content of what you have entered to make it clearer or to add or delete information.
3. Test	Test the worksheet for errors. Several sets of real or sample data are used as the input, and the resulting output is verified. The input data should include a full range of possible values for each data item to ensure the worksheet can function successfully under all possible conditions.
4. Format	Enhance the appearance of the worksheet to make it more readable or attractive. This step is usually performed when the worksheet is near completion. It includes many features such as boldface text, italic, and color.

As the complexity of the worksheet increases, the importance of following the design process increases. Even for simple worksheets like the one you will create in this lab the design process is important.

During the planning phase, you have spoken with the Café manager regarding the purpose of the workbook and the content in general. The primary purpose is to develop a forecast for sales and expenses for the next year. Evan first wants you to develop a worksheet for the first quarter forecast and then extend it by quarters for the year. After reviewing past budgets and consulting with Evan, you have designed the basic layout for the first quarter forecast for the Café as shown below.

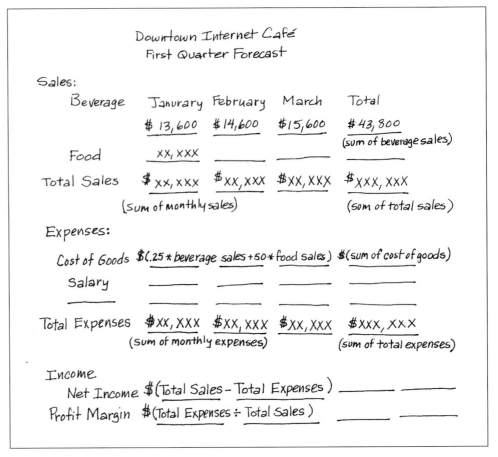

Downtown Internet Café
First Quarter Forecast

Sales:

	Janurary	February	March	Total
Beverage	$ 13,600	$14,600	$15,600	$ 43,800 (sum of beverage sales)
Food	XX,XXX			
Total Sales	$ xx,xxx (sum of monthly sales)	$xx,xxx	$xx,xxx	$xxx,xxx (sum of total sales)

Expenses:

Cost of Goods $(.25 * beverage sales + 50 * food sales) $(sum of cost of goods)
Salary _____

| Total Expenses | $xx,xxx (sum of monthly expenses) | $xx,xxx | $xx,xxx | $xxx,xxx (sum of total expenses) |

Income

Net Income $(Total Sales - Total Expenses) _____
Profit Margin $(Total Expenses ÷ Total Sales) _____

Entering and Editing Data

Now that you understand the purpose of the workbook and have a general idea of the content, you are ready to begin entering the data. You enter data by moving to the cell where you want the data displayed and typing the entry using the keyboard.

As you can see, the budget contains both descriptive text entries and numeric data. These are two types of entries you can make in a worksheet.

concept 2

Text and Numeric Entries

2 The information or data you enter in a cell can be text, numbers, or formulas. **Text** entries can contain any combination of letters, numbers, spaces, and any other special characters. **Number** entries can include only the digits 0 to 9 and any of the special characters, + − ( ) , . / $ % Σ =. Number entries can be used in calculations. An entry that begins with an equal sign (=) is a **formula**. Formula entries perform calculations using numbers or data contained in other cells. The resulting value from formulas is a **variable** value because it can change if the data it depends on changes. In contrast, a number entry is a **constant** value. It does not begin with an equal sign and does not change unless you change it directly by typing in another entry.

Entering Text

First you will enter the worksheet headings. Row and column **headings** are entries that are used to create the structure of the worksheet and describe other worksheet entries. Generally, headings are text entries. The column headings in this worksheet consist of the three months (January through March) and a total (sum of entries over three months) located in columns B through E. To enter data in a worksheet, you must first select the cell where you want the entry displayed. The column heading for January will be entered in cell B2.

1 ● **Move to B2.**

● **Type J.**

Your screen should be similar to Figure 1.9

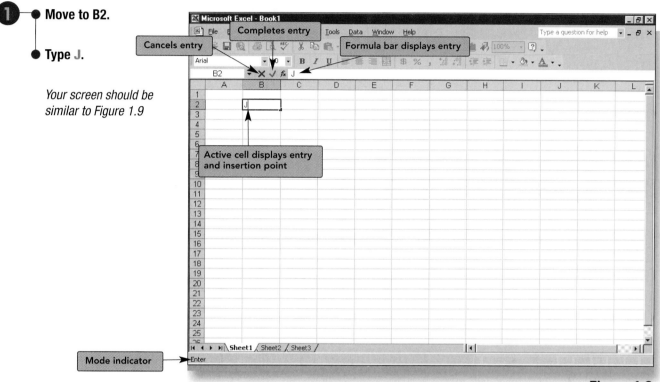

Figure 1.9

Several changes have occurred in the window. As you type, the entry is displayed both in the active cell and in the formula bar. An insertion point appears in the active cell and marks your location in the entry. Two new buttons, ☒ and ☑, appear in the formula bar. They can be used with a mouse to complete your entry or cancel it.

Notice also that the mode displayed in the status bar has changed from Ready to Enter. This notifies you that the current mode of operation in the worksheet is entering data. To continue entering the heading,

2 ● Type **anuary.**

Your screen should be similar to Figure 1.10

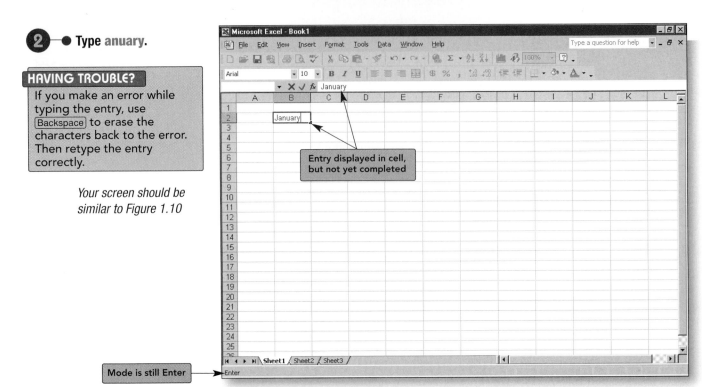

Figure 1.10

Although the entry is displayed in both the active cell and the formula bar, you need to press the ←Enter key or click ☑ to complete your entry. If you press Esc or click ☒, the entry is cleared and nothing appears in the cell. Since your hands are already on the keyboard, it is quicker to press ←Enter than it is to use the mouse to click ☑.

3 ● Press ←Enter.

Your screen should be similar to Figure 1.11

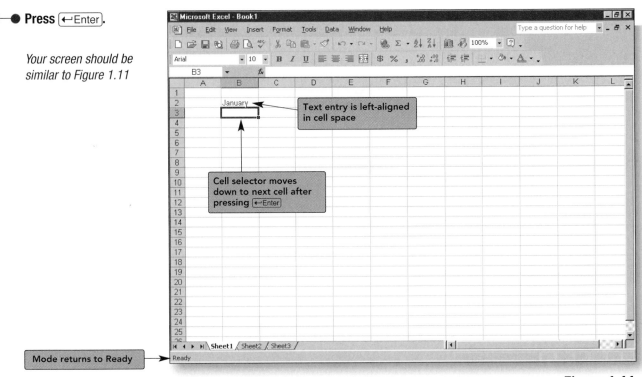

Figure 1.11

The entry January is displayed in cell B2, and the mode has returned to Ready. In addition, the cell selector has moved to cell B3. Whenever you use the ←Enter key to complete an entry, the cell selector moves down one cell.

Notice that the entry is positioned to the left side of the cell space. The positioning of cell entries in the cell space is called **alignment**. This is a default setting included in the default workbook template you are using. You will learn more about this feature later in the lab.

Clearing an Entry

After looking at the entry, you decide you want the column headings to be in row 3 rather than in row 2. This will leave more space above the column headings for a worksheet title. The Delete key can be used to clear the contents from a cell. To remove the entry from cell B2 and enter it in cell B3,

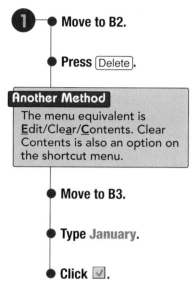

1 ● Move to B2.

● Press Delete.

Another Method

The menu equivalent is Edit/Clear/Contents. Clear Contents is also an option on the shortcut menu.

● Move to B3.

● Type January.

● Click ☑.

Your screen should be similar to Figure 1.12

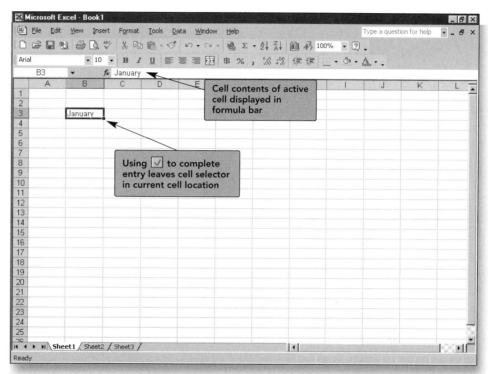

Figure 1.12

The cell selector remains in the active cell when you use ☑ to complete an entry. Because the cell selector is positioned on a cell containing an entry, the contents of the cell are displayed in the formula bar.

Editing an Entry

You would like to change the heading from January to JAN. An entry in a cell can be entirely changed in the Ready mode or partially changed or edited in the Edit mode. To use the Ready mode, you move the cell selector to the cell you want to change and retype the entry the way you want it to appear. As soon as a new character is entered, the existing entry is cleared.

Generally, however, if you need to change only part of an entry, it is quicker to use the Edit mode. To change to Edit mode, double-click on the cell whose contents you want to edit.

① ● Double-click B3.

Your screen should be similar to Figure 1.13

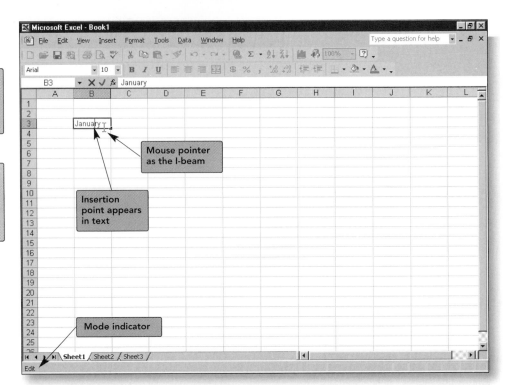

Figure 1.13

The status bar shows that the new mode of operation is Edit. The insertion point appears in the entry, and the mouse pointer changes to an I-beam when positioned on the cell. The mouse pointer can now be used to move the insertion point in the entry by positioning the I-beam and clicking.

In addition, in the Edit mode, the following keys can be used to move the insertion point:

Key	Action
Home	Moves insertion point to beginning of entry
End	Moves insertion point to end of entry
→	Moves insertion point one character right
←	Moves insertion point one character left

Once the insertion point is appropriately positioned, you can edit the entry by removing the incorrect characters and typing the correct characters. The [Delete] key erases characters at the insertion point, and the [Backspace] key erases characters to the left of the insertion point. You will change this entry to JAN.

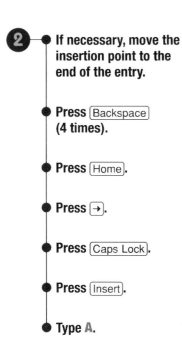

2 ● If necessary, move the insertion point to the end of the entry.

● Press [Backspace] (4 times).

● Press [Home].

● Press [→].

● Press [Caps Lock].

● Press [Insert].

● Type **A**.

Your screen should be similar to Figure 1.14

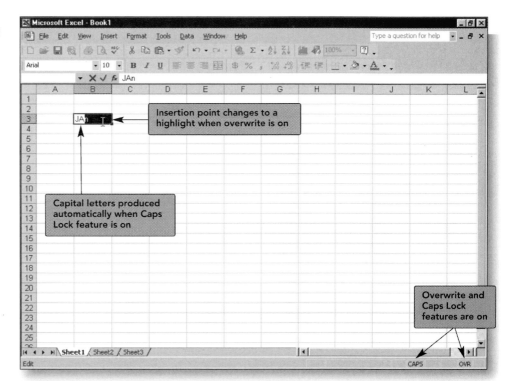

Capital letters produced automatically when Caps Lock feature is on

Insertion point changes to a highlight when overwrite is on

Overwrite and Caps Lock features are on

Figure 1.14

Additional Information
The Caps Lock indicator light on your keyboard is lit when this feature is on.

The four characters at the end of the entry were deleted using [Backspace]. Turning on the Caps Lock feature produced an uppercase letter A without having to hold down [⇧Shift]. Finally, by pressing [Insert] the program switched from inserting text to overwriting text as you typed. The insertion point changes to a highlight to show the character will be replaced. The status bar displays CAPS and OVR to let you know these features are on.

3 ● Type **N**.

● Press [←Enter].

Your screen should be similar to Figure 1.15

Additional Information
Overwrite is automatically turned off when you leave Edit mode or if you press [Insert] again.

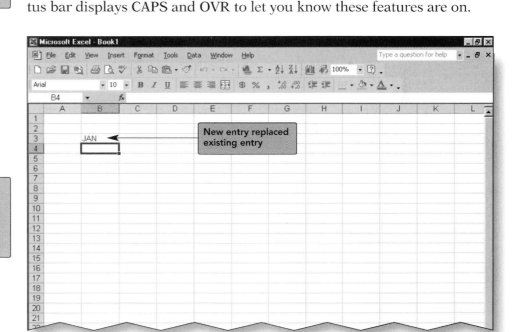

New entry replaced existing entry

Figure 1.15

The new heading JAN is entered into cell B3, replacing January. As you can see, editing will be particularly useful with long or complicated entries.

Next, you will enter the remaining three headings in row three. You can also complete an entry by moving to any other worksheet cell.

4 ● Move to C3.

● Type **FEB**.

● Press → or Tab ⇄ or click D3.

● Complete the column headings by entering **MAR** in cell D3 and **TOTAL** in cell E3.

● When you are done, turn off Caps Lock.

Your screen should be similar to Figure 1.16

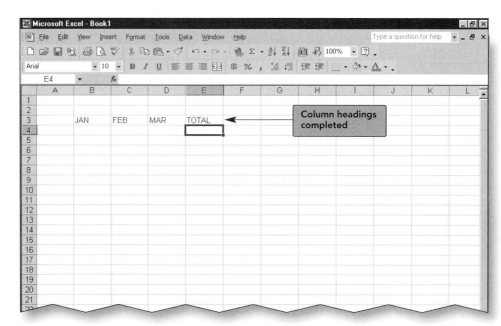

Column headings completed

Figure 1.16

The column headings are now complete for the first quarter.

Using AutoCorrect

As soon as you complete an entry in a cell, Excel checks the entry for accuracy. This is part of the automatic correcting feature of Excel.

concept 3

AutoCorrect

3 The **AutoCorrect** feature makes some basic assumptions about the text you are typing and, based on these assumptions, automatically corrects the entry. The AutoCorrect feature automatically inserts proper capitalization at the beginning of sentences and in the names of days of the week. It will also change to lowercase letters any words that were incorrectly capitalized due to the accidental use of the Caps Lock key. In addition, it also corrects many common typing and spelling errors automatically.

One way the program automatically makes corrections is by looking for certain types of errors. For example, if two capital letters appear at the beginning of a word, the second capital letter is changed to a lowercase letter. If a low-

ercase letter appears at the beginning of a sentence, the first letter of the first word is capitalized. If the name of a day begins with a lowercase letter, the first letter is capitalized.

Another way the program makes corrections is by checking all entries against a built-in list of words that are commonly spelled incorrectly or typed incorrectly. If it finds the entry on the list, the program automatically replaces the error with the correction. For example, the typing error "aboutthe" is automatically changed to "about the" because the error is on the AutoCorrect list. You can also add words that you want to be automatically corrected to the AutoCorrect list. Words you add are added to the list on the computer you are using and will be available to anyone who uses the machine after you.

Above the column headings, in rows 1 and 2, you want to enter a title for the worksheet. While entering the title, you will intentionally misspell two words to demonstrate how the AutoCorrect feature works.

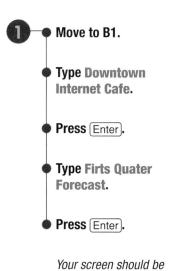

Move to B1.

Type Downtown Internet Cafe.

Press Enter.

Type Firts Quater Forecast.

Press Enter.

Your screen should be similar to Figure 1.17

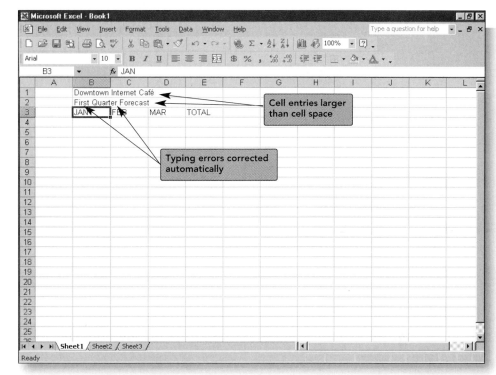

Figure 1.17

The two typing errors were automatically corrected when you completed the entry. When a text entry is longer than the cell's column width, Excel will display as much of the entry as it can. If the cell to the right is empty, the whole entry will be displayed. If the cell to the right contains an entry, the overlapping part of the entry is not displayed.

Next, the row headings need to be entered into column A of the worksheet. The row headings and what they represent are shown on the next page.

Heading	Represents
Sales	
Beverage	Income from sales of drinks (espresso, gourmet coffee, cold drinks)
Food	Income from sales of sandwiches and salads
Internet	Income from Internet connection time charges
Merchandise	Income from sales of Café tee shirts, mugs, and so forth
Total Sales	Sum of all sales
Expenses	
Cost of Goods	Cost of beverage and food items sold
Salary	Personnel expenses
Computers	Monthly payment for computer hardware
Lease	Monthly lease expense
Miscellaneous	Monthly expenses for T1 line, phone, electricity, water, trash removal, etc.
Income	
Net Income	Total sales minus total expenses
Profit Margin	Net income divided by total sales

2 ● Complete the row headings for the Sales portion of the worksheet by entering the following headings in the indicated cells:

Cell	Heading
A4	**Sales**
A5	**Beverage**
A6	**Food**
A7	**Internet**
A8	**Merchandise**
A9	**Total Sales**

HAVING TROUBLE?
Remember to press Enter or an arrow key to complete the last entry.

Your screen should be similar to Figure 1.18

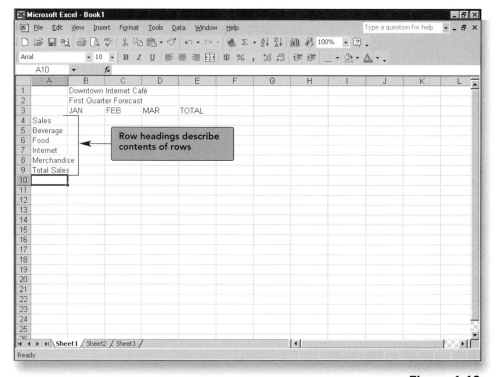

Figure 1.18

Entering Numbers

Next, you will enter the expected beverage sales numbers for January through March into cells B5 through D5. As you learned earlier, number entries can include the digits 0 to 9 and any of these special characters: + – ( ), . / $ % Σ =. When entering numbers, it is not necessary to type the comma to separate thousands or the currency ($) symbol. You will learn about adding these symbols shortly.

You will enter the expected beverage sales for January first.

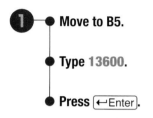

● **Move to B5.**

● **Type 13600.**

● **Press ←Enter.**

Your screen should be similar to Figure 1.19

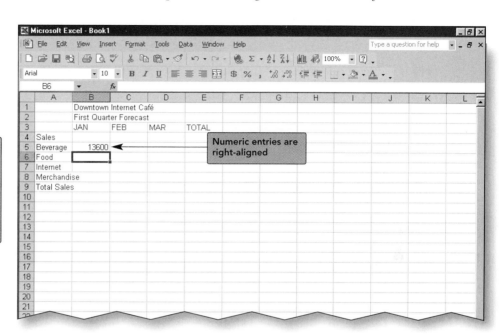

Figure 1.19

Unlike text entries, Excel displays number entries right-aligned in the cell space by default.

● **In the same manner, enter the January sales numbers for the remaining items using the values shown below.**

Cell	Number
B6	7100
B7	3600
B8	3100

● **Move to A8.**

Your screen should be similar to Figure 1.20

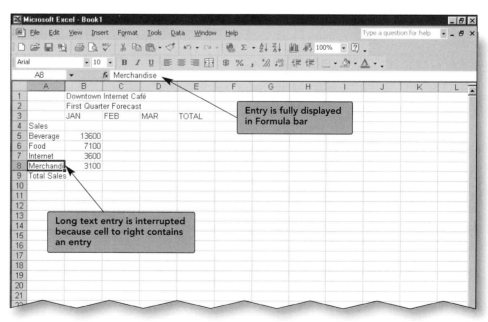

Figure 1.20

After entering the numbers for January in column B, any long headings in column A were cut off or interrupted. Notice that the entry in cell A8 is no longer completely displayed. It is a long text entry and because the cell to the right (B8) now contains an entry, the overlapping part of the entry is shortened. However, the entire entry is fully displayed in the Formula bar. Only the display of the entry in the cell has been shortened.

Changing Column Widths

To allow the long text entries in column A to be fully displayed, you can increase the column's width.

concept 4

Column Width

4 | The size or width of a column controls how much information can be displayed in a cell. A text entry that is larger than the column width will be fully displayed only if the cells to the right are blank. If the cells to the right contain data, the text is interrupted. On the other hand, when numbers are entered in a cell, the column width is automatically increased to fully display the entry.

The default column width setting in the default workbook template is 8.43. The number represents the average number of digits that can be displayed in a cell using the standard type style. The column width can be any number from 1 to 255.

When the worksheet is printed, it appears as it does currently on the screen. Therefore, you want to increase the column width to display the largest entry. Likewise, you can decrease the column width when the entries in a column are short.

Dragging the Column Boundary

Additional Information
You can also adjust the size of any row by dragging the row divider line or by using Format/Row/Height.

The column width can be quickly adjusted by dragging the boundary line located to the right of the column letter. Dragging it to the left decreases the column width, while dragging it to the right increases the width. As you drag, a temporary column reference line shows where the new column will appear and a ScreenTip displays the width of the column.

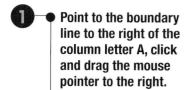

Point to the boundary line to the right of the column letter A, click and drag the mouse pointer to the right.

HAVING TROUBLE?
Make sure the mouse pointer changes to ✛ before you drag the column boundary line to size the column.

When the ScreenTip displays 15.00, release the mouse button.

Another Method
The menu equivalent is Format/Column/Width.

Your screen should be similar to Figure 1.21

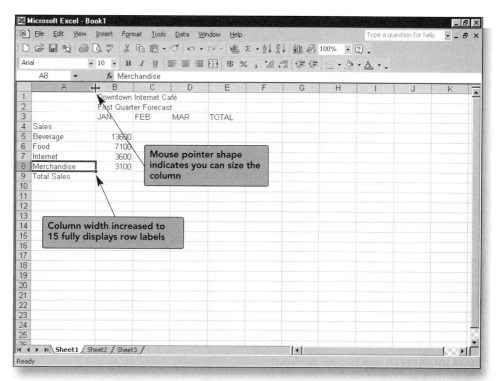

Mouse pointer shape indicates you can size the column

Column width increased to 15 fully displays row labels

Figure 1.21

Now, however, the column width is wider than needed.

Using AutoFit

Another way to change the column width is to automatically adjust the width to fit the column contents.

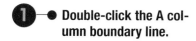

Double-click the A column boundary line.

HAVING TROUBLE?
Make sure the mouse pointer changes to ✛ before you double-click on the column boundary line.

Another Method
The menu equivalent is Format/Column/AutoFit Selection.

Your screen should be similar to Figure 1.22

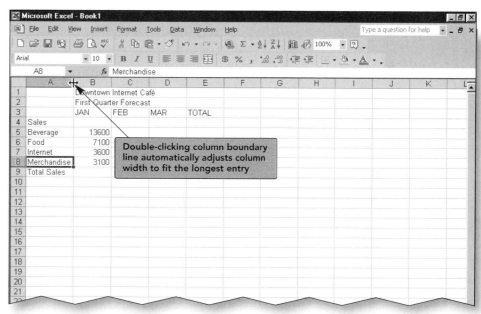

Double-clicking column boundary line automatically adjusts column width to fit the longest entry

Figure 1.22

The column width is sized to just slightly larger than the longest cell contents.

Saving, Closing, and Opening Workbooks

You have a meeting you need to attend shortly, so you want to save your work to a file and close the file. As you enter and edit data to create a new workbook, the changes you make are immediately displayed onscreen and are stored in your computer's memory. However, they are not permanently stored until you save your work to a file on a disk. Once a workbook is saved as a file, it can be closed and opened again at a later time to be further edited.

As a backup against the accidental loss of work due to power failure or other mishap, Office XP includes an AutoRecover feature. When this feature is on, as you work you may see a pulsing disk icon briefly appear in the status bar. This indicates the program is saving your work to a temporary recovery file. The time interval between automatic saving can be set to any period you specify; the default is every 10 minutes. When you start up again, the recovery file is automatically opened containing all changes you made up to the last time it was saved by AutoRecover. You then need to save the recovery file. If you do not save it, it is deleted when closed. While AutoRecover is a great feature for recovering lost work, it should not be used in place of regularly saving your work.

Saving a New Workbook

You will save the work you have done so far on the workbook. The Save or Save As commands on the File menu are used to save files. The Save command or the 🖫 Save button will save the active file using the same file name by replacing the contents of the existing file with the document as it appears on your screen. The Save As command allows you to save a file with a new file name or to a new location. This leaves the original file unchanged.

Additional Information

When a workbook is saved for the first time, either Save or Save As can be used.

1 ● Choose **F**ile/Save **A**s.

Your screen should be similar to Figure 1.23

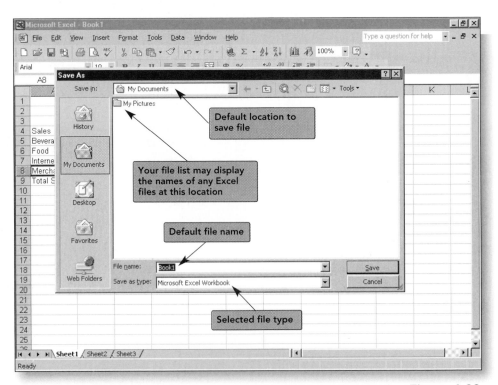

Figure 1.23

This Save As dialog box is used to specify the location to save the file and the file name. The Save In drop-down list box displays the default folder as the location where the file will be saved, and the File Name text box displays the proposed file name. The file list box displays the names of any Excel workbook files in the default location. Only Excel workbook files are listed, because the selected file type in the Save As Type list box is Excel Workbook. First you need to change the location where the file will be saved.

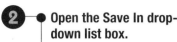

2 ● **Open the Save In drop-down list box.**

● **Select the appropriate location to save the file.**

HAVING TROUBLE?

If you are saving to a floppy disk and an error message is displayed, check that your disk is properly inserted in the drive and click ▭OK▭.

Your screen should be similar to Figure 1.24

Additional Information

If your system uses Windows NT, My Network Places is Network Neighborhood; in Windows 98, it is Web Folders.

Additional Information

If your dialog box displays the extension, this is a function of your Windows setup.

Additional Information

In addition to the .xls file type, Excel workbooks can also be saved in several different file formats that have different file extensions depending upon the format.

Additional Information

Windows documents can have up to 215 characters in the file name. Names can contain letters, numbers, and spaces; the symbols \, /, ?, :, *, ", < and > cannot be used.

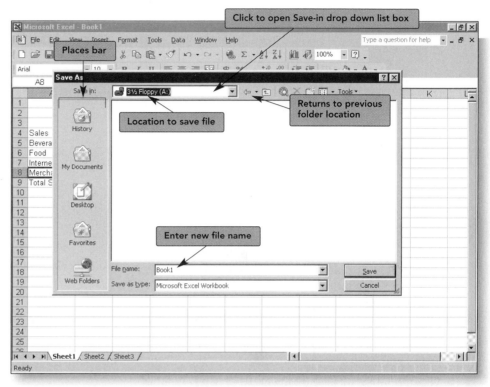

Figure 1.24

If the location you are saving to does not contain other Excel files, your file list will be empty as shown here. Otherwise, your file list may display Excel file names. You can also select the location to save your file from the Places bar along the left side of the dialog box. The icons bring up a list of recently accessed files and folders, the contents of the My Documents and Favorites folder, the Windows desktop, and folders that reside on a network or Web through My Network Places. Selecting a folder from one of these lists changes to that location. You can also click the ⬅ button in the toolbar to return to folders that were previously opened.

Next, you need to enter a file name and specify the file type. The File Name box displays the default file name, Book1. The Save as Type box displays Excel workbook as the default format in which the file will be saved. Workbooks are identified by the file extension .xls. The file type you select determines the file extension that will be automatically added to the file name when the file is saved. You will change the file name to Forecast.

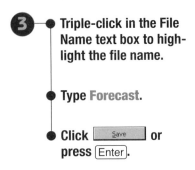

New file name

3
- Triple-click in the File Name text box to highlight the file name.

- Type **Forecast**.

- Click [Save] or press [Enter].

Your screen should be similar to Figure 1.25

Closes workbook file

Figure 1.25

The new file name is displayed in the application window title bar. The worksheet data that was on your screen and in the computer's memory is now saved at the location you specified in a new file called Forecast.

Closing a Workbook

You are now ready to close the workbook file.

1
- Click ☒ Close Window (in the menu bar).

Because you did not make any changes to the document since saving it, the document window is closed immediately and the Excel window displays an empty workspace. If you had made additional changes, Excel would ask if you wanted to save the file before closing it. This prevents the accidental closing of a file that has not been saved first.

Note: If you are running short on lab time, this is an appropriate place to end your session.

Opening an Existing Workbook

After attending your meeting, you continued working on the Café forecast. To see what has been done so far, you will open the workbook file named ex01_Forecast2.

1 ● Choose **V**iew/Tas**k** Pane.

● Click 🖆 More Workbooks (in the task pane).

Another Method

The menu equivalent is **F**ile/**O**pen and the keyboard shortcut is Ctrl + O. You can also click 🖆 Open in the Standard toolbar.

Additional Information

The **F**ile/**N**ew command or ☐ Blank Workbook on the New Workbook task pane opens a blank new workbook.

Your screen should be similar to Figure 1.26

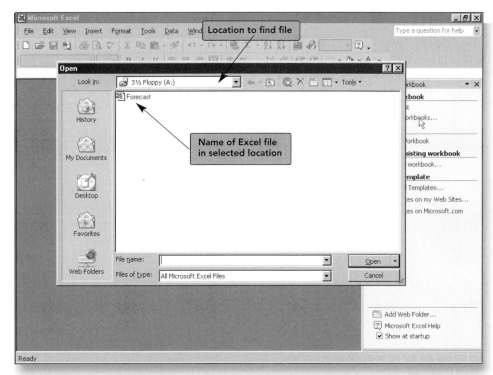

Figure 1.26

In the Open dialog box, you specify the location and name of the file you want to open. The Look In drop-down list box displays the last specified location, in this case the location where you saved the Forecast workbook. The large list box displays the names of all Excel workbooks with the file extensions displayed in the Files of type box. As in the Save As dialog box, the Places bar can be used to quickly access recently used files. When selecting a file to open, it may be helpful to see a preview of the file first. To do this, you can change the dialog box view.

2 ● If necessary, select the location containing your data files from the Look In drop-down list box.

● Open the  Views drop-down list.

● Choose Preview.

● Select ex01_Forecast2.

Your screen should be similar to Figure 1.27

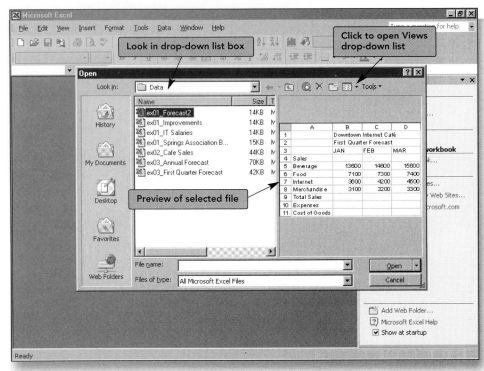

Figure 1.27

A preview of the selected file is displayed in the right pane of the dialog box. To return the view to the list of file names and open this file,

3 ● Open the  Views drop-down list.

● Choose List.

● Select ex01_Forecast2.

● Click 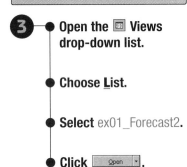 Open .

Your screen should be similar to Figure 1.28

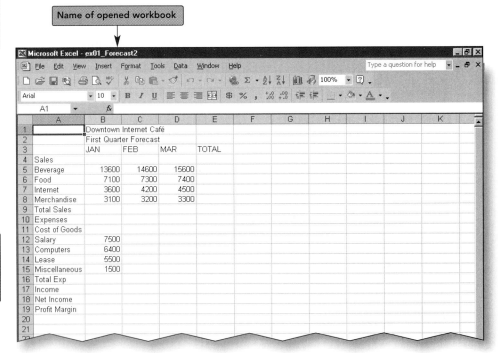

Figure 1.28

The workbook is opened and displayed in the workbook window. The workbook contains the additional sales values for February and March, the expense row headings, and several of the expense values for the month of January.

Duplicating Cell Contents

Next, you want to enter the estimated expenses for salary, computers, lease, and miscellaneous for February and March. They are the same as the January expense numbers. Because these values are the same, instead of entering the same number repeatedly into each cell you can quickly copy the contents of one cell to another. You also want to move information from one location in the worksheet to another.

concept 5

Copy and Move

5 The contents of worksheet cells can be duplicated (copied) or moved to other locations in the worksheet or between worksheets, saving you time by not having to retype the same information. An entry that is copied leaves the original, called the **source** or **copy area**, and inserts a duplicate at a new location, called the **destination** or **paste area**. A selection that is moved is removed or cut from the original location in the source and inserted at the destination.

When a selection is moved or copied, the selection is stored in the system Clipboard, a temporary Windows storage area in memory. The system Clipboard contents are then inserted at the new location specified by the location of the insertion point.

Office XP also includes an Office Clipboard that can store up to 24 items that have been cut or copied. This allows you to insert multiple items from various Office files and paste all or part of the collection of items into another file.

Using Copy and Paste

When using Copy and Paste, you first use the Copy command to copy the cell contents to the system Clipboard. Then you move to the new location where you want the contents copied and use the Paste command to insert the system Clipboard contents into the selected cells. Be careful when pasting to the new location because any existing entries are replaced.

To use the Copy command, you first must select the cell or cells in the source containing the data to be copied. You will copy the value in cell B12 into cells C12 and D12.

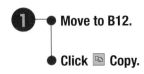

● Move to B12.

● Click 🔲 Copy.

Another Method

The menu equivalent is Edit/Copy and the shortcut key is Ctrl + C. Copy is also available on the shortcut menu.

Your screen should be similar to Figure 1.29

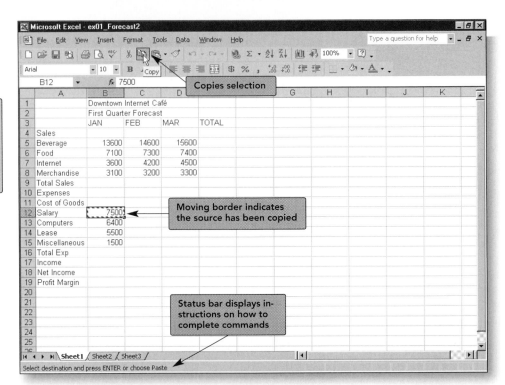

Figure 1.29

A moving border identifies the source and indicates that the contents have been copied to the system Clipboard. The instructions displayed in the status bar tell you to select the destination where you want the contents copied. You will copy it to cell C12.

● Move to C12.

● Click 🔲 Paste.

Another Method

The menu equivalent is Edit/Paste and the shortcut key is Ctrl + V. Paste is also available on the shortcut menu.

Your screen should be similar to Figure 1.30

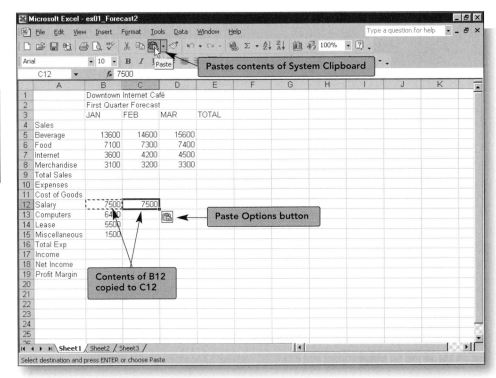

Figure 1.30

The contents of the system Clipboard are inserted at the specified destination location. Each time the paste command is used, the 🔲 Paste Options button is available. Clicking on the button opens the Paste Options menu that allows you to control how the information you are pasting is inserted.

3 ● **Click  Paste Options.**

Your screen should be similar to Figure 1.31

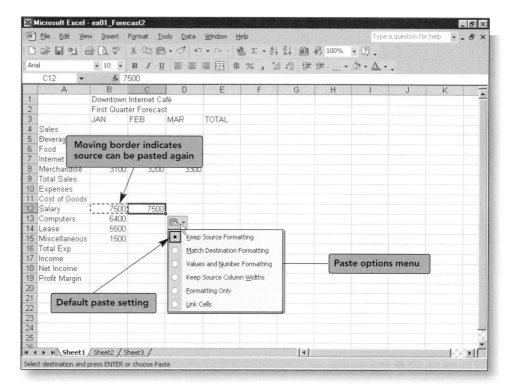

Figure 1.31

The selected option, Keep Source Formatting, will insert the copy exactly as it appears in the source. This is the default paste setting and is appropriate for this and most situations.

4 ● **Click outside the menu to close it.**

Additional Information

You can cancel a moving border and clear the System Clipboard contents by pressing Esc.

The moving border is still displayed indicating the system Clipboard still contains the copied entry. Now you can complete the data for the Salary row by pasting the value again from the system Clipboard into cell D12. While the moving border is still displayed, you can also simply press ⏎Enter to paste. However, as this method clears the contents of the system Clipboard immediately, it can only be used once.

5 ● Move to D12.

● Press ⏎Enter.

Your screen should be similar to Figure 1.32

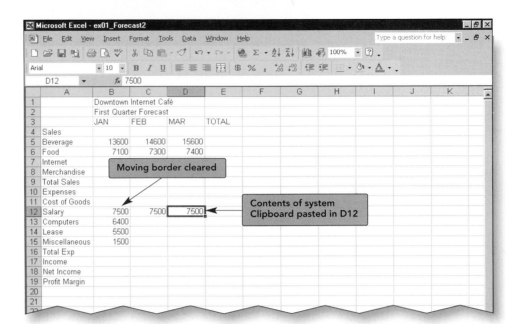

Moving border cleared

Contents of system Clipboard pasted in D12

Figure 1.32

The contents of the system Clipboard are inserted at the specified destination location and the moving border is cleared indicating the system Clipboard is empty.

Selecting a Range

Now you need to copy the Computers value in cell B13 to February and March. You could copy and paste the contents individually into each cell. It is much faster, however, to select a paste area that consists of multiple cells, called a range, and paste the contents to all cells in the selection at once.

concept 6

Range

6 A selection consisting of two or more cells is a **range**. The cells in a range can be adjacent or nonadjacent. An **adjacent range** is a rectangular block of adjoining cells. A **nonadjacent range** is two or more selected cells or ranges that are not adjoining. In the example shown below, the shaded areas show valid adjacent and nonadjacent ranges.

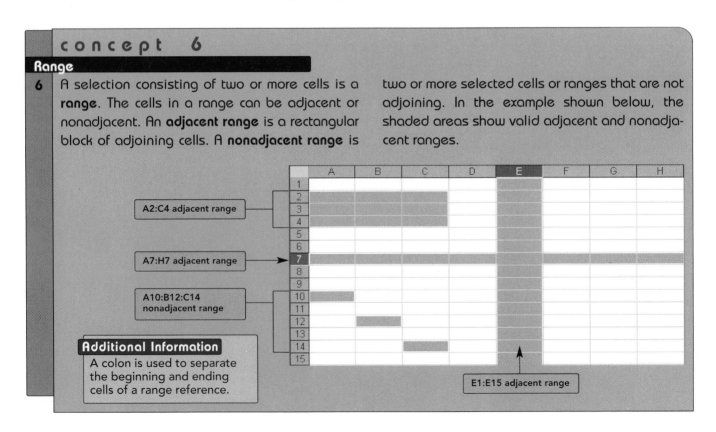

A2:C4 adjacent range

A7:H7 adjacent range

A10:B12:C14 nonadjacent range

E1:E15 adjacent range

Additional Information
A colon is used to separate the beginning and ending cells of a range reference.

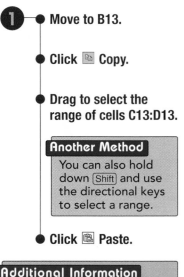

To complete the data for the Computer row, you want to copy the value in cell B13 to the system Clipboard and then copy the system Clipboard contents to the adjacent range of cells C13 through D13. To select an adjacent range, drag the mouse from one corner of the range to the other. If the range is large, it is often easier to select the range by clicking on the first cell of the range, then hold down ⬆Shift while clicking on the last cell of the range.

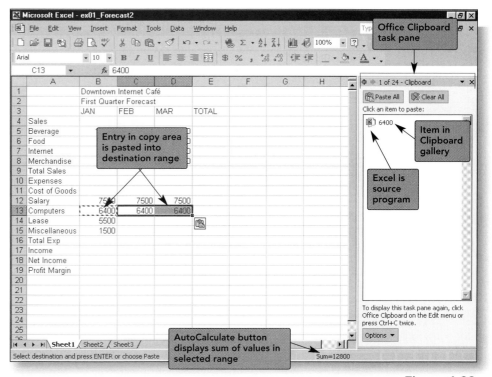

Figure 1.33

The destination range is highlighted and identified by a dark border surrounding the selected cells. The entry copied from cell B13 was pasted into the selected destination range. Also notice the AutoCalculate button in the status bar is now active. This button displays the sum of values in a selected range of cells. It can also display the average, count, minimum, or maximum values in a range by selecting the appropriate option from the button's shortcut menu.

Also, because this is the second consecutive copy you have performed in the workbook, the Office Clipboard task pane automatically opened. As items are copied, an entry representing the copied item is displayed in the

Clipboard gallery. The newest item appears at the top of the gallery. Each entry includes an icon representing the source Office program and a portion of copied text. Because the previous item you copied was cleared from the System Clipboard, only one item is displayed in the gallery. You can click an item in the gallery to paste it or use Paste All to paste all items in the gallery.

Using the Fill Handle

Next you will copy the January Lease expenses to cells C14 through D14 and Miscellaneous expenses to cells C15 through D15. You can copy both values at the same time across the row by first specifying a range as the source. Another way to copy is to drag the **fill handle**, the black box in the lower-right corner of the selection.

1 ● Drag to select cells B14:B15.

● Point to the fill handle and when the mouse pointer is a +, drag the mouse to extend the selection to cells C14:D15.

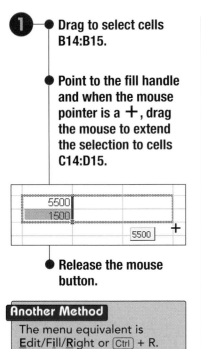

● Release the mouse button.

Another Method

The menu equivalent is Edit/Fill/Right or Ctrl + R.

Your screen should be similar to Figure 1.34

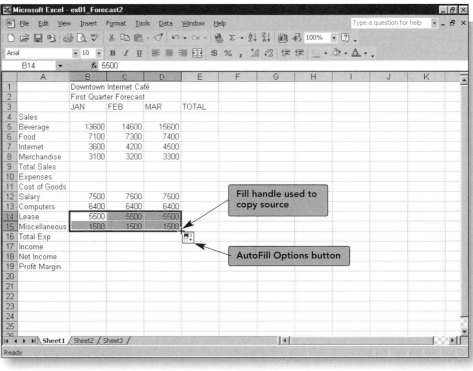

Figure 1.34

The range of cells to the right of the source is filled with the same value as in the source cell. The Fill command does not copy the source to the system Clipboard and therefore an item for the copied selection does not appear in the Office Clipboard task pane gallery. Because the Office Clipboard task pane is no longer needed, it closes automatically. Additionally, you cannot paste the source multiple times. The AutoFill Options button menu commands can be used to modify how the fill operation was performed.

Inserting Copied Cells

You also decide to include another row of month headings above the expense columns to make the worksheet data easier to read. To do this quickly, you can insert copied data between existing data. To indicate where to place the copied text, you move the cell pointer to the upper-left cell of the area where you want the selection inserted and specify the direction you want to shift the surrounding cells.

1 ● Copy the contents of cells A3:E3.

● Move to A10.

● Choose **Insert/Copied Cells.**

● If necessary, select **Shift Cells Down** from the Insert Paste dialog box.

● Click OK on the Task Pane to close it.

● Press Esc to clear the moving border.

Your screen should be similar to Figure 1.35

Additional Information

You can insert cut selections between existing cells by choosing Cut **C**ells from the **I**nsert menu.

Additional Information

Holding down Ctrl while dragging a selection copies it to the new location.

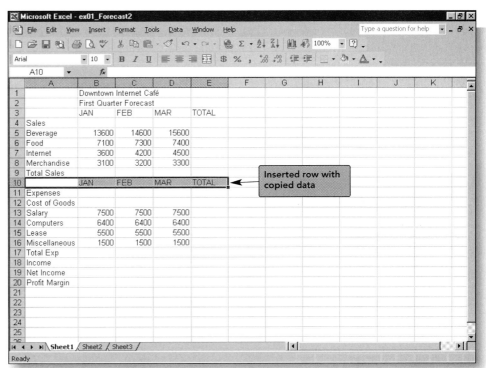

Figure 1.35

The copied data is inserted into the existing row (10) and all entries below are moved down one row.

Moving Entries

You also decide the profit margin row of data would stand out more if a blank row separated it from the net income row. You could remove the cell contents using Edit/Cut and then paste the contents from the system Clipboard into the new location. Alternatively, you can drag the cell border to move the cell contents. Dragging is quickest and most useful when the distance between cells is short and they are visible within the window, whereas Cut and Paste is best for long-distance moves.

1 ● **Move to cell A20.**

● **Point to the border of the selection and when the mouse pointer shape is ⬚, drag the selection down one row to cell A21 and release the mouse button.**

Additional Information

As you drag, an outline of the cell selection appears and the mouse pointer displays the cell reference to show its new location in the worksheet.

● **Choose File/Save As and save the changes you have made to the workbook as** Forecast3.

Your screen should be similar to Figure 1.36

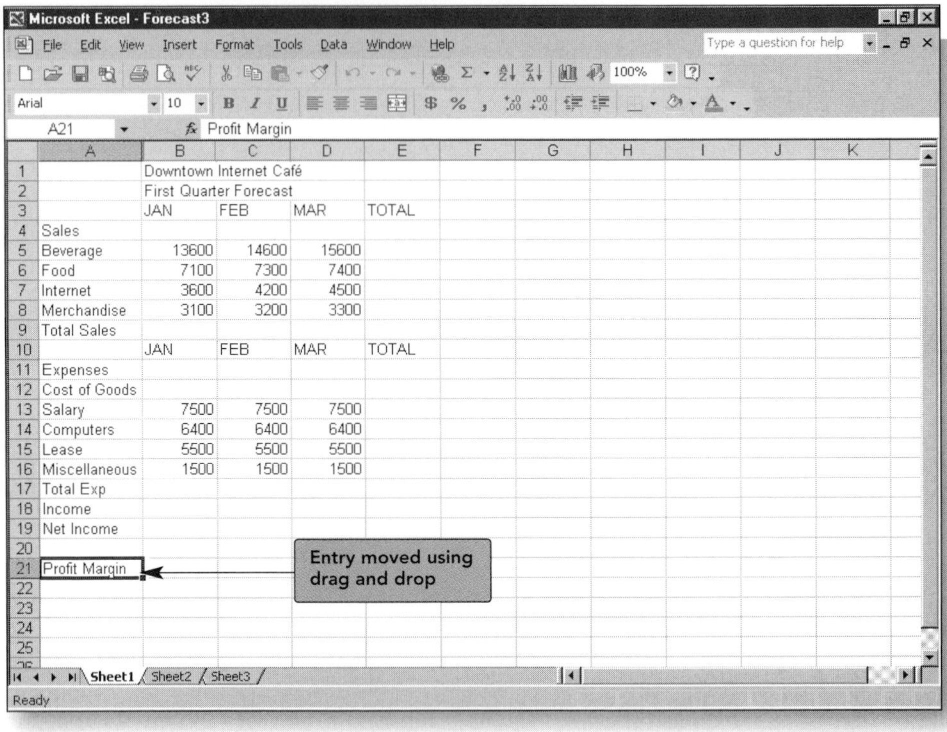

Figure 1.36

The cell contents was moved into cell A21 and cleared from the original cell.

Review of Copying and Moving Methods

To review, you have learned three methods to copy or move an entry:

1. Use the Copy, Cut and Paste commands: Edit/Copy (Ctrl + C) or ▣, Edit/Cut (Ctrl + X) or ✂, and Edit/Paste (Ctrl + V) or ▣.

2. Use the Edit/Fill command: Right, Left, Up, or Down or drag the fill handle.

3. Drag the cell border of the selection to move. Hold down Ctrl while dragging a selection to copy.

When you use the Copy and Cut commands, the contents are copied to the system Clipboard and can be copied to any location in the worksheet, another workbook, or another application multiple times. When you use Edit/Fill or drag the fill handle, the destination must be in the same row or column as the source, and the source is not copied to the system Clipboard. Dragging the cell border to move or copy also does not copy the source to the system Clipboard.

Working with Formulas

The remaining entries that need to be made in the worksheet are formula entries.

concept 7

Formulas

7 A formula is an equation that performs a calculation on data contained in a worksheet. A formula always begins with an equal sign (=) and uses the following arithmetic **operators** to specify the type of numeric operation to perform: + (addition), – (subtraction), / (division), * (multiplication), % (percent), ^ (exponentiation).

In a formula that contains more than one operator, Excel calculates the formula from left to right and performs the calculation in the following order: percent, exponentiation, multiplication and division, and addition and subtraction (see Example A). If a formula contains operators with the same precedence (for example, addition and subtraction), they are again evaluated from left to right. The order of precedence can be overridden by enclosing the operation you want performed first in parentheses (see Example B). When there are multiple sets of parentheses, Excel evaluates them working from the innermost set of parentheses out.

Example A: =5*4–3   Result is 17 (5 times 4 to get 20, and then subtract 3 for a total of 17)

Example B: =5*(4–3)   Result is 5 (4 minus 3 to get 1, and then 1 times 5 for a total of 5)

The values on which a numeric formula performs a calculation are called **operands**. Numbers or cell references can be operands in a formula. Usually cell references are used, and when the numeric entries in the referenced cell(s) change, the result of the formula is automatically recalculated.

Entering Formulas

The first formula you will enter will calculate the total Beverage sales for January through March (cell E5) by summing the numbers in cells B5 through D5. You will use cell references in the formula as the operands and the + arithmetic operator to specify addition. A formula is entered in the cell where you want the calculated value to be displayed. As you enter the formula, to help you keep track of the cell references Excel identifies the referenced cell by adding a color to the cell border and using the same color for the cell reference in the formula.

① ● Move to E5.

● Type =b5+c5+d5.

Additional Information

Cell references can be typed in either uppercase or lowercase letters. Spaces between parts of the formula are optional.

● Press [Ctrl] + [←Enter]
or click ☑.

HAVING TROUBLE?

If you enter a formula incorrectly, Excel displays an error in the cell or a message box proposing a correction.

Your screen should be similar to Figure 1.37

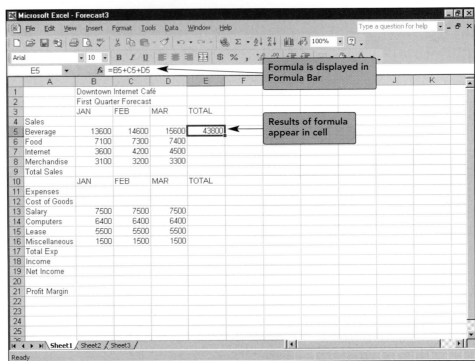

Figure 1.37

The number 43800 is displayed in cell E5 and the formula that calculates this value is displayed in the formula bar.

Copying Formulas

The formulas to calculate the total sales for rows 5 through 8 can be entered next. Just as you can with text and numeric entries, you can copy formulas from one cell to another.

① ● Copy the formula in cell E5 to cells E6 through E8 using any of the copying methods.

● Move to E6.

Your screen should be similar to Figure 1.38

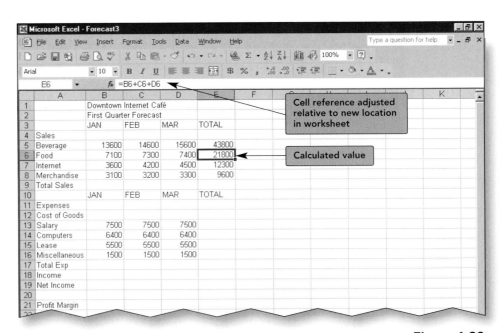

Figure 1.38

The calculated result, 21800 is displayed in the cell. The formula displayed in the formula bar is =B6+C6+D6. The formula to calculate the Food total sales is not an exact duplicate of the formula used to calculate the Beverage total sales (=B5+C5+D5). Instead, the cells referenced in the formula have been changed to reflect the new location of the formula in row 6. This is because the references in the formula are relative references.

concept 8

Relative Reference

8 A **relative reference** is a cell or range reference in a formula whose location is interpreted by Excel in relation to the position of the cell that contains the formula. When a formula is copied, the referenced cells in the formula automatically adjust to reflect the new worksheet location. The relative relationship between the referenced cell and the new location is maintained. Because relative references automatically adjust for the new location, the relative references in a copied formula refer to different cells than the references in the original formula. The relationship between cells in both the copied and pasted formula is the same although the cell references are different.

For example, in the figure here, cell A1 references the value in cell A4 (in this case, 10). If the formula in A1 is copied to B2, the reference for B2 is adjusted to the value in cell B5 (in this case, 20).

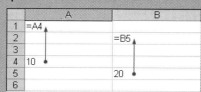

2 ● Move to cell E7 and then to cell E8.

Your screen should be similar to Figure 1.39

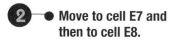

If you move cells containing formulas, the formulas are not adjusted relative to their new worksheet location.

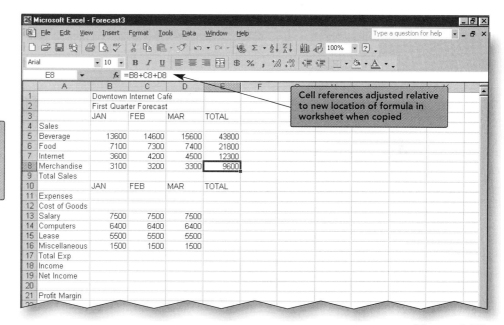

Cell references adjusted relative to new location of formula in worksheet when copied

Figure 1.39

The formulas in these cells have also changed to reflect the new row location and to appropriately calculate the total based on the sales.

Entering Functions

Next you will calculate the monthly total sales. The formula to calculate the total sales for January needs to be entered in cell B9 and copied across the row. You could use a formula similar to the formula used to calculate the category sales in column E. The formula would be =B5+B6+B7+B8. However, it is faster and more accurate to use a function.

concept 9

Functions

1   **Functions** are prewritten formulas that perform certain types of calculations automatically. The **syntax** or rules of structure for entering all functions is:

=function name (argument1, argument2,...)

The function name identifies the type of calculation to be performed. Most functions require that you enter one or more arguments following the function name. An **argument** is the data the function uses to perform the calculation. The type of data the function requires depends upon the type of calculation being performed. Most commonly, the argument consists of numbers or references to cells that contain numbers. The argument is enclosed in parentheses, and commas separate multiple arguments. If a function starts the formula, enter an equal sign before the function name (=SUM(D5:F5)/25).

Excel includes several hundred functions divided into nine categories. Some common functions and the results they calculate are shown in the following table.

Category	Function	Calculates
Financial	PMT	Calculates the payment for a loan based on constant payments and a constant interest rate
	PV	Returns the present value of an investment; the total amount that a series of future payments is worth now
Time & Date	TODAY	Returns the serial number that represents today's date
	DATE	Returns the serial number of a particular date
	NOW	Returns the serial number of the current date and time
Math & Trig	SUM	Adds all the numbers in a range of cells
	ABS	Returns the absolute value of a number, a number without its sign
Statistical	AVERAGE	Returns the average (arithmetic mean) of its arguments
	MAX	Returns the largest value in a set of values; ignores logical values and text
Lookup & Reference	COLUMNS	Returns the number of columns in an array or reference
	CHOOSE	Chooses a value or action to perform from a list of values, based on an index number

Category	Function	Calculates
Database	DSUM	Adds the numbers in the field (column) or records in the database that match the conditions you specify
	DAVERAGE	Averages the values in a column in a list or database that match conditions you specify
Text	DOLLAR	Converts a number to text, using currency format
	UPPER	Converts text to uppercase
Logical	IF	Returns one value if a condition you specify evaluates to True and another value if it evaluates to False
	AND	Returns True if all its arguments are True; returns False if any arguments are False
Information	ISLOGICAL	Returns True if value is a logical value, either True or False
	ISREF	Returns True if value is a reference

You will use the SUM function to calculate the total sales for January. Because the SUM function is the most commonly used function, it has its own toolbar button.

● Move to B9.

● Click Σ AutoSum.

Another Method

Pressing [Alt] + = is the keyboard shortcut for AutoSum.

Your screen should be similar to Figure 1.40

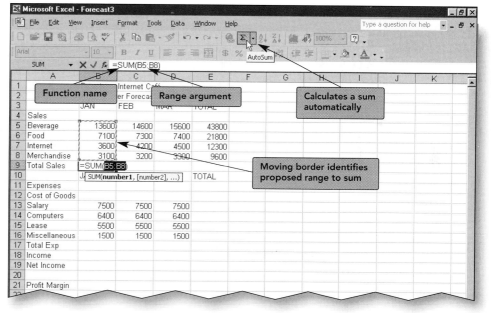

Figure 1.40

Additional Information

The AutoSum button can also calculate a grand total if your worksheet contains subtotals. Select a cell below or to the right of a cell that contains a subtotal and then click Σ AutoSum.

Excel automatically proposes a range based upon the data above or to the left of the active cell. The name of the function followed by the range argument enclosed in parentheses is displayed in the formula bar. To accept the proposed range and enter the function,

2 ● **Click** ☑ **Enter.**

*Your screen should be
similar to Figure 1.41*

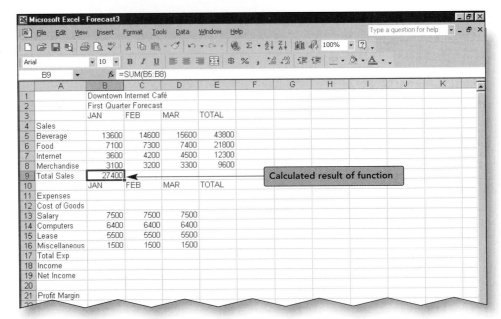

Figure 1.41

The result, 27400, calculated by the SUM function is displayed in cell B9.
Next you need to calculate the total sales for February and March and the
Total column.

3 ● **Copy the function from
cell B9 to cells C9
through E9.**

● **Move to C9.**

*Your screen should be
similar to Figure 1.42*

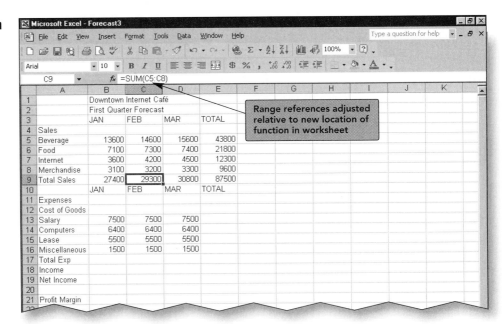

Figure 1.42

The result calculated by the function, 29300, is displayed in cell C9 and the
copied function is displayed in the formula bar. The range reference in the
function adjusted relative to its new cell location because it is a relative
reference.

Using Pointing to Enter a Formula

Next you will enter the formula to calculate the cost of goods sold. These numbers are estimated by using a formula to calculate the number as a percent of sales. As a general rule, the Café calculates beverage expenses at 25 percent of beverage sales and food expenses at 50 percent of food sales.

Rather than typing in the cell references for the formula, you will enter them by selecting the worksheet cells. In addition, to make the process of entering and copying entries even easier, you can enter data into the first cell of a range and have it copied to all other cells in the range at the same time by using [Ctrl] + [←Enter] to complete the entry. You will use this feature to enter the formulas to calculate the beverage expenses for January through March. This formula needs to first calculate the beverage cost of goods at 25 percent and add it to the food cost of goods calculated at 50 percent.

1 ● Select B12:D12.

● Type =.

● Click cell B5.

Additional Information

Even when a range is selected, you can still point to specify cells in the formula. You can also use the direction keys to move to the cell.

Your screen should be similar to Figure 1.43

Mode indicator

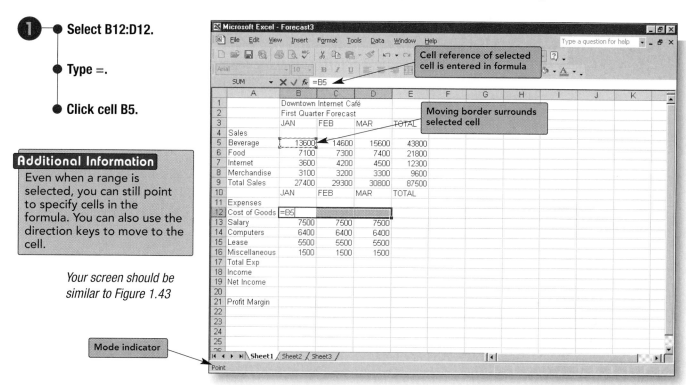

Figure 1.43

Notice that the status bar displays the current mode as Point. This tells you the program is allowing you to select cells by highlighting them. The cell reference, B5, is entered following the = sign. You will complete the formula by entering the percentage value to multiply by and adding the Food percentage to the formula.

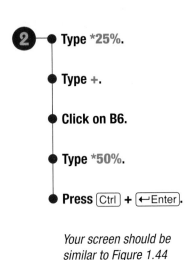

2 ● Type *25%.

● Type +.

● Click on B6.

● Type *50%.

● Press Ctrl + ←Enter.

Your screen should be similar to Figure 1.44

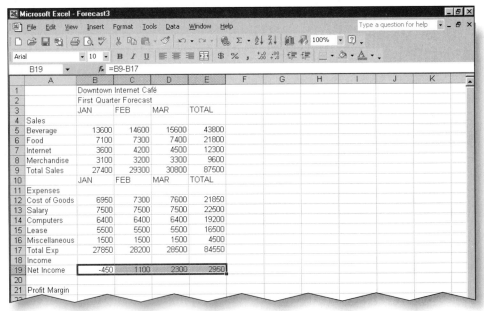

Formula entered into all cells of range

Figure 1.44

The formula to calculate the January cost of goods expense was entered in cell B12 and copied to all cells of the selected range. You can now calculate the total expenses in row 17 and column E. To do this quickly, you will pre-select the range and use the Σ AutoSum button. Then you will enter the formula to calculate the net income. Net income is calculated by subtracting total expenses from total sales.

Additional Information

The cells in the selected range can be adjacent or nonadjacent.

3 ● Select B12 through E17.

● Click Σ AutoSum.

● In a similar manner, enter sum functions to calculate the expenses in column E.

● Select B19 through E19.

● Enter the formula =B9–B17.

● Press Ctrl + ←Enter.

Your screen should be similar to Figure 1.45

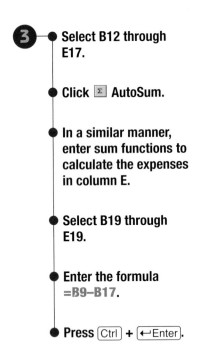

Figure 1.45

The formula is quickly entered into all cells of the range. The final formula you need enter is to calculate the profit margin.

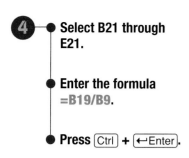

4 • **Select B21 through E21.**

• **Enter the formula =B19/B9.**

• **Press** `Ctrl` + `←Enter`.

Your screen should be similar to Figure 1.46

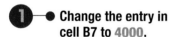

Figure 1.46

The profit margins are calculated and displayed in cells B20 through E20.

Recalculating the Worksheet

Now that you have created the worksheet structure and entered some sample data for the forecasted sales for the first quarter, you want to test the formulas to verify they are operating correctly. A simple way to do this is to use a calculator to verify that the correct result is displayed. You can then further test the worksheet by changing values and verifying that all cells containing formulas that reference the value are appropriately recalculated.

After considering the sales estimates for the three months, you decide that the estimated Internet sales for January are too low and you want to increase this number from 3600 to 4000.

1 • **Change the entry in cell B7 to 4000.**

Your screen should be similar to Figure 1.47

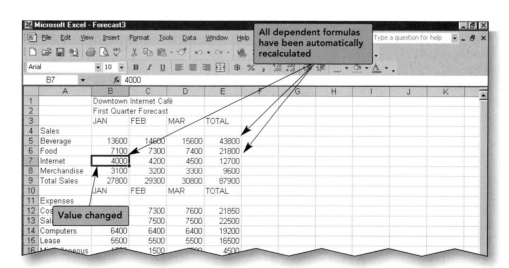

Figure 1.47

The Internet total in cell E7 has been automatically recalculated. The number displayed is now 12700. Likewise, the January total in cell B9 and the grand total in cell E9 have increased by 400 to reflect the change in cell B7.

concept 10

Recalculation

10 Whenever a number in a referenced cell in a formula changes, Excel automatically **recalculates** all formulas that are dependent on the changed value. Because only those formulas directly affected by a change in the data are recalculated, the time it takes to recalculate the workbook is reduced. Without this feature, in large worksheets it could take several minutes to recalculate all formulas each time a number is changed in the worksheet. Recalculation is one of the most powerful features of electronic worksheets.

The formulas in the worksheet are correctly calculating the desired result. The Sales portion of the worksheet is now complete.

Inserting Rows

Finally, you realize you forgot to include a row for the Advertising expenses. To add this data, you will insert a blank row below the Lease row. To indicate where you want to insert a single blank row, move the cell pointer to the row immediately below the row where you want the new row inserted. If you want to insert multiple rows, select a range of rows and Excel inserts the same number of rows you selected in the range.

Additional Information

To delete a row or column, move to it and choose Edit/Delete/Entire Row or Entire Column.

1
- Move to A15.
- Choose Insert/Rows.
- Enter the label Advertising in cell A15 and the value 1000 in cells B15 through D15.
- Copy the function from cell E14 to E15 to calculate the Total Advertising expense.
- Move to cell B18.
- Click 💾 Save to save the worksheet using the same file name.

Your screen should be similar to Figure 1.48

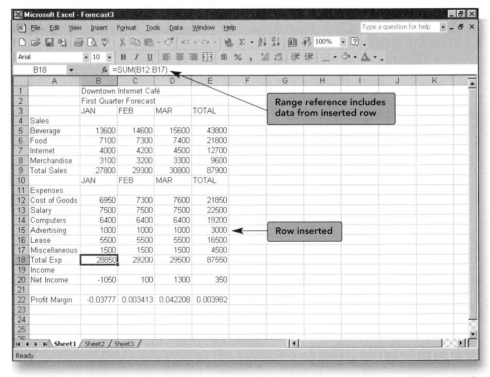

Figure 1.48

The range in the formula to calculate monthly total expenses in row 18 has been revised to include the data in the inserted row. Additionally, the net income in row 20 and profit margin in row 22 have been recalculated to reflect the change in data.

Formatting the Worksheet

Now that many of the worksheet values are entered, you want to improve the appearance of the worksheet by changing the format of the headings. **Format** controls how information is displayed in a cell and includes such features as font (different type styles and sizes), color, patterns, borders, and **number formats** such as commas and dollar signs. Applying different formats greatly improves both the appearance and readability of the data in a worksheet.

Changing Cell Alignment

You decide the column headings would look better if they were right-aligned in their cell spaces. Then they would appear over the numbers in the column. Alignment is a basic format setting that is used in most worksheets.

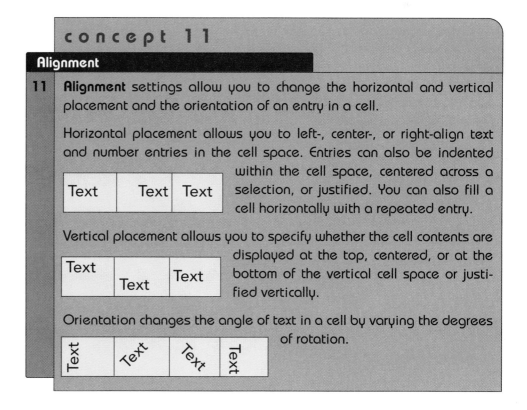

concept 11

Alignment

11 **Alignment** settings allow you to change the horizontal and vertical placement and the orientation of an entry in a cell.

Horizontal placement allows you to left-, center-, or right-align text and number entries in the cell space. Entries can also be indented within the cell space, centered across a selection, or justified. You can also fill a cell horizontally with a repeated entry.

Vertical placement allows you to specify whether the cell contents are displayed at the top, centered, or at the bottom of the vertical cell space or justified vertically.

Orientation changes the angle of text in a cell by varying the degrees of rotation.

First you will change the column heading in cell B3 to right-aligned.

① • **Move to cell B3.**

• **Choose Format/C<u>e</u>lls.**

Another Method
The shortcut key is
[Ctrl] + 1. Format Cells
is also an option on
the shortcut menu.

• **Open the Alignment
tab.**

*Your screen should be
similar to Figure 1.49*

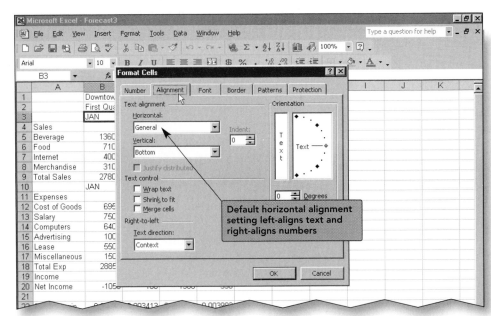

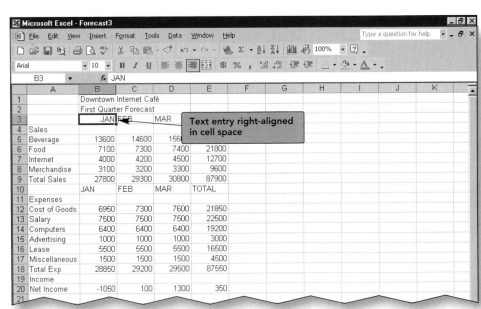

Figure 1.49

The Alignment tab shows the default workbook template alignment settings. The horizontal alignment setting is General. This setting left-aligns text entries and right-aligns number entries. The vertical alignment is set to bottom for both types of entries and the orientation is set to zero degrees rotation from the horizontal position. You want to change the horizontal alignment of the entry to right-aligned.

② • **Open the Horizontal
drop-down list box.**

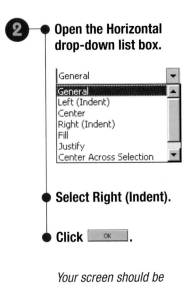

• **Select Right (Indent).**

• **Click** OK .

*Your screen should be
similar to Figure 1.50*

Figure 1.50

A quicker way to change the alignment is to use the Formatting toolbar or keyboard shortcuts shown on the next page.

Formatting toolbar	Keyboard	Action
≣	Ctrl + L	Left align entry
≣	Ctrl + C	Center entry
≣	Ctrl + J	Right align entry

You can quickly align a range of cells by selecting the range and then using the command or button. A quick way to select a range of filled cells is to hold down ⇧Shift and double-click on the edge of the active cell in the direction in which you want the range expanded. For example, to select the range to the right of the active cell, you would double-click the right border. You will use this method to select and right-align the remaining column entries.

Additional Information

If you do not hold down ⇧Shift while double-clicking on a border, the cell selector moves to the last-used cell in the direction indicated.

3 ● **Move to cell C3.**

● **Hold down ⇧Shift and double-click the right cell border of cell C3.**

HAVING TROUBLE?
The mouse pointer must be ⬚ when you click the cell border.

● **Click ≣ Align Right.**

● **In a similar manner, right align the entries in row 10.**

Your screen should be similar to Figure 1.51

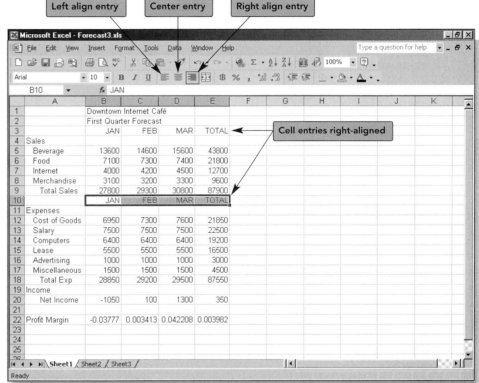

Figure 1.51

The entries in the selected range are right-aligned in their cell spaces.

Indenting Entries

Next you would like to indent the row headings in cells A5 through A8 and A12 through A17 from the left edge of the cell. You want to indent the headings in both ranges at the same time. To select nonadjacent cells or cell ranges, after selecting the first cell or range hold down Ctrl while selecting each additional cell or range. You will select the cells and indent their contents.

Additional Information
You can also select entire nonadjacent rows or columns by holding down Ctrl while selecting the rows or columns.

1 ● **Select A5 through A8.**

● **Hold down** `Ctrl`.

● **Select A12 through A17.**

● **Release** `Ctrl`.

● **Click** 🔲 **Increase Indent.**

Another Method

The menu equivalent is Format/Cells/Alignment/Horizontal/Left(Indent)/1.

Your screen should be similar to Figure 1.52

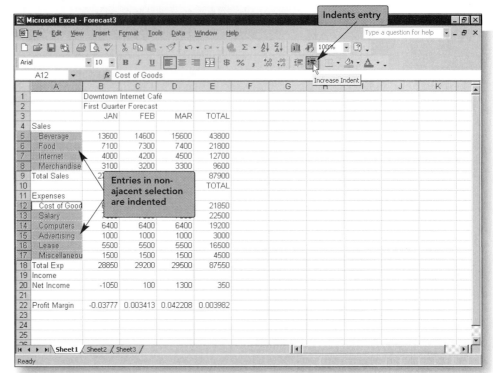

Figure 1.52

Each entry in the selected range is indented two spaces from the left edge of the cell. You would also like to indent the Total Sales, Total Exp, and Net Income headings four spaces.

2 ● **Select A9, A18, and A20.**

● **Click** 🔲 **Increase Indent twice.**

Your screen should be similar to Figure 1.53

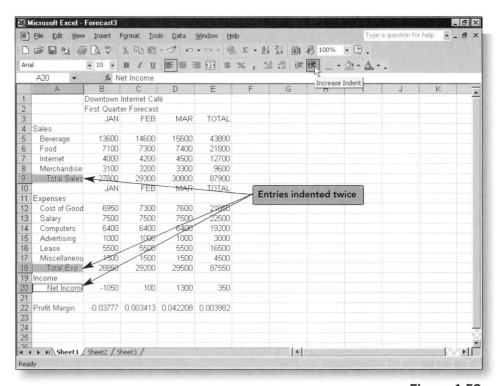

Figure 1.53

Centering across a Selection

Next you want to center the worksheet titles across columns A through E so they are centered over the worksheet data.

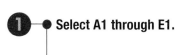

Select A1 through E1.

Click 🔳 Merge and Center.

Another Method

The menu equivalent is Format/Cells/Alignment/Horizontal/Center Across Selection/Merge cells.

Your screen should be similar to Figure 1.54

Another Method

You could also use Format/Cells/Alignment/Horizontal/Center Across Selection to center the contents across a range. The cells however, are not merged and the cell contents to be centered must be in the leftmost cell of the selected range.

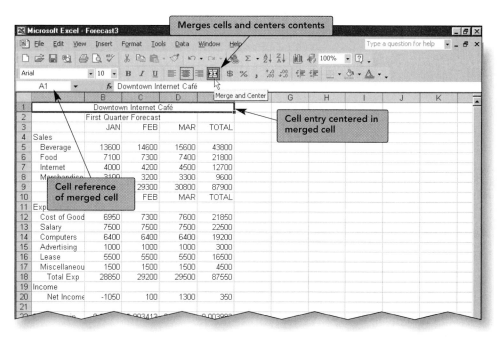

Figure 1.54

The contents of the range are centered in the range. Additionally, the five cells in the selection have been combined into a single large **merged cell**. The cell reference for a merged cell is the upper-left cell in the original selected range, in this case A1. When creating a merged cell and centering the contents, only the contents of the upper-leftmost data in the selected range are centered. If other cells in the range contained data, it would be deleted.

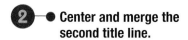

Center and merge the second title line.

Your screen should be similar to Figure 1.55

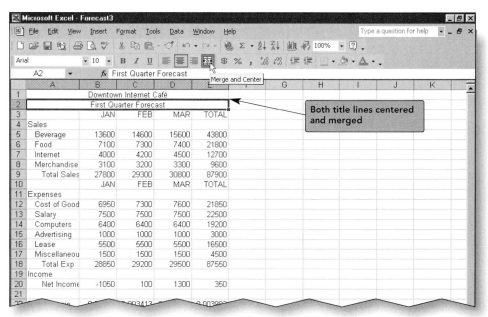

Figure 1.55

Once cells have been merged, you can split them back into their original cells by selecting the merged cell and clicking 🔳 to unmerge the cells.

Changing Fonts and Font Styles

Finally, you want to improve the worksheet appearance by enhancing the appearance of the title. One way to do this is to change the font and font size used in the title.

concept 12

Fonts

12 A **font**, also commonly referred to as a **typeface**, is a set of characters with a specific design. The designs have names such as Times New Roman and Courier. Using fonts as a design element can add interest to your document and give readers visual cues to help them find information quickly.

There are two basic types of fonts, serif and sans serif. **Serif** fonts have a flair at the base of each letter that visually leads the reader to the next letter. Two common serif fonts are Roman and Times New Roman. Serif fonts generally are used in paragraphs. **Sans serif** fonts do not have a flair at the base of each letter. Arial and

Helvetica are two common sans serif fonts. Because sans serif fonts have a clean look, they are often used for headings in documents. It is good practice to use only two types of fonts in a document, one for text and one for headings. Too many styles can make your document look cluttered and unprofessional.

Each font has one or more sizes. **Size** is the height and width of the character and is commonly measured in **points**, abbreviated pt. One point equals about 1/72 inch, and text in most documents is 10 pt or 12 pt.

Here are several examples of the same text in various fonts and sizes.

Typeface	Font Size (12 pt/18 pt)
Arial (Sans Serif)	This is 12 pt. This is 18 pt.
Courier New (Serif)	This is 12 pt. This is 18 pt.
Times New Roman (Serif)	This is 12 pt. This is 18 pt.

1 ● **Select A1 and A2.**

● **Open the** [Times New Roman] **Font drop-down list box.**

Another Method
The menu equivalent is Format/Cells/Font/Font.

Your screen should be similar to Figure 1.56

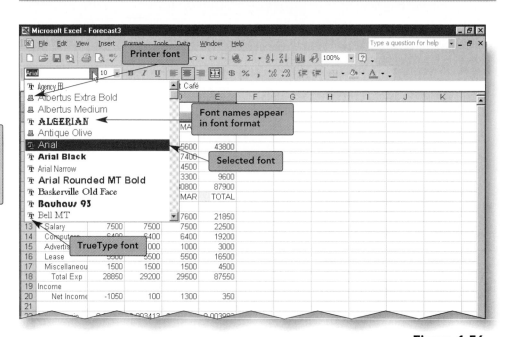

Figure 1.56

The Font drop-down menu displays examples of the available fonts on your system in alphabetical order. The default worksheet font, Arial, is highlighted. Notice the TT preceding the font name. This indicates the font is a TrueType font. TrueType fonts appear onscreen as they will appear when printed. They are installed when Windows is installed. Fonts that are preceded with a blank space or ⚏ are printer fonts. These fonts are supported by your printer and are displayed as closely as possible to how they will appear onscreen, but may not match exactly when printed.

2 ● **Scroll the list and select Times New Roman.**

Your screen should be similar to Figure 1.57

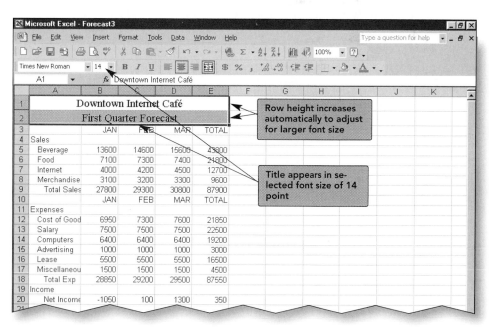

Figure 1.57

The title appears in the selected typeface and the Font button displays the name of the font in the active cell. Next you will increase the font size to 14.

3 ● **Open the [10] Font Size drop-down list box.**

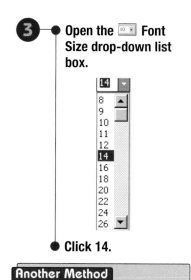

● **Click 14.**

Another Method

The menu equivalent is Format/Cells/Font/Size.

Your screen should be similar to Figure 1.58

Figure 1.58

Notice that the height of the row has increased to accommodate the larger font size of the heading.

Applying Character Effects

In addition to changing font and font size, you can apply different **character effects** to enhance the appearance of text. The table below describes some of the effects and their uses.

Format	Example	Use
Bold	**Bold**	Adds emphasis
Italic	*Italic*	Adds emphasis
Underline	Underline	Adds emphasis
Strikethrough	~~Strikethrough~~	Indicates words to be deleted
Superscript	"To be or not to be."[1]	Used in footnotes and formulas
Subscript	H_2O	Used in formulas
Color	**Color Color Color**	Adds interest

You want to add bold, italic, and underlines to several worksheet entries. First you will bold the two title lines that are already selected.

1 ● **Click** **B** **Bold.**

Another Method

The menu equivalent is Format/Cells/Font/Font Style/Bold and the keyboard shortcut is Ctrl + B.

Your screen should be similar to Figure 1.59

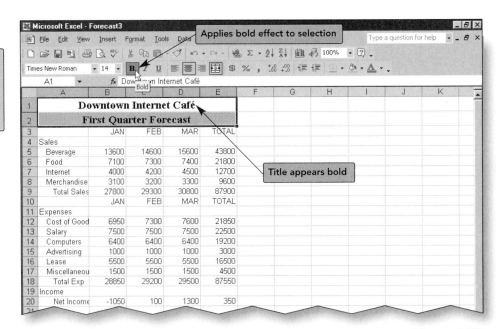

Figure 1.59

Next you would like to bold, underline, and italicize some of the other entries in the worksheet.

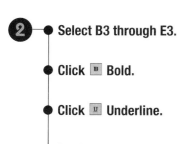

2 ● **Select B3 through E3.**

● **Click** B **Bold.**

● **Click** U **Underline.**

● **Bold and italicize the entries in cells A5 through A8.**

Another Method

The menu equivalent for underline is F**o**rmat/C**e**lls/ Font/**U**nderline/Single or Ctrl + U and for italic is F**o**rmat/C**e**lls/Font/F**o**nt Style/Italic or Ctrl + I.

Your screen should be similar to Figure 1.60

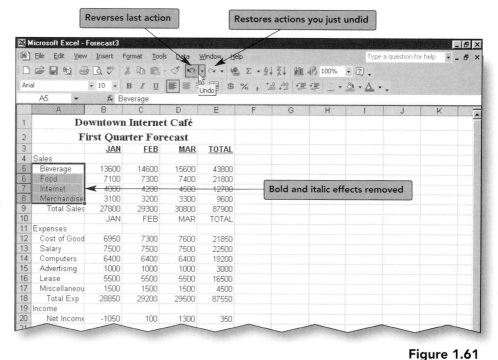

Adds Italic effect

Adds underline effect

Bold and underline applied to labels

Bold and italic applied to labels

Figure 1.60

Using Undo

Sometimes formatting changes you make do not have the expected result. In this case, you feel that the sales category names would look better without the formatting. To quickly undo the last two actions you performed,

1 ● **Open the** 🔄 **Undo drop-down list.**

● **Move the mouse pointer down the list to highlight the Italic and Bold actions.**

Another Method

The menu equivalent is **E**dit/ **U**ndo or Ctrl + Z. You can also click 🔄 repeatedly to undo the actions in the list one by one.

Your screen should be similar to Figure 1.61

Reverses last action

Restores actions you just undid

Bold and italic effects removed

Figure 1.61

Additional Information

The menu equivalent is **E**dit/**R**edo or Ctrl + Y.

The two actions you selected are undone. Undo reverses the selected actions regardless of the current cell pointer location. If you change your mind after you Undo an action, the 🔄 Redo button is available so that you can restore the action you just undid.

Using Format Painter

You do think, however, that the Total Sales, Total Exp, and Net Income labels would look good in bold. You will bold the entry in cell A9 and then copy the format from A9 to the other cells using Format Painter. This feature applies the formats associated with the current selection to new selections. To turn on the feature, move the insertion point to the cell whose formats you want to copy and click the  Format Painter button. Then you select the cell you want the formats applied to. The format is automatically applied to an entire cell contents simply by clicking on the cell. If you double-click the  Format Painter button, you can apply the format multiple times. You will also format the labels in row 10.

①

● **Apply bold to cell A9.**

● **With cell A9 selected, double-click  Format Painter.**

Additional Information

When Format Painter is on, the mouse pointer appears as 🖌️⌶.

● **Click A18.**

● **Click A20.**

● **Click  Format Painter to turn it off.**

Another Method

You can also press Esc to turn off Format Painter.

● **Use Format Painter to copy the format from cell B3 to cells B10 through E10.**

Your screen should be similar to Figure 1.62

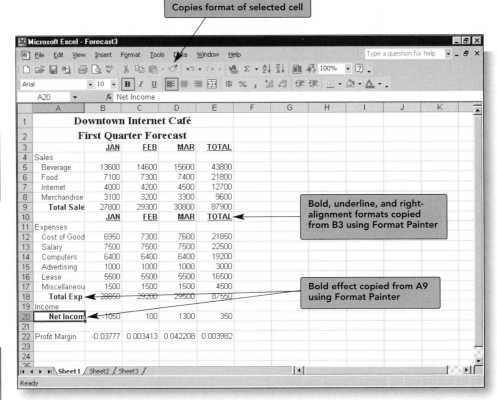

Figure 1.62

The formatting was quickly added to each cell as it was selected.

Formatting Numbers

You also want to improve the appearance of the numbers in the worksheet by changing their format.

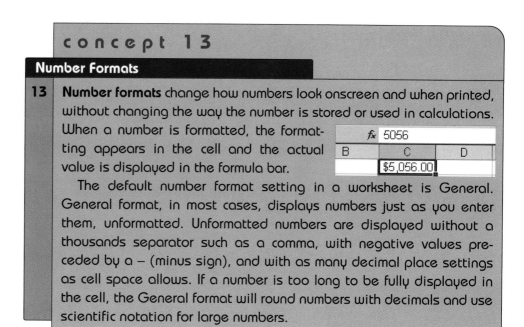

concept 13

Number Formats

13 **Number formats** change how numbers look onscreen and when printed, without changing the way the number is stored or used in calculations. When a number is formatted, the formatting appears in the cell and the actual value is displayed in the formula bar.

The default number format setting in a worksheet is General. General format, in most cases, displays numbers just as you enter them, unformatted. Unformatted numbers are displayed without a thousands separator such as a comma, with negative values preceded by a – (minus sign), and with as many decimal place settings as cell space allows. If a number is too long to be fully displayed in the cell, the General format will round numbers with decimals and use scientific notation for large numbers.

First you will change the number format of cells B5 through E8 to display dollar signs, commas, and decimal places.

1 ● **Select cells B5 through E9.**

● **Choose Format/Cells.**

Another Method

The keyboard shortcut is Ctrl + 1.

● **If necessary, open the Number tab.**

● **From the Category list box, select Currency.**

Your screen should be similar to Figure 1.63

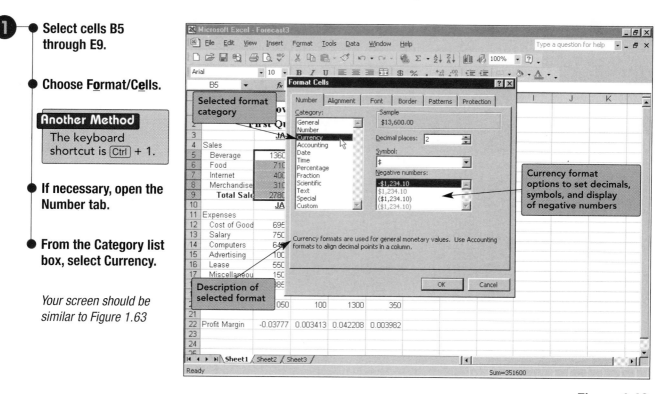

Figure 1.63

The Currency category includes options that allow you to specify the number of decimal places, how negative numbers will appear, and whether a currency symbol such as a dollar sign will be displayed.

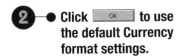

2 ● Click [OK] to use the default Currency format settings.

Your screen should be similar to Figure 1.64

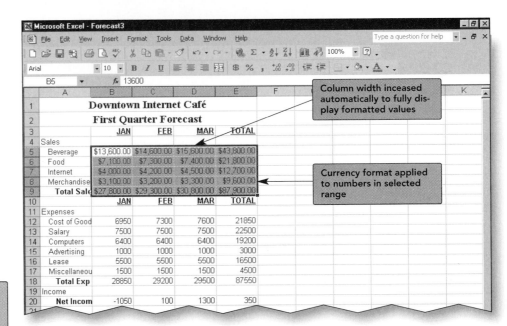

Figure 1.64

The number entries in the selected range appear with a currency symbol, comma, and two decimal places. The column widths increased automatically to fully display the formatted values.

A second format category that displays numbers as currency is Accounting. You will try this format next on the same range. Additionally, you will specify zero as the number of decimal places since all the values are whole values.

3 ● Choose Format/Cells/ Accounting.

● Reduce the decimal places to 0.

● Click [OK].

Your screen should be similar to Figure 1.65

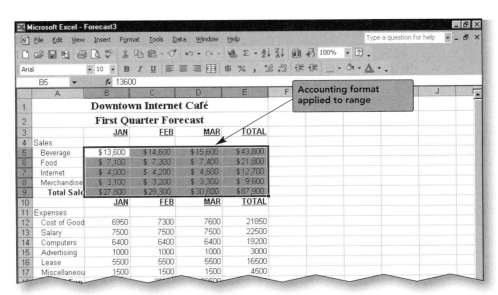

Figure 1.65

The numbers now appear in Accounting format. The primary difference between the Accounting and the Currency formats is that the Accounting format aligns numbers at the decimal place and places the dollar sign in a column at the left edge of the cell space. In addition, it does not allow you to select different ways of displaying negative numbers but displays them in black in parentheses. You decide the Accounting format will make it easier to read the numbers in a column.

Using Styles

You want to apply the same format to the expense range of cells. Another way to apply number formats is to select a predefined format style.

concept 14

Styles

14 A **style** consists of a combination of formats that have been named and that can be quickly applied to a selection. Excel includes six predefined styles, or you can create your own custom styles. Normal is the default style used in the Book template. It sets the number format to General and controls other format settings that are applied to all entries, including font type, font size, alignment, and indentation.

Examples of the six predefined styles are shown on the right. Notice the two Currency styles. They will display dollar signs, commas, and two or zero decimal places, just as if you had selected these formats from the Format Cells dialog box.

Style	Example
Normal	89522
Comma	89,522.00
Comma [0]	89,522
Currency	$ 89,522.00
Currency [0]	$ 89,522
Percent	89.52200%

● **Drag to select the range B12 through E20.**

● **Choose F<u>o</u>rmat/<u>S</u>tyle.**

Your screen should be similar to Figure 1.66

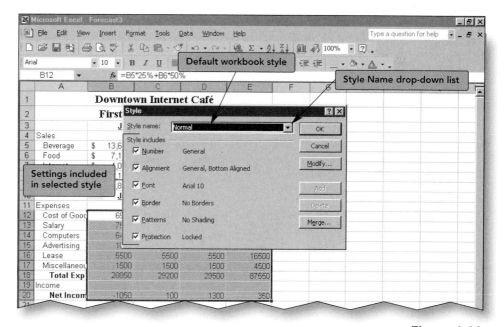

Figure 1.66

The Style dialog box displays the name of the default workbook style, Normal, in the Style Name list box. The check boxes in the Style Includes area of the dialog box show the options that are included in this style and a description or sample. You want to use the Currency $ style.

2 ● **Open the Style Name drop-down list box.**

● **Select Currency $.**

● **Click** OK **.**

Additional Information

Using $ Currency Style on the Formatting toolbar applies the Accounting number format with two decimal places.

Your screen should be similar to Figure 1.67

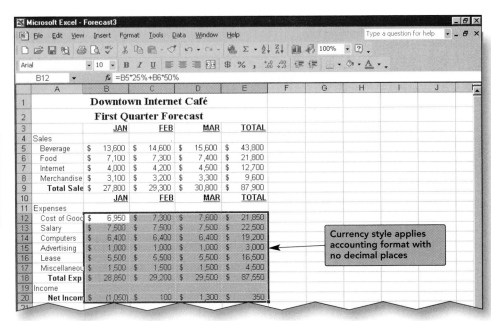

Figure 1.67

The Currency $ style applies the Accounting number format with zero decimal places.

Finally, you want the Profit Margin values to be displayed as percentages with two decimal places.

3 ● **Select B22 through E22.**

● **Click % Percent Style.**

Another Method

The menu equivalent is Format/Style/Percent.

● **Click Increase decimal twice.**

Another Method

You could also use Format/Cells/Percentage/Decimal Places/2.

Your screen should be similar to Figure 1.68

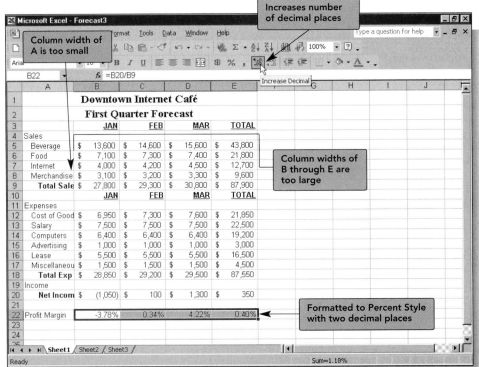

Figure 1.68

Now that the numbers are displayed as a percentage and the number of decimal places has been decreased, the column widths are larger than they need to be. Because Excel does not automatically reduce column widths, you need to make this change yourself. Additionally, you want column A to fully display the row headings. You will use the AutoFit feature to adjust the column widths for all cells in columns A through E.

4 ● **Click the A column letter and drag to the right to expand the selection to include column E.**

● **Double-click any column border line in the selection to AutoFit the selection.**

Additional Information

You could also press Ctrl + A or click the button at the intersection of the row numbers and column letters to select the entire worksheet and then double-click on any border line to AutoFit the column width of all columns containing entries.

Your screen should be similar to Figure 1.69

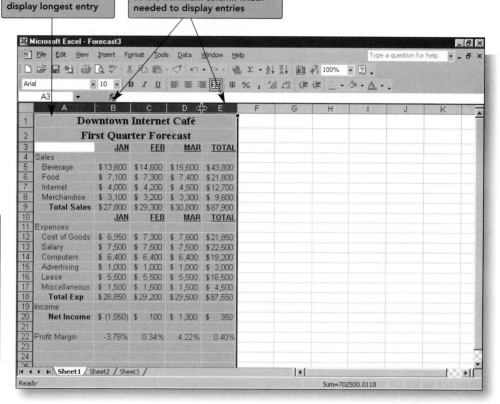

Figure 1.69

The width of columns B through E automatically decreased to the minimum column width needed to fully display the entries. The width of column A increased to accommodate the longest entry.

Adding Color

The last formatting change you would like to make to the worksheet is to add color to the text and to the background of selected cells. First you will change the color of the text.

1 ● Select A1 through A2.

● Open the  Font Color palette.

● Select a color of your choice.

Your screen should be similar to Figure 1.70

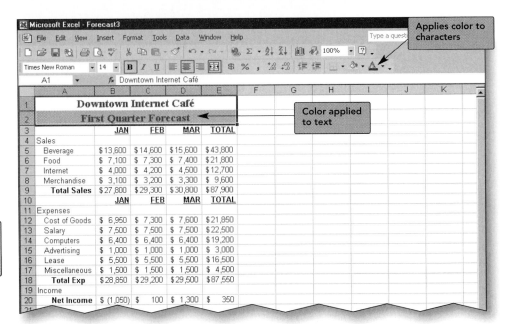

Figure 1.70

The selected color appears in the button and can be applied again simply by clicking the button. Next you will change the cell background color, also called the fill color.

2 ● Open the  Fill Color palette.

● Select a color of your choice.

● Apply the same font color, fill color, and bold to cell A4.

● Use Format Painter to quickly copy the format from cell A4 to cells A11, A19, and A22.

● Apply the same fill color to B4 through E4, B11 through E11, B19 through E19, and B22 through E22.

Your screen should be similar to Figure 1.71

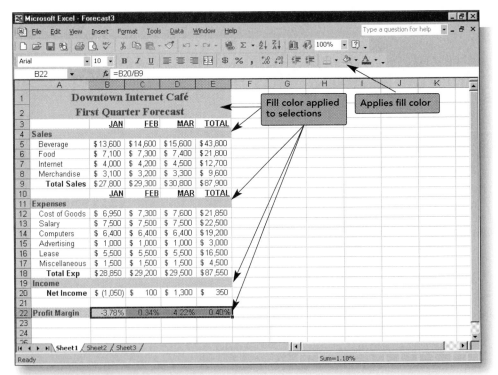

Figure 1.71

Working with Graphics

Finally you want to add a graphic to add interest. A ClipArt image is one of several different graphic objects that can be added to an Excel document.

Inserting Graphics

You want to insert a graphic to the right of the data in the worksheet. Graphic files can be obtained from a variety of sources. Many simple drawings called **clip art** are available in the Clip Organizer that comes with Office XP. You can also create graphic files using a scanner to convert any printed document, including photographs, to an electronic format. Most images that are scanned are stored as Windows bitmap files (.bmp). All types of graphics, including clip art, photographs, and other types of images, can be found on the Internet. These files are commonly stored as .jpg or .pcx files. Keep in mind that any images you locate on the Internet may be copyrighted and should only be used with permission. You can also purchase CDs containing graphics for your use.

You decide to use the Clip Organizer to find a suitable graphic.

1 • Move to F3.

• Choose **I**nsert/**P**icture/**C**lip Art.

Your screen should be similar to Figure 1.72

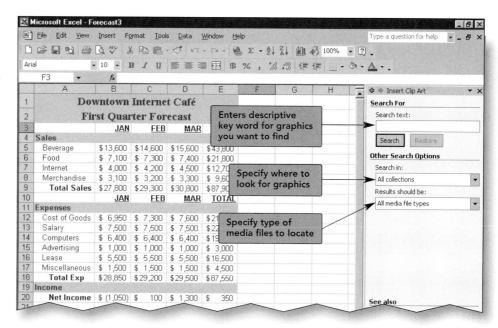

Figure 1.72

The Insert Clip Art task pane appears in which you can enter a key word, a word or phrase that is descriptive of the type of graphic you want to locate. The graphics in the Clip Organizer are organized by topic and are identified with several keywords that describe the graphic. You can also specify the locations to search and the type of media files, such as clip art, movies, photographs or sound, to display in the search results. You want to find clip art and photographs of computers.

2 ● **In the Search Text box, type computer.**

● **Open the Results Should Be drop-down list.**

● **Select Photographs and Clip Art.**

● **Deselect all other options and click outside the drop-down list to close it.**

● **Click** Search .

Your screen should be similar to Figure 1.73

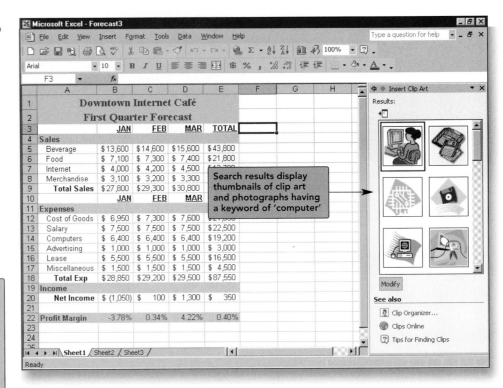

Figure 1.73

The Clip Organizer displays **thumbnails**, miniature images, of all clip art and photographs that are identified with the keyword "computer." You want to use a graphic showing people and a computer.

3 ● Scroll the list and point to the thumbnail of the computer and two people (see Figure 1.74).

● Click on the thumbnail to insert it.

● Click ☒ in the task pane title bar to close it.

HAVING TROUBLE?
If this graphic is not available in the Clip Organizer, choose Insert/Picture/From File and select Internet.wmf from your data file location.

Another Method
You could also choose Insert from the graphics shortcut menu to insert it in the worksheet.

Your screen should be similar to Figure 1.74

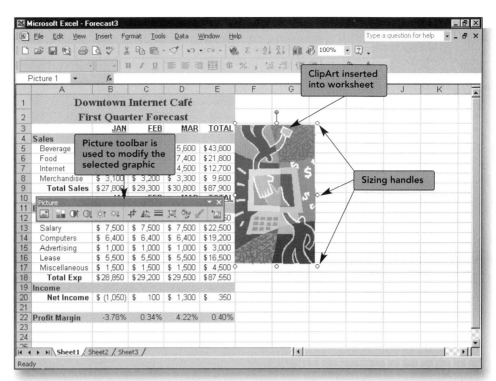

Figure 1.74

Additional Information
A selected graphic object can be deleted by pressing Del.

HAVING TROUBLE?
If the Picture toolbar is not displayed, right-click on any toolbar to open the Shortcut menu and select Picture, or use View/Toolbars/Picture.

Sizing Graphics

The ClipArt image is inserted in the document at the current cell. Once a graphic object is inserted into the workbook, it can be manipulated in many ways. You can change its size, add borders or shading, or move it to another location including in the margin, in headers and footers, or on top of or below other objects. It cannot, however, be placed behind the worksheet data.

You want to reduce the size of the graphic and move it to the top row of the worksheet. The picture is surrounded by eight boxes, called **sizing handles**, indicating it is a selected object and can now be sized and moved anywhere in the document. The handles are used to size the object. A graphic object is moved by dragging it to the new location.

The Picture toolbar is also automatically displayed. Its buttons are used to modify the selected picture object. Your Picture toolbar may be floating or docked along an edge of the window, depending on where it was when last used.

1 ● **Point to the lower-right corner handle.**

● **Drag the mouse inward to reduce the size of the graphic until the bottom of the graphic is even with row 12.**

● **Point to the graphic and drag upward to move the graphic to row 1 of columns F and G.**

● **Click outside the graphic to deselect it.**

● **Add the same background fill color as in the other areas of the worksheet to cells F1:G22.**

Your screen should be similar to Figure 1.75

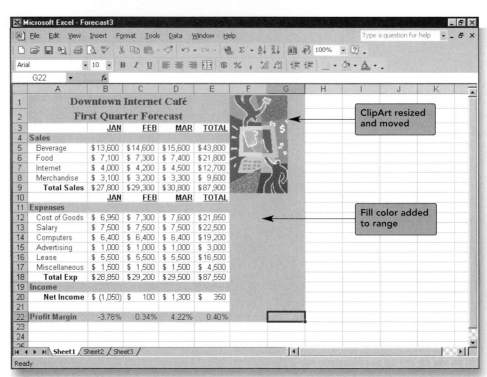

Figure 1.75

The three-month forecast is now complete.

Entering the Date

Now that the worksheet is complete, you want to include your name and the date in the worksheet as documentation.

1 ● Enter your first initial and last name in cell A24.

● Enter the current date in cell B24 in the format mm/dd/yy (for example, 10/10/02).

● Move to B24.

● Click ▣ Save to save the worksheet changes.

Another Method
You can quickly insert the current date using [Ctrl] + ;.

Your screen should be similar to Figure 1.76

Additional Information
Dates, like other numeric entries, can be formatted to display in many different ways. Use Format/Cells/Number/Category/Date to change the date format.

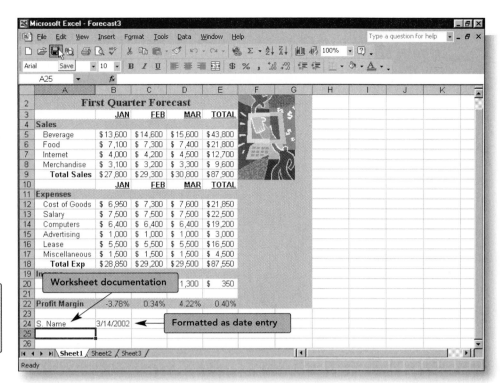

Figure 1.76

Excel automatically recognized your entry as a date and formatted the entry using the short date format. If you had preceded the date entry with =, Excel would have interpreted it as a formula and a calculation of division would have been performed on the numbers.

Excel stores all dates as serial numbers with each day numbered from the beginning of the century; the date serial number 1 corresponds to the date January 1, 1900, and the integer 65380 is December 31, 2078. The integers are assigned consecutively beginning with 1 and ending with 65,380. They are called **date numbers**. Conversion of the date to a serial number allows dates to be used in calculations.

Previewing and Printing a Workbook

If you have printer capability, you can print a copy of the worksheet. To save time and unnecessary printing and paper waste, it is always a good idea to preview onscreen how the worksheet will appear when printed.

① → ● Click 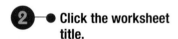 **Print Preview.**

Another Method

The menu equivalent is File/Print Preview.

Your screen should be similar to Figure 1.77

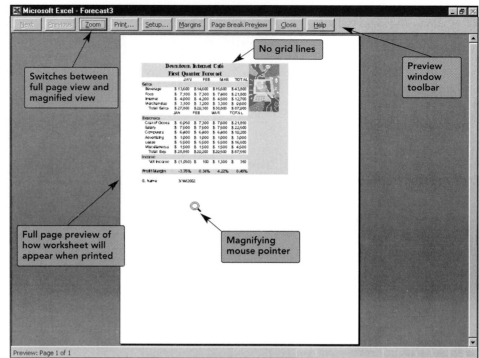

Figure 1.77

Additional Information

If you have a monochrome printer, the preview appears in shades of gray as it will appear when printed.

The print preview window displays the worksheet as it will appear on the printed page. Notice that the row and column lines are not displayed and will not print. The worksheet looks good and does not appear to need any further modifications immediately.

The preview window also includes its own toolbar. While previewing, you can change from full-page view to a magnified view using [Zoom] or by clicking on the preview page.

② → ● **Click the worksheet title.**

Additional Information

The area you click on is the area that will display in the preview window.

Your screen should be similar to Figure 1.78

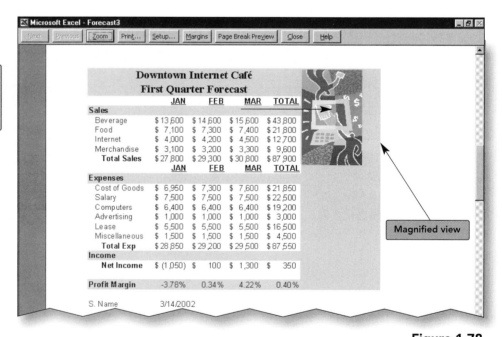

Figure 1.78

The worksheet is displayed in the actual size it will appear when printed. Now you are ready to print the worksheet.

3 ● Click on the worksheet again to return to full-page view.

● Click [Print...].

Your screen should be similar to Figure 1.79

Another Method

You can also use <u>F</u>ile/<u>P</u>rint or the keyboard shortcut [Ctrl] + P from the worksheet window. Clicking 🖨 Print on the Standard toolbar will send the workbook directly to the printer.

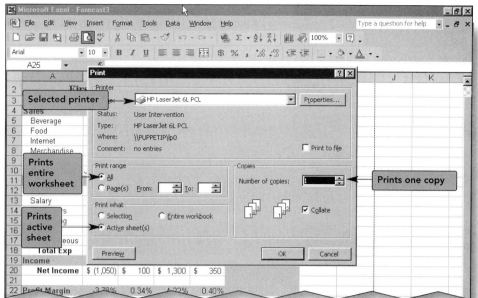

Figure 1.79

Note: Please consult your instructor for printing procedures that may differ from the following directions.

From the Print dialog box, you need to specify the printer you will be using and the document settings. The printer that is currently selected is displayed in the Name drop-down list box in the Printer section of the dialog box.

The Print Range area lets you specify how much of the worksheet you want printed. The range options are described in the following table:

Option	Action
All	Prints the entire worksheet
Pages	Prints pages you specify by typing page numbers in the text box
Selection	Prints selected range only
Active Sheet	Prints the active worksheet
Entire Workbook	Prints all worksheets in the workbook

The default settings of All and Active sheet are correct. In the Copies section, the default setting of one copy of the worksheet is acceptable.

4

- **If necessary, make sure your printer is on and ready to print.**
- **If you need to change the selected printer to another printer, open the Name drop-down list box and select the appropriate printer.**
- **Click OK.**

The printed copy should be similar to the document shown here.

> **Additional Information**
> If you do not have a color printer, the colors appear as shades of gray.

Downtown Internet Café
First Quarter Forecast

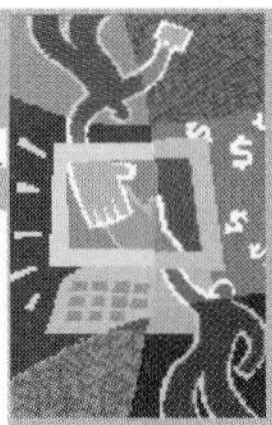

	JAN	FEB	MAR	TOTAL
Sales				
Beverage	$ 13,600	$ 14,600	$ 15,600	$ 43,800
Food	$ 7,100	$ 7,300	$ 7,400	$ 21,800
Internet	$ 4,000	$ 4,200	$ 4,500	$ 12,700
Merchandise	$ 3,100	$ 3,200	$ 3,300	$ 9,600
Total Sales	$ 27,800	$ 29,300	$ 30,800	$ 87,900
	JAN	FEB	MAR	TOTAL
Expenses				
Cost of Goods	$ 6,950	$ 7,300	$ 7,600	$ 21,850
Salary	$ 7,500	$ 7,500	$ 7,500	$ 22,500
Computers	$ 6,400	$ 6,400	$ 6,400	$ 19,200
Advertising	$ 1,000	$ 1,000	$ 1,000	$ 3,000
Lease	$ 5,500	$ 5,500	$ 5,500	$ 16,500
Miscellaneous	$ 1,500	$ 1,500	$ 1,500	$ 4,500
Total Exp	$ 28,850	$ 29,200	$ 29,500	$ 87,550
Income				
Net Income	$ (1,050)	$ 100	$ 1,300	$ 350
Profit Margin	-3.78%	0.34%	4.22%	0.40%

S. Name 3/14/2002

Exiting Excel 2002

The Exit command in the File menu is used to quit the Excel program. Alternatively, you can click the ☒ Close button in the application window title bar. If you attempt to close the application without first saving the workbook, Excel displays a warning asking if you want to save your work. If you do not save your work and you exit the application, all changes you made from the last time you saved are lost.

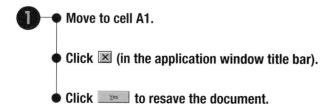

- Move to cell A1.

- Click ☒ (in the application window title bar).

- Click Yes to resave the document.

Additional Information

Excel saves the file with the cell selector in the same cell it is in when saved.

LAB 1
Creating and Editing a Worksheet

Template (EX1.12)

A template is a workbook file that includes predefined settings that can be used as a pattern to create many common types of workbooks.

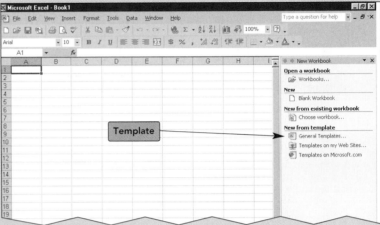

Text and Numeric Entries (EX1.14)

The information or data you enter in a cell can be text, numbers, or formulas.

AutoCorrect (EX1.20)

The AutoCorrect feature makes some basic assumptions about the text you are typing and, based on these assumptions, automatically corrects the entry.

Column Width (EX1.24)

The size or width of a column controls how much information can be displayed in a cell.

Copy and Move (EX1.31)

The contents of worksheet cells can be duplicated (copied) or moved to other locations in the worksheet or between worksheets, saving you time by not having to retype the same information.

Range (EX1.34)

A selection consisting of two or more cells on a worksheet is a range.

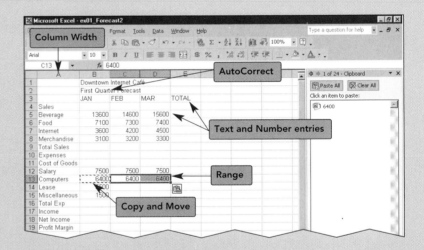

Formulas (EX1.39)

A formula is an equation that performs a calculation on data contained in a worksheet.

Relative Reference (EX1.41)

A relative reference is a cell or range reference in a formula whose location is interpreted by Excel in relation to the position of the cell that contains the formula.

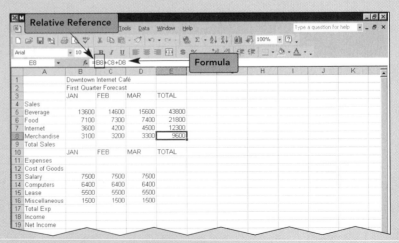

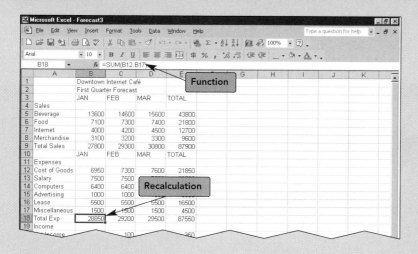

Functions (EX1.42)

Functions are prewritten formulas that perform certain types of calculations automatically.

Recalculation (EX1.48)

Excel automatically recalculates formulas whenever a change occurs in a referenced cell.

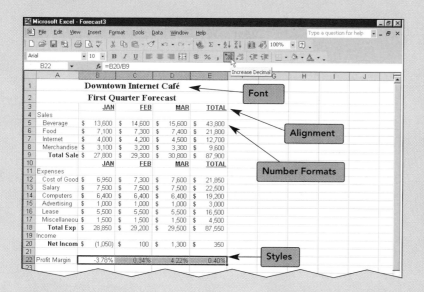

Alignment (EX1.49)

Alignment settings allow you to change the horizontal and vertical placement and the orientation of an entry in a cell.

Fonts (EX1.54)

Fonts consist of typefaces, point sizes, and styles that can be applied to characters to improve their appearance.

Number Formats (EX1.59)

Number formats affect how numbers look onscreen and when printed.

Styles (EX1.61)

A style consists of a combination of formats that have been named and that can be quickly applied to a selection.

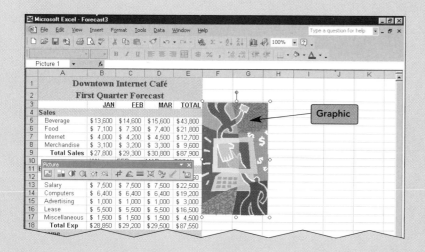

Graphics (EX1.65)

A graphic is a non-text element or object, such as a drawing or picture, that can be added to a document.

key terms

active cell   EX1.7
active sheet   EX1.8
adjacent range   EX1.34
alignment   EX1.17
argument   EX1.42
AutoCorrect   EX1.20
cell   EX1.7
cell selector   EX1.7
character effects   EX1.56
clip art   EX1.65
column   EX1.7
column letter   EX1.7
constant   EX1.14
copy area   EX1.31
date number   EX1.69
defaults   EX1.12
destination   EX1.31
drawing object   EX1.65
embedded object   EX1.65
fill handle   EX1.36
font   EX1.54
format   EX1.49

Formatting toolbar   EX1.5
formula   EX1.14
formula bar   EX1.5
functions   EX1.42
graphic   EX1.65
heading   EX1.15
merged cell   EX1.53
Name box   EX1.5
nonadjacent range   EX1.34
number   EX1.14
number formats   EX1.49
object   EX1.65
operand   EX1.39
operator   EX1.39
paste area   EX1.31
picture   EX1.65
point   EX1.54
range   EX1.34
reference   EX1.8
recalculate   EX1.48
relative reference   EX1.41
row   EX1.7

row number   EX1.7
sans serif   EX1.54
serif   EX1.54
sheet tab   EX1.8
size   EX1.54
sizing handle   EX1.67
source   EX1.31
spreadsheet   EX1.7
Standard toolbar   EX1.5
style   EX1.61
syntax   EX1.42
tab scroll button   EX1.8
task pane   EX1.5
template   EX1.12
text   EX1.14
thumbnail   EX1.66
typeface   EX1.54
variable   EX1.14
workbook   EX1.6
workbook window   EX1.6
worksheet   EX1.7

mous skills

The Microsoft Office User Specialist (MOUS) certification program is designed to measure your proficiency in performing basic tasks using the Office XP applications. Getting certified demonstrates that you have the skills and provides a valuable industry credential for employment. After completing this lab, you have learned the following Microsoft Office User Specialist skills:

Skill	Description	Page
Working with Cells and Cell Data	Insert, delete, and move cells	EX1.36,1.53
	Enter and edit cell data including text, numbers and formulas	EX1.15–1.23,1.39–1.44, 1.54
Managing Workbooks	Manage workbook files and folders	EX1.28
	Save workbooks using different names and file formats	EX1.26
Formatting and Printing Worksheets	Apply and modify cell formats	EX1.54
	Modify row and column formats	EX1.48
	Modify column and row settings	EX1.24
	Apply styles	EX1.61
	Preview and print worksheets and workbooks	EX1.69
Creating and Revising Formulas	Create and revise formulas	EX1.39
	Use statistical, date and time, financial, and logical functions	EX1.42
Creating and Modifying Graphics	Create, modify, and position graphics	EX1.65

command summary

Command	Shortcut Key	Button	Action
File/Open <file name>	Ctrl + O	☞	Opens an existing workbook file
File/Close		☒	Closes open workbook file
File/Save <file name>	Ctrl + S	🖫	Saves current file on disk using same file name
File/Save As <file name>			Saves current file on disk using a new file name
File/Print Preview		🔍	Displays worksheet as it will appear when printed
File/Print	Ctrl + P	🖨	Prints a worksheet
File/Exit		☒	Exits Excel
Edit/Undo	Ctrl + Z	↺ ▾	Undoes last editing or formatting change
Edit/Redo	Ctrl + Y	↻ ▾	Restores changes after using Undo
Edit/Copy	Ctrl + C	🗐	Copies selected data to Clipboard
Edit/Office Clipboard			Displays Office Clipboard task pane
Edit/Paste	Ctrl + V	🗐	Pastes selections stored in Clipboard
Edit/Fill			Fills selected cells with contents of source cell
Edit/Clear/Contents	Delete		Clears cell contents
Edit/Delete/Entire Row			Deletes selected rows

command summary (continued)

Command	Shortcut Key	Button	Action
<u>E</u>dit/<u>D</u>elete/Entire <u>c</u>olumn			Deletes selected columns
<u>V</u>iew/<u>T</u>oolbars			Displays or hides selected toolbar
<u>I</u>nsert/Copied C<u>e</u>lls			Inserts row and copies text from Clipboard
<u>I</u>nsert/<u>R</u>ows			Inserts a blank row
<u>I</u>nsert/<u>C</u>olumns			Inserts a blank column
<u>I</u>nsert/<u>P</u>icture/<u>F</u>rom File			Inserts picture at insertion point from disk
F<u>o</u>rmat/C<u>e</u>lls/Number/Currency			Applies Currency format to selection
F<u>o</u>rmat/C<u>e</u>lls/Number/Accounting		$	Applies Accounting format to selection
F<u>o</u>rmat/C<u>e</u>lls/Number/Date			Applies Date format to selection
F<u>o</u>rmat/C<u>e</u>lls/Number/Percent		%	Applies Percent format to selection
F<u>o</u>rmat/C<u>e</u>lls/Number/Decimal places		.00 .00	Increases or decreases the number of decimal places associated with a number value
F<u>o</u>rmat/C<u>e</u>lls/Alignment/<u>H</u>orizontal/Left (Indent)			Left-aligns entry in cell space
F<u>o</u>rmat/C<u>e</u>lls/Alignment/<u>H</u>orizontal/Center			Center-aligns entry in cell space
F<u>o</u>rmat/C<u>e</u>lls/Alignment/<u>H</u>orizontal/Right			Right-aligns entry in cell space
F<u>o</u>rmat/C<u>e</u>lls/Alignment/<u>I</u>ndent			Indents cell entry
F<u>o</u>rmat/C<u>e</u>lls/Alignment/ <u>H</u>orizontal/Center Across Selection			Centers cell contents across selected cells
F<u>o</u>rmat/C<u>e</u>lls	Ctrl + 1		Changes font and attributes of cells
F<u>o</u>rmat/C<u>e</u>lls/Font/F<u>o</u>nt Style/Bold	Ctrl + B	B	Bolds selected text
F<u>o</u>rmat/C<u>e</u>lls/Font/F<u>o</u>nt Style/Italic	Ctrl + I	I	Italicizes selected text
F<u>o</u>rmat/C<u>e</u>lls/Font/<u>U</u>nderline/Single	Ctrl + U	U	Underlines selected text
F<u>o</u>rmat/C<u>e</u>lls/Font/<u>C</u>olor		A ·	Adds color to text
F<u>o</u>rmat/C<u>e</u>lls/Patterns/<u>C</u>olor		·	Adds color to cell background
F<u>o</u>rmat/<u>R</u>ow/He<u>i</u>ght			Changes height of selected rows
F<u>o</u>rmat/<u>C</u>olumn/<u>W</u>idth			Changes width of columns
F<u>o</u>rmat/<u>C</u>olumn/<u>A</u>utofit Selection			Changes column width to match widest cell entry
F<u>o</u>rmat/<u>S</u>tyle			Applies selected style to selection

Terminology

screen identification

In the following worksheet, several items are identified by letters. Enter the correct term for each item in the space provided.

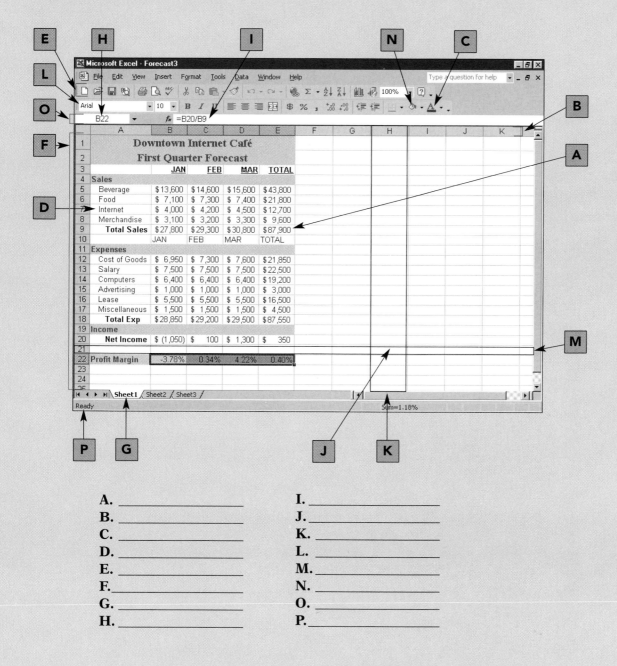

A. _____   I. _____
B. _____   J. _____
C. _____   K. _____
D. _____   L. _____
E. _____   M. _____
F. _____   N. _____
G. _____   O. _____
H. _____   P. _____

matching

Match the lettered item on the right with the numbered item on the left.

1. source   _____   **a.** undoes last action

2. *   _____   **b.** a set of characters with a specific design

3. ▦   _____   **c.** the cell you copy from

4. font   _____   **d.** two or more worksheet cells

5. .xls   _____   **e.** a cell reference

6. ↶▾   _____   **f.** enters a sum function

7. =C19+A21   _____   **g.** an arithmetic operator

8. range   _____   **h.** merges cells and centers entry

9. D11   _____   **i.** a formula summing two cells

10. Σ   _____   **j.** Excel workbook file name extension

multiple choice

Circle the correct response to the questions below.

1. Row and column _____ are entries that are used to create the structure of the worksheet and describe other worksheet entries.
   a. cells
   b. headings
   c. objects
   d. formats

2. _____ entries can contain any combination of letters, numbers, spaces, and any other special characters.
   a. Number
   b. Variable
   c. Constant
   d. Text

3. The _____ feature automatically corrects common typing errors as they are made.
   a. AutoFix
   b. Fixit
   c. AutoComplete
   d. AutoCorrect

4. The _____ is a small black square, located in the lower-right corner of the selection, used to create a series or copy to adjacent cells.
   a. scroll bar
   b. sheet tab
   c. sizing handle
   d. fill handle

5. The values on which a numeric formula performs a calculation are called:
   a. operators
   b. operands
   c. accounts
   d. data

6. Whenever a formula containing _____ references is copied, the referenced cells are automatically adjusted.
   a. relative
   b. automatic
   c. fixed
   d. variable

7. A(n)_____ is a box used to size a selected object.
   a. sizing handle
   b. cell selector
   c. operand
   d. fill handle

8. _____ can be applied to selections to add emphasis or interest to a document.
   a. Alignments
   b. Pictures
   c. Character effects
   d. Text formats

9. The currency number format can display:
   a. dollar signs
   b. commas
   c. decimal places
   d. all the above

10. The integers assigned to the days from January 1, 1900, through December 31, 2099, that allow dates to be used in calculations are called:
    a. date numbers
    b. syntax
    c. number formats
    d. reference

lab exercises

true/false

Circle the correct answer to the following questions.

1. Formulas are used to create, edit, and position graphics.   True   False
2. The default column width setting in Excel is 15.0.   True   False
3. A nonadjacent range is two or more selected cells or ranges that are adjoining.   True   False
4. A formula is an entry that performs a calculation.   True   False
5. When a formula containing relative references is copied, the cell references in the copied formula refer to different cells than the references in the original formula.   True   False
6. Formulas are prewritten statements that perform certain types of calculations automatically.   True   False
7. Recalculation is one of the most powerful features of electronic worksheets.   True   False
8. Font settings allow you to change the horizontal and vertical placement and the orientation of an entry in a cell.   True   False
9. Number formats affect how numbers look onscreen and when printed.   True   False
10. A drawing object is created using a special drawing program that is not included with Excel.   True   False

Concepts

fill-in

Complete the following statements by filling in the blanks with the correct terms.

1. The _____ controls how much information can be displayed in a cell.

2. _____ affect how numbers look onscreen and when printed.

3. _____ placement allows you to specify whether the cell contents are displayed at the top, centered, or at the bottom of the vertical cell space.

4. Pictures are inserted as _____ objects.

5. The _____ feature decreases the recalculation time by only recalculating dependent formulas.

6. By default, text entries are _____ -aligned and number entries are _____ -aligned.

7. A(n) _____ in a formula automatically adjusts for the new location when copied.

8. The values on which a numeric formula performs a calculation are called _____.

9. Without _____ recalculation, large worksheets would take several minutes to recalculate all formulas each time a number was changed.

10. A(n) _____ is the data the function uses to perform the calculation.

discussion questions

1. Discuss four steps in developing a workbook. Why is it important to follow these steps?

2. What types of entries are used in worksheets? Discuss the uses of each type of entry.

3. Discuss how formulas and functions are created. Why are they the power behind workbooks?

4. Discuss the formatting features presented in the lab. Why are they important to the look of the worksheet?

Hands-On Exercises

step-by-step

Park Improvement Bid Analysis

★ **1.** Kelly Fitzgerald is an analyst for the city parks and recreation department. One of her responsibilities is to collect and analyze data on future improvements. She has compiled a list of the parks that are scheduled for improvements for the next year and the project bids for each. Follow the directions below to complete the worksheet shown here.

Park Improvement Bids
Calendar Year 2005

Park	Bid 1	Bid 2	Bid 3	Bid 4
West Avenue	$127,000	$154,200	$135,700	$142,800
Amigo	154,500	251,000	202,500	220,300
Canyon Creek	13,600	18,900	15,500	14,700
Mountain View	1,300	2,500	1,800	1,600
East Hill	129,100	154,300	128,500	133,400
Maple Grove	1,200	1,500	1,400	1,600
Thompson-West	10,300	14,200	11,500	10,200
Marshall Way	19,300	19,900	18,900	22,300
Green Mountain	10,200	11,500	12,600	12,500
Blue Bird Pass	29,100	32,500	25,700	28,900
Total	$495,600	$660,500	$554,100	$588,300

Student Name
Date

a. Open the workbook ex01_Improvements.

b. Modify the label in cell B2 so that the first letter of each word is capitalized. Increase the font size to 14 point. Center both title lines across columns A through E.

c. Bold and center the titles in row 5.

d. Adjust the column widths so that all the data is fully displayed.

e. In row 16, enter a function to total the Bid 1 and Bid 2 columns.

f. Format the numbers in rows 6 and 16 using the Currency style with zero decimal places and the numbers in rows 7 through 15 using the Comma style with zero decimal places.

g. Kelly has just received the last two bids. Enter the following data in the cells indicated.

Row	Col D	Col E
5	Bid 3	Bid 4
6	135700	142800
7	202500	220300
8	15500	14700
9	1800	1600
10	128500	133400
11	1400	1600
12	11500	10200
13	18900	22300
14	12600	12500
15	25700	28900

h. Format the data to match the style of the corresponding information in columns B and C.

i. Copy the total function to calculate the total for the new bids.
j. Insert a blank row above the Total row.
k. Add font and fill colors to the worksheet, as you like.
l. Insert a Clip Art graphic of your choice from the Clip Organizer. Size and position it appropriately to fit the worksheet.
m. Enter your name and the current date on separate rows just below the worksheet.
n. Move to cell A1. Save the workbook as Park Improvements. Preview and print the worksheet.

Job Trends Analysis Worksheet

★ 2. Lisa Sutton is an employment analyst working for the state of New Jersey. One of her responsibilities is to collect and analyze data on future job opportunities in the state. Lisa has compiled a list of the jobs that are expected to offer the most new positions. Follow the directions below to complete the worksheet shown here.

a. Open the workbook ex01_New Positions.

b. Modify the label in cell B2 so that the first letter of each word is capitalized; move the label in cell B2 to A2; move the label in cell B3 to A3; center the titles across the columns A through D; and finally, increase the font size to 14 point.

c. Format the numbers in column B as number with a comma to separate thousands and 0 decimal places. Format the numbers in column C as currency with dollar signs and two decimal places. Format the numbers in column D as percent with one decimal place.

d. Insert a new row below row 3 and a new row below row 6.

e. Bold the titles in rows 5 and 6. Underline the titles in row 6. Adjust the column widths so that all the data is fully displayed.

f. Add font and fill colors to the worksheet as you like.

g. Insert a Clip Art graphic of your choice from the Clip Organizer. Size and position it appropriately to fit the page.

h. Enter your name and the current date on separate rows just below the worksheet.

i. Move to cell A1. Save the workbook as Jobs. Preview and print the worksheet.

Comparative U.S. Families at Poverty Level

★ ★ **3.** Mark Ernster works for an agency that provides help to families in poverty. He has been doing some research on the percent of families that fall into this category. He has started a worksheet with data from the years 1990–1999. Follow the directions below to complete the worksheet shown here.

a. Open the workbook ex01_Poverty Level.

b. Edit the title in cell D2 so that the first letter of each word is upper-case except the words 'of' and 'or'. Center the title across columns A through J. Increase the font size to 14 and bold and apply a font color of your choice to the title.

c. Center-align and underline the column headings in row 4. Left-align cells A5 through A14.

d. Calculate the average for the Official percentage in cell B15 using the Average function (=Average(B5:B14)). Format the cell as a percentage with two decimal places. Copy the formula to cells C15 through J15.

e. Next, you would like to calculate the percent of change from 1990 to 1999. Enter the label **Percent Change** in cell A16. Enter the formula **=(B14-B5)/B15** in cell B16. Format the cell as a percentage with two decimal places. Copy the formula to cells C16 through J16.

Percentage of Families At or Below Poverty Level

	Official	NAS	NAS-U	DES	DES-U	NGA	NGA-U	DCM	DCM-U
1990	13.5%	13.7%	16.1%	13.6%	16.7%	13.8%	16.6%	13.6%	16.4%
1991	14.2%	14.5%	16.9%	14.4%	17.6%	14.6%	17.3%	14.3%	17.3%
1992	14.8%	15.1%	17.6%	15.1%	18.3%	15.2%	18.2%	15.0%	18.0%
1993	15.1%	15.8%	18.3%	15.8%	19.0%	15.8%	18.6%	15.7%	18.8%
1994	14.6%	14.6%	17.0%	14.6%	17.5%	14.6%	17.3%	14.5%	17.5%
1995	13.8%	13.8%	16.3%	13.8%	16.9%	13.9%	16.6%	13.8%	16.8%
1996	13.7%	13.6%	16.0%	13.6%	16.7%	13.5%	16.2%	13.7%	16.6%
1997	13.3%	13.3%	15.4%	13.3%	16.0%	13.3%	15.8%	13.3%	15.9%
1998	12.7%	12.5%	14.4%	12.5%	15.1%	12.3%	14.6%	12.5%	15.0%
1999	11.8%	11.7%	13.8%	11.8%	14.3%	11.7%	14.0%	11.9%	14.4%
Average	13.75%	13.86%	16.18%	13.85%	16.81%	13.87%	16.52%	13.83%	16.67%
Percent Change	-12.59%	-14.60%	-14.29%	-13.24%	-14.37%	-15.22%	-15.66%	-12.50%	-12.20%

Legend
Official U.S. government
NAS   National Academy of Sciences methodology - standardized
NAS-U   National Academy of Sciences methodology - unstandardized
DES   Different Equivalence Scale: uses three parameters to adjust thresholds by family size, presence of children and family structure (but otherwise similar to NAS) - standardized
DES-U   Different Equivalence Scale: uses three parameters to adjust thresholds by family size, presence of children and family structure (but otherwise similar to NAS) - unstandardized
NGA   No Geographic Adjustment (but otherwise similar to NAS) - standardized
NGA-U   No Geographic Adjustment (but otherwise similar to NAS) - unstandardized
DCM   Different Child Care Method: assigns fixed amounts of child care expenditures to families based on the number and ages of children present (but otherwise similar to NAS) - standardized
DCM-U   Different Child Care Method: assigns fixed amounts of child care expenditures to families based on the number and ages of children present (but otherwise similar to NAS) - unstandardized

Student Name
Date

f. Format the data in cells B5 through J14 as a percentage with one decimal place. Best-fit columns B through J.

g. Adjust the width of column A to fully display the labels.

h. Insert a blank row between rows 14 and 15 and another between rows 16 and 17.

i. Add fill colors to the worksheet as you like.

j. Insert the picture ex01_family. Size and position it to fit on the left side of the title.

k. Enter your name and the current date on separate rows just below the legend.

l. Move to cell A1. Save and replace the workbook as Poverty Level. Preview and print the worksheet.

Information Technology Job and Salary Analysis

★★ **4.** Jake Bell is a writer for a local television station. The station is planning a series about information technology. In his research on this topic, he has found some interesting data on information technology jobs and salaries. He has entered this data into a worksheet but still needs to format the data and perform some analysis of the information. Follow the directions below to complete the worksheet shown here.

a. Open the workbook ex01_IT Salaries.

b. Adjust the width of column A to fully display the row labels.

c. Center the title in row 2 over the worksheet columns A through F. Format the title in row 2 to Tahoma 14 point. Apply a font color and fill color of your choice to row 2.

d. Bold and center the column labels in row 4.

e. Format the data in B6 through D15 using the Comma style and no decimal places.

f. Insert a new column between C and D. Calculate the % of change from 1995 to 1999. Format the data as a percentage with two decimal places. (*Hint:* Subtract the 1995 value from the 1999 value and divide the result by the 1995 value.)

g. Calculate the % of change from 1999 to 2000 in column F. Format the data as a percentage with two decimal places.

h. Label the new columns in row 4 **% Change**. Enter **1995–1999** in cell D5 and **1999–2000** in cell F5. Format the headings appropriately. Best-fit the columns to display the labels. Change the widths of columns B, C, and E to the same width as columns D and F.

i. Insert a blank row above row 6.

j. Insert the Disks Clip Art graphic (located in the Computer category of the Clip Organizer or ex01_Disks from your data files) to the right and left of the title on the worksheet. Adjust the size and location of the pictures as necessary.

k. Apply a fill color of your choice behind all rows of the worksheet (except row 2, which already contains a fill color.)

l. Enter your name and the current date on separate rows below the worksheet.

m. Move to cell A1. Save and replace the workbook file as IT Salaries. Preview and print the worksheet.

Information Technology Median Salaries

Management Level	1995	1999	% Change 1995 - 1999	2000	% Change 1999 - 2000
CIO/Vice President	102,500	146,400	42.83%	158,000	7.92%
IS Director	76,650	106,500	38.94%	113,700	6.76%
Manager, Sys. Analysis& Prog.	69,950	91,100	30.24%	97,100	6.59%
Manager, Sys. Prog./Tech. Support	66,200	89,700	35.50%	95,800	6.80%
Network Manager LAN/WAN	56,300	85,200	51.33%	92,100	8.10%
Sys. Analyst/Prog./Proj. Leader	48,250	72,200	49.64%	77,900	7.89%
Database Admin. Manager	64,500	89,000	37.98%	96,500	8.43%
Manager Telecommunications	67,450	79,100	17.27%	84,800	7.21%
Data Center Manager	62,800	73,600	17.20%	77,400	5.16%
PC Work Station Manager	44,650	59,400	33.03%	63,100	6.23%

Student Name
Date

Homeowners Association Projected Budget

★ ★
★

5. Stuart Philips is president of the Garden Springs Homeowners Association. The Association is planning a large improvement project and wants to project how much there is likely to be in the cash budget after expenses. Using last year's final budget numbers, he wants to create a projected budget for 2004. Follow the directions below to complete the worksheet shown here.

a. Open the workbook file ex01_Springs Budget. Adjust the width of column A to fully display the labels.

b. In column C, calculate a 5 percent increase for all the income numbers for the year 2004. Calculate a 10 percent increase in Administrative and Maintenance expenditures, and a 15 percent increase in Miscellaneous expenditures.

c. Format the data with the Accounting number format.

d. In column D, calculate the totals for Total Income, Total Administrative, Total Maintenance, and Total Expenditures for 2004. In column E, calculate the Total Cash Balance by subtracting the total income from the total expenditures for 2004.

e. Indent the row label subheads and further indent the items under each subhead. Right-align the total labels except for the Total Cash Balance.

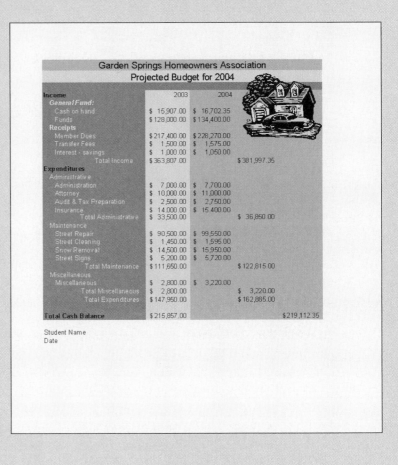

f. Delete rows 13 and 14.

g. Change the font type, size, and color of the worksheet title lines to a format of your choice. Center the titles across columns A through E.

h. Apply character effects and color of your choice to the worksheet.

i. Insert a Clip Art image of your choice from the Clip Organizer. Position and size it to fit the worksheet.

j. Enter your name and the current date on separate rows just below the worksheet.

k. Move to cell A1. Save the workbook file as Springs Projected Budget. Preview and print the worksheet.

Tracking Your Grades

★ ★ **1.** A worksheet can be used to track your grades in a class or for each semester. Design and create a worksheet to record your grades in any class. The worksheet should include grades for at least four test scores showing the number of points you earned on each test and the number of possible points. Include an appropriate title, row and column headings, and formulas to calculate your total points earned and total possible points. Include a formula to calculate your percent. Format the worksheet appropriately using features presented in this lab. Enter real or sample data for the four tests. Include your name and date above the worksheet. Save the workbook as Class Grades and print the worksheet.

Creating a Personal Budget

★ ★ **2.** Create a personal three-month budget using a worksheet. Enter an appropriate title and use descriptive labels for your monthly expenses (food, rent, car payments, insurance, credit card payments, etc.). Enter your monthly expenses (or, if you prefer, any reasonable sample data). Use formulas to calculate total expenses for each month and to calculate the average monthly expenditures for each expense item. Enhance the worksheet using features you learned in this lab. Enter your name and the current date on separate rows just below the worksheet. Save the workbook as Personal Budget. Preview and print the worksheet.

Tracking Sales

★ ★ **3.** Trevor Grey is the new owner and manager of a small custom publishing company. He has four salespeople (Kevin, April, Karen, and Sam) and is planning an intense marketing campaign for the next month. Using the steps in the planning process, plan and create a worksheet for Trevor that can be used to record and analyze sales for that month.

Weekly sales data for each employee will be entered into the worksheet. Using that data, the worksheet will calculate the total monthly sales for each person. Additionally, it will calculate the total weekly sales for the company. Write a short paragraph describing how you used each of the planning steps. Enter sample data in the worksheet. Include your name and the current date on separate rows just below the worksheet. Save the workbook as Weekly Sales. Preview and print the worksheet.

Job Analysis

★ ★ ★ **4.** Use the library and/or the Web to locate information on employment opportunities and salary trends related to your area of study. Create a worksheet to display information relating to job titles, years of experience, and starting and top salaries for positions in your field. Calculate the median salary (the average of the starting and the top salary). Enhance the worksheet using features you learned in this lab. Enter your name and the current date on separate rows just below the worksheet. Save the workbook as Job Analysis. Preview and print the worksheet.

Membership Analysis

★ ★ **5.** LifeStyle Fitness Club wants to analyze their membership growth for the past 3 years. Design and
★   create a worksheet to record the membership enrollment for three years in the three membership
categories: Single, Family, and Senior. Include an appropriate title, row and column headings, and
formulas to calculate total enrollment by category and by year. Include a formula to calculate the
percent growth over the three years. Format the worksheet appropriately using features presented
in this tutorial. Enter sample data for the three years. Include your name and date above the
worksheet. Save the workbook as Membership and print the worksheet.

on the web

Design, planning and testing are very important steps in the development of an accurate
worksheet. A poorly designed worksheet can lead to serious errors in the analysis of data. Use the
Web to find information about spreadsheet errors and spreadsheet design. Write a short paper
summarizing your findings. Include proper citations for your sources. If you are using a word
processor to write the report, save the document as Spreadsheet Design.

Charting Worksheet Data

LAB 2

objectives

After completing this lab, you will know how to:

1.	Select a chart data range.
2.	Change the type of chart.
3.	Move the chart location.
4.	Format chart elements.
5.	Add chart titles and move the legend.
6.	Create a combination chart.
7.	Change worksheet data.
8.	Add data labels, text boxes, and arrows.
9.	Create, explode, and rotate a pie chart.
10.	Apply patterns and color.
11.	Size and align a sheet on a page.
12.	Add predefined headers and footers.
13.	Document, preview, and print a workbook.

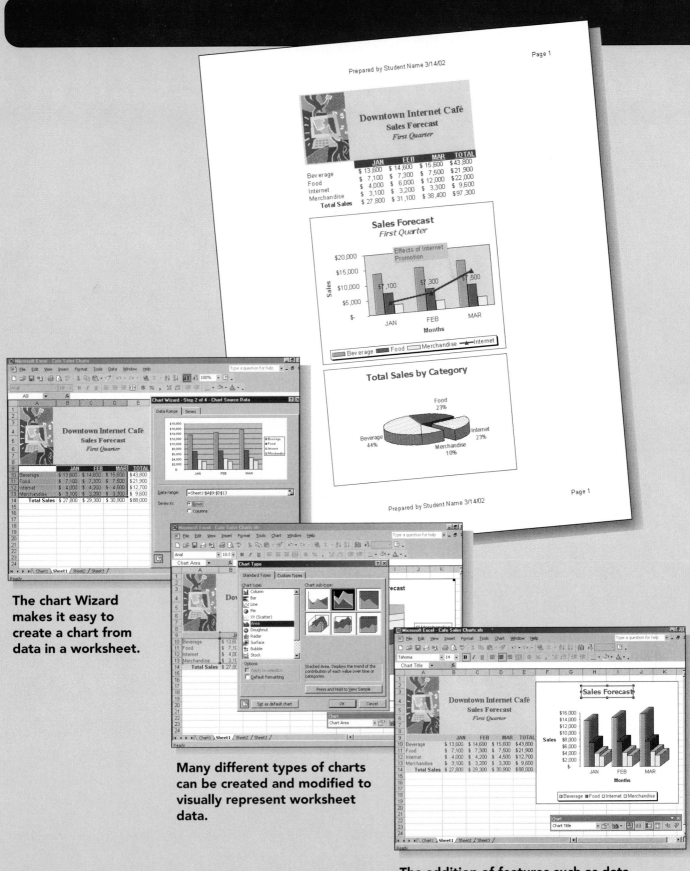

The chart Wizard makes it easy to create a chart from data in a worksheet.

Many different types of charts can be created and modified to visually represent worksheet data.

The addition of features such as data labels, text boxes, arrows, and color add emphasis to the chart.

Downtown Internet Café

After creating the first quarter forecast for the Downtown Internet Café, you contacted several other Internet cafes to inquire about their startup experiences. You heard many exciting success stories! Internet connections attract more customers and the typical customer stays longer at an Internet café than at a regular café. As a result, they end up spending more money.

You now believe that your initial sales estimates are too low. You too should be able to increase sales dramatically. In addition to sales of coffee and food items to customers, the Café also derives sales from charging for Internet connection time. In your discussions with other Internet café managers, you have found that Internet connection sales account for ap-

proximately 25 percent of their total sales. You would like to launch an aggressive advertising campaign to promote the new Internet aspect of the Downtown Internet Café. You believe that the campaign will lead to an increase in sales not only in Internet connection time but also in food and beverage sales.

To convince Evan, you need an effective way to illustrate the sales growth you are forecasting. In this lab, you will learn to use Excel 2002's chart-creating and formatting features to produce several different charts of your sales estimates, as shown on the preceding page.

The following concepts will be introduced in this lab:

1	**Chart** A chart is visual representation of data that is used to convey information in an easy-to-understand and attractive manner. Different types of charts are used to represent data in different ways.
2	**Chart Elements** Chart elements consist of a number of parts that are used to graphically display the worksheet data.
3	**Chart Objects** A chart object is a graphic object that is created using charting features included in Excel. A chart object can be inserted into a worksheet or into a special chart sheet.
4	**Group** Because it consists of many separate objects, a chart object is a group. A group is two or more objects that behave as a single object when it is moved or sized.
5	**Data Label** Data labels provide additional information about a data marker.
6	**Text Box** A text box is a rectangular object in which you type text. Text boxes can be added to a sheet or an embedded chart.
7	**Header and Footer** Lines of text displayed above the top margin or below the bottom margin of each page are called headers and footers.

Learning About Charts

Creating charts of the sales projections makes it easy to visually understand numeric data. Excel 2002 can create many types of charts from data in a worksheet.

You have decided to chart the sales forecast data for the Downtown Internet Café to better see the sales trends. The sales data is in a separate workbook file.

1 ● **Open the file**
ex02_Cafe Sales.

Your screen should be similar to Figure 2.1

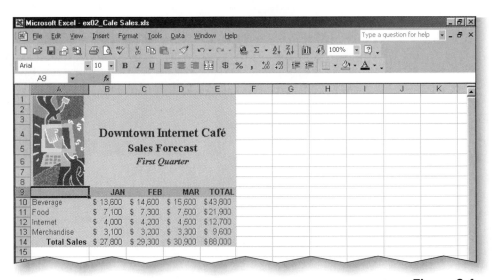

Figure 2.1

Although the worksheet shows the sales data for each category, it is hard to see how the different categories change over time. To make it easier to see the sales trends, you decide to create a chart of this data.

Charts

1 A **chart** is visual representation of data that is used to convey information in an easy-to-understand and attractive manner. Different types of charts are used to represent data in different ways. The type of chart you create depends on the type of data you are charting and the emphasis you want the chart to impart.

Excel 2002 can produce 14 standard types of graphs or charts, with many different sub-types for each standard type. In addition, Excel includes professionally designed built-in custom charts that include additional formatting and chart refinements. The basic chart types and how they represent data are described in the following table.

Type	Description	Type	Description
	Area charts show the magnitude of change over time by emphasizing the area under the curve created by each data series.		Radar charts display a line or area chart wrapped around a central point. Each axis represents a set of data points.
	Bar charts display data as evenly spaced bars. The categories are displayed along the Y axis and the values are displayed horizontally, placing more emphasis on comparisons and less on time.		XY (scatter) charts are used to show the relationship between two ranges of numeric data.
	Column charts display data as evenly spaced bars. They are similar to bar charts, except that categories are organized horizontally and values vertically to emphasize variation over time.		Surface charts display values as what appears to be a rubber sheet stretched over a 3-D column chart. These are useful for finding the best combination between sets of data.
	Line charts display data along a line. They are used to show changes in data over time, emphasizing time and rate of change rather than the amount of change.		Bubble charts compare sets of three values. It is like a scatter chart with the third value displayed as the size of bubble markers.
	Pie charts display data as slices of a circle or pie. They show the relationship of each value in a data series to the series as a whole. Each slice of the pie represents a single value in the series.		A stock chart is a high-low-close chart. It requires three series of values in this order.
			Cylinder charts display values with a cylindrical shape.
			Cone charts display values with a conical shape.
	Doughnut charts are similar to pie charts except that they can show more than one data series.		Pyramid charts display values with a pyramid shape.

Creating a Single Data Series Chart

All charts are drawn from data contained in a worksheet. To create a new chart, you select the worksheet range containing the data you want displayed as a chart plus any row or column headings you want used in the chart. Excel then translates the selected data into a chart based upon the shape and contents of the worksheet selection.

A chart consists of a number of parts that are important to understand so that you can identify the appropriate data to select in the worksheet.

concept 2

Chart Elements

2 A chart consists of a number of parts or elements that are used to graphically display the worksheet data. In a two-dimensional chart, the selected worksheet data is visually displayed within the X- and Y-axis boundaries. The **X axis**, also called the **category axis**, is the bottom boundary line of the chart and is used to label the data being charted, such as a point in time or a category. The left boundary line of the chart is the **Y axis**, also called the **value axis**. This axis is a numbered scale whose numbers are determined by the data used in the chart. Typically the X-axis line is the horizontal line and the Y-axis line is the vertical line. In 3-D charts there can also be an additional axis, called the **Z axis**, which allows you to compare data within a series more easily. This axis is the vertical axis. The X and Y axes delineate the horizontal surface of the chart.

Other basic elements of a 2-dimensional chart are:

Element	Description
category names	Labels that correspond to the headings for the worksheet data that is plotted along the X axis.
plot area	The area within the X- and Y-axis boundaries where the chart appears
data series	Related data points that are distinguished by different colors or patterns
data marker	A bar, dot, or other symbol that represents one number from the worksheet.
chart gridlines	Lines extending from the axis line across the plot area that make it easier to read the chart data.
legend	A box that identifies the chart data series
chart title	A descriptive label displayed above the charted data that explains the contents of the chart.
category-axis title	A descriptive label displayed along the X axis
value-axis title	A descriptive label displayed along the Y axis

The basic parts of a two-dimensional chart are shown in the figure below.

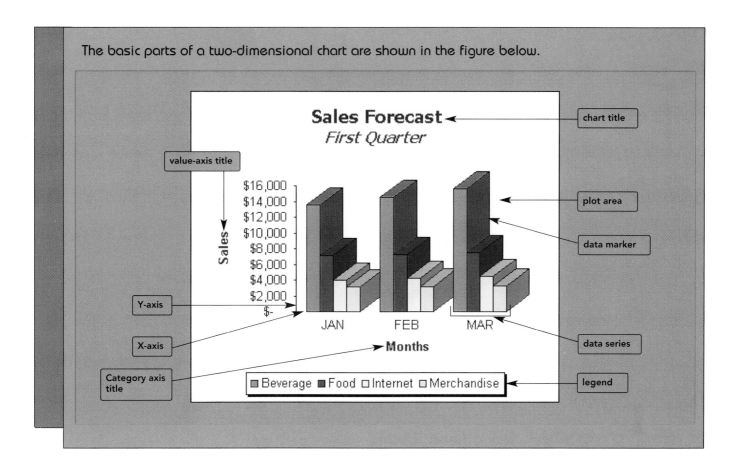

Selecting the Data to Chart

The first chart you want to create will show the total sales pattern over the three months. This chart will use the month labels in cells B9 through D9 to label the X-axis. The numbers to be charted are in cells B14 through D14. In addition, the label Total Sales in cell A14 will be used as the chart legend, making the entire range A14 through D14.

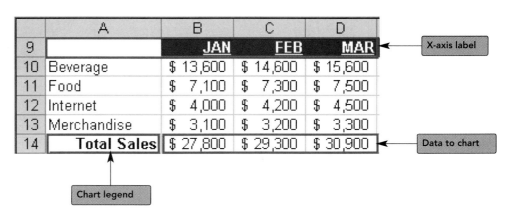

Notice that the two ranges, B9 through D9 and A14 through D14, are not adjacent and are not the same size. When plotting nonadjacent ranges in a chart, the selections must form a rectangular shape. To do this, the blank cell A9 will be included in the selection. You will specify the range and create the chart.

1 ● **Select A9 through D9.**

● **Hold down** [Ctrl].

● **Select A14 through D14.**

Your screen should be similar to Figure 2.2

Selected non-adjacent ranges

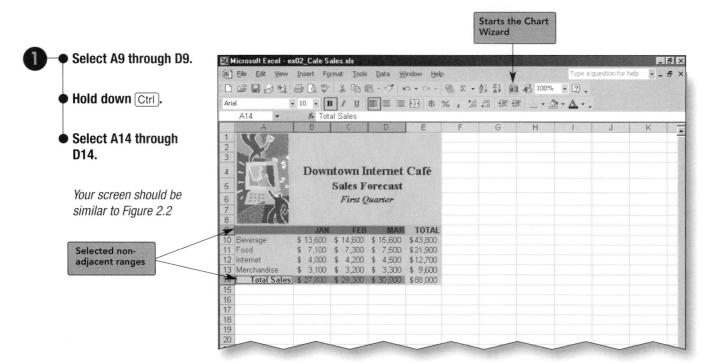

Figure 2.2

Additional Information

Office XP includes many different Wizards that provide step-by-step guidance to help you quickly perform many complicated tasks.

Using Chart Wizard

Next you will use the Chart Wizard to help you create the chart. Chart Wizard is an interactive program that guides you through the steps to create a chart by asking you questions and creating a chart based on your responses.

1 ● **Click**  **Chart Wizard.**

Another Method

The menu equivalent is Insert/Chart.

● **Move the Chart Wizard dialog box to the right to see as much of the worksheet as possible.**

HAVING TROUBLE?

Drag the title bar of the dialog box to move it.

Your screen should be similar to Figure 2.3

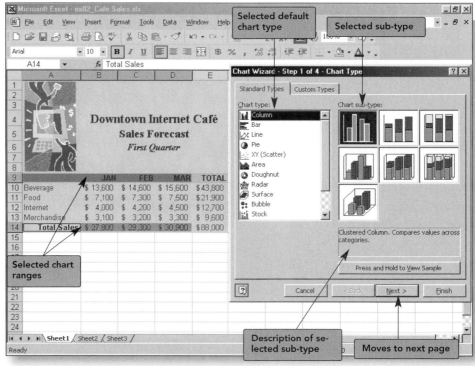

Figure 2.3

The first step is to select the chart type from the Chart Type list box. The default chart type is a column chart. Each type of chart includes many variations. The variations associated with the column chart type are displayed as buttons in the Chart Sub-type section of the dialog box. The default column sub-type is a clustered column. A description of the selected sub-type is displayed in the area below the sub-type buttons. You will use the default column chart type and move to the next step.

2 ● Click Next > .

Your screen should be similar to Figure 2.4

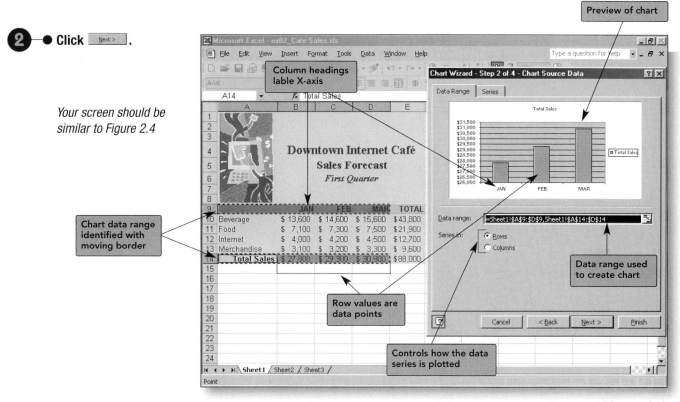

Figure 2.4

In the second Chart Wizard dialog box, you specify the data range on the worksheet you want to plot. Because you selected the data range before starting the Chart Wizard, the range is correctly displayed in the Data range text box. In addition, the data range is identified with a moving border in the worksheet. The dialog box also displays a preview of the chart that will be created using the specified data and selected chart type.

The two Series In options change how Excel plots the data series from the rows or columns in the selected data range. The orientation Excel uses by default varies depending upon the type of chart selected and the number of rows and columns defined in a series. The worksheet data range that has the greater number of rows or columns appears along the X-axis and the smaller number is charted as the data series. When the data series is an equal number of rows and columns, as it is in this case, the default is to plot the rows. The first row defines the X-axis category labels and the second row the plotted data. The content of the first cell in the second row is used as the legend text. To accept the default settings,

3 ● Click  .

● If necessary, open the Titles tab.

Your screen should be similar to Figure 2.5

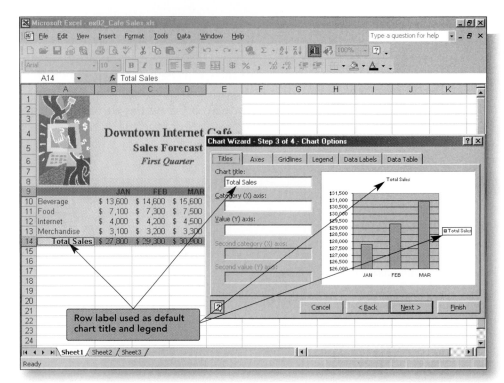

Figure 2.5

In the step 3 dialog box, you can turn some standard options on and off and change the appearance of chart elements such as a legend and titles. To clarify the data in the chart, you will add a more descriptive chart title as well as titles along the X and Y axes. As you add the titles, the preview chart will update to display the new settings.

4 ● In the Chart Title text box, replace the default title with Downtown Internet Cafe Sales.

● Press Tab ⇥.

HAVING TROUBLE?
Do not use ←Enter after typing the title text as this is the same as clicking Next >. Click < Back if needed to return to the previous Wizard step.

● In the Category (X) Axis text box, enter Months.

● In the Value (Y) Axis text box, enter Total Sales.

Your screen should be similar to Figure 2.6

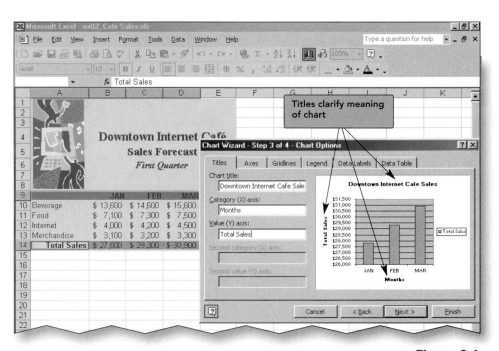

Figure 2.6

The titles clearly describe the information displayed in the chart. Now, because there is only one data range, and the category title fully explains this data, you decide to clear the display of the legend.

5 ● **Open the Legend tab.**

● **Click Show Legend to clear the checkmark.**

Your screen should be similar to Figure 2.7

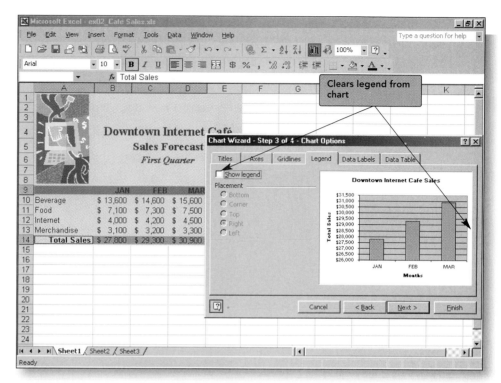

Figure 2.7

The legend is removed and the chart area resized to occupy the extra space.

6 ● Click .

*Your screen should be
similar to Figure 2.8*

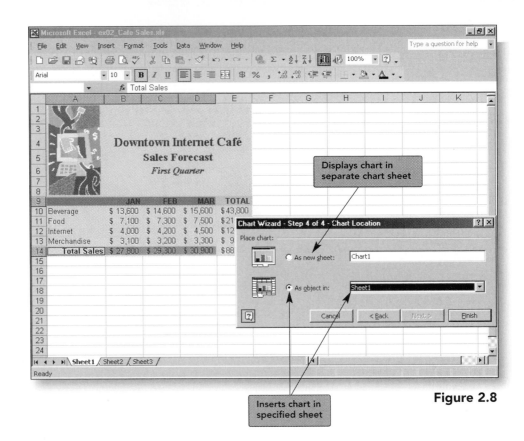

Figure 2.8

In the last step, you specify where you want the chart displayed in the worksheet. A chart can be displayed in a separate chart sheet or as an object in an existing sheet.

---

concept 3

Chart Objects

3 A **chart object** is a graphic object that is created using charting features included in Excel. A chart object can be inserted into a worksheet or into a special chart sheet.

Charts that are inserted into a worksheet are embedded objects. An **embedded chart** becomes part of the sheet in which it is inserted and is saved as part of the worksheet when you save the workbook file. Like all graphic objects, an embedded chart object can be sized and moved in a worksheet. A worksheet can contain multiple charts.

A chart that is inserted into a separate chart sheet is also saved with the workbook file. Only one chart can be added to a chart sheet and it cannot be sized and moved.

You would like this chart displayed as an object in the Sales worksheet. This is the default selection. You have provided all the information needed by the Wizard to create the chart.

---

7 ● Click [Finish].

● **If necessary, move the Chart toolbar to the bottom right corner of the window.**

HAVING TROUBLE?

If your chart toolbar is not automatically displayed, open it by selecting it from the toolbar shortcut menu. Move toolbars by dragging the title bar of the floating toolbar or the move handle ▯ of a docked toolbar.

Your screen should be similar to Figure 2.9

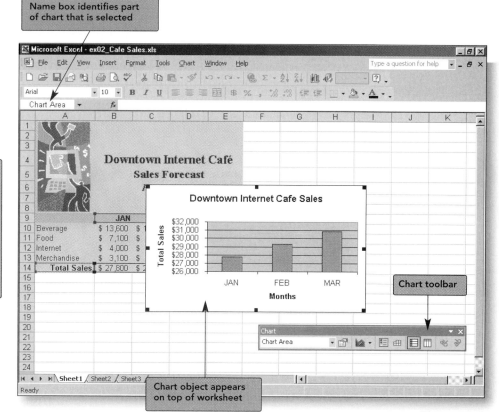

Name box identifies part of chart that is selected

Chart object appears on top of worksheet

Figure 2.9

The chart with the settings you specified using the Chart Wizard is displayed on the worksheet. It covers some of the worksheet data because it is a separate chart object that can be moved and sized within the worksheet.

Notice that the Name box displays Chart Area. The Name box identifies the part of the chart that is selected, in this case the entire chart and all its contents.

Also notice that the Chart toolbar is automatically displayed whenever a chart is selected. The Chart toolbar contains buttons for the most frequently used chart editing and formatting features. These buttons are identified below.

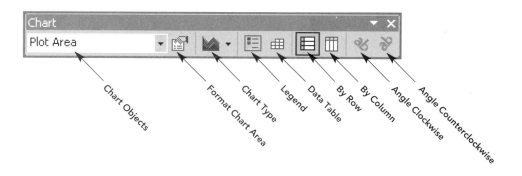

Chart Objects

Format Chart Area

Chart Type

Legend

Data Table

By Row

By Column

Angle Clockwise

Angle Counterclockwise

Moving and Sizing a Chart

You want to move the chart so that it is displayed to the right of the worksheet data. In addition, you want to increase the size of the chart. A selected chart object is moved by pointing to it and dragging it to a new location. When you move the mouse pointer into the selected chart object, it will display a chart tip to advise you of the chart element that will be affected by your action. When moving the entire chart, the chart tip must display Chart Area.

1 ● **Move the mouse pointer to different elements within the chart and note the different chart ScreenTips that appear.**

● **With the chart ScreenTip displaying Chart Area, drag the chart object so that the upper-left corner is in cell F4.**

Additional Information

The mouse pointer changes to a ✛ while dragging to move an object.

Your screen should be similar to Figure 2.10

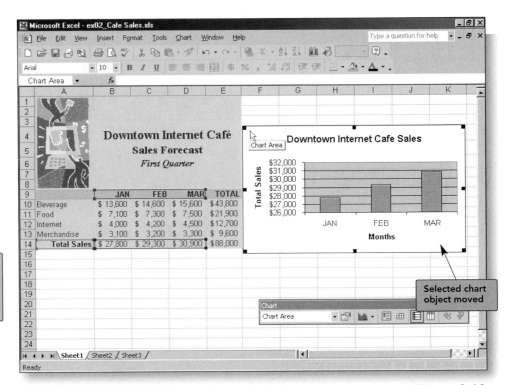

Figure 2.10

Next you will increase the size of the chart by dragging a sizing handle. This is the same as sizing a graphic object.

Point to the lower-center sizing handle, hold down Alt, and drag the chart box down until it is displayed over cells F4 through K20.

Your screen should be similar to Figure 2.11

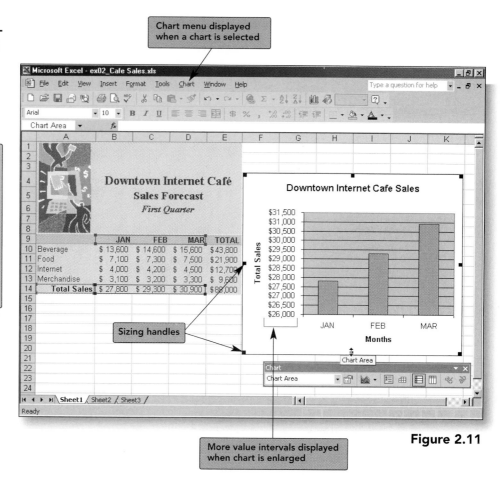

Chart menu displayed when a chart is selected

Sizing handles

More value intervals displayed when chart is enlarged

Figure 2.11

As you enlarge the chart, more value intervals are displayed along the Y axis, making the data in the chart easier to read. Additionally, the fonts in the chart scale proportionally as you resize the chart. The chart includes standard formats that are applied to the selected chart sub-type, such as a shaded background in the plot area and blue columns.

It is now easy to see how the worksheet data you selected is represented in the chart. Each column represents the total sales for that month in row 14. The month labels in row 9 have been used to label the X axis category labels. The range or scale of values along the Y axis is determined from the data in the worksheet. The upper limit is the maximum value in the worksheet rounded upward to the next highest interval.

Changing the Chart Location

Although this chart compares the total sales for the three months, you decide you are more interested in seeing a comparison for the sales categories. You could delete this chart simply by pressing Delete while the chart is selected. Instead, however, you will move it to a separate worksheet in case you want to refer to it again.

When a chart is selected, the Data menu changes to the Chart menu. In addition, many of the commands under the other menus change to commands that apply to charts only. The Chart menu contains commands that can be used to modify the chart.

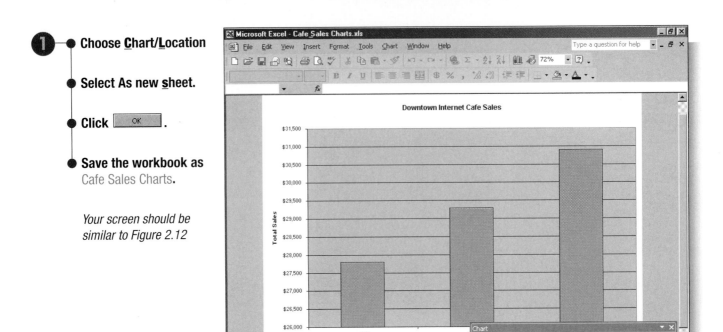

1 ● **Choose Chart/Location**

● **Select As new sheet.**

● **Click** [OK] .

● **Save the workbook as**
Cafe Sales Charts.

*Your screen should be
similar to Figure 2.12*

Chart displayed in
separate sheet

Figure 2.12

The column chart is now an object displayed in a separate chart sheet. Generally, you display a chart in a chart sheet when you want the chart displayed separately from the associated worksheet data. The chart is still automatically linked to the worksheet data from which it was created.

The new chart sheet named Chart1 was inserted to the left of the worksheet, Sheet1. The Chart sheet is the active sheet, or the sheet you are currently viewing and working in.

Creating a Multiple Data Series Chart

Now you are ready to continue your analysis of sales trends. You want to create a second chart to display the sales data for each category for the three months. You could create a separate chart for each category and then compare the charts; however, to make the comparisons between the categories easier, you will display all the categories on a single chart.

The data for the three months for the four categories is in cells B10 through D13. The month headings (X-axis data series) are in cells B9 through D9, and the legend text is in the range A10 through A13.

1
● **Click the Sheet1 tab.**

● **Select A9 through D13.**

● **Click 📊 Chart Wizard.**

● **Click** Next > **.**

Your screen should be similar to Figure 2.13

Selected data range

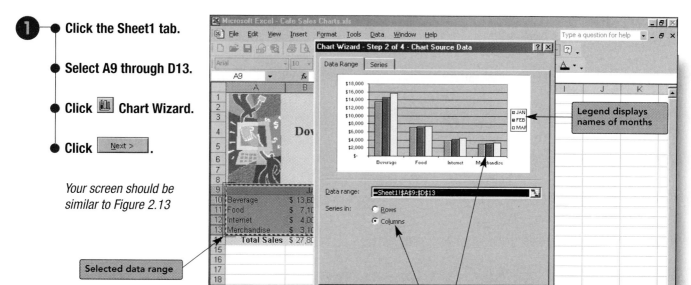

Series plotted by columns

Figure 2.13

When plotting the data for this chart, the Chart Wizard selected Columns as the data series orientation because there are fewer columns than rows in the data range. This time, however, you want to change the data series to Rows so that the months are along the X axis.

2
● **Select Rows.**

Your screen should be similar to Figure 2.14

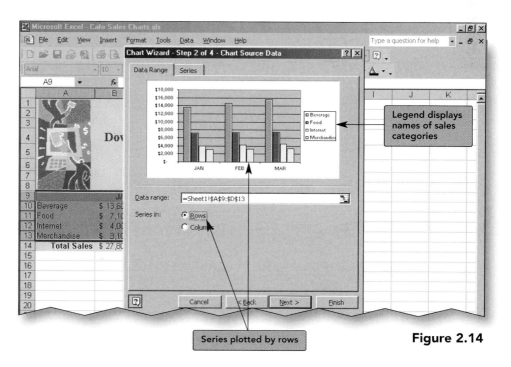

Series plotted by rows

Figure 2.14

The sample chart is redrawn with the new orientation. The column chart now compares the sales by month rather than by category. The Legend displays the names of the sales categories. Next, you will specify the chart titles and finish the chart.

3 ● Click Next > .

● **Open the Titles tab. Enter the following titles:**

Title	Entry
Chart	**Sales Forecast**
Category	**Months**
Value	**Sales**

● Click Finish .

● **Move and size the chart until it covers cells F2 through K19.**

Your screen should be similar to Figure 2.15

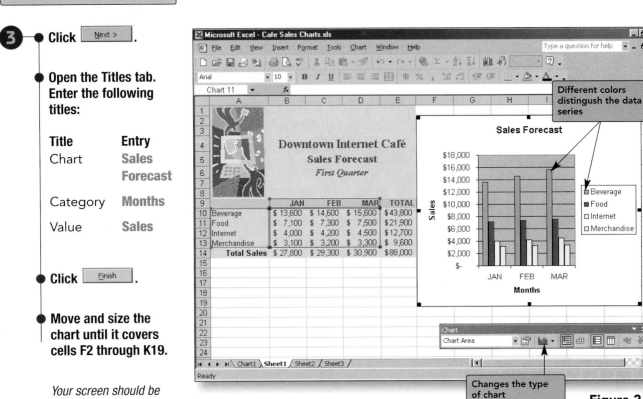

Figure 2.15

A different column color identifies each data series and the legend identifies the categories. The column chart shows that sales in all categories are increasing, with the greatest increase occurring in beverage sales.

Changing the Chart Type

Next you would like to see how the same data displayed in the column chart would look as a line chart. A line chart displays data as a line and is commonly used to show trends over time. This is easily done by changing the chart type using the Chart Type button on the Chart toolbar.

1 ● **Open the** 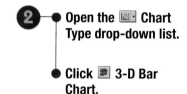 **Chart Type drop-down list.**

Another Method

The menu equivalent is Chart/Chart Type.

● **Click** ⬜ **Line Chart.**

Your screen should be similar to Figure 2.16

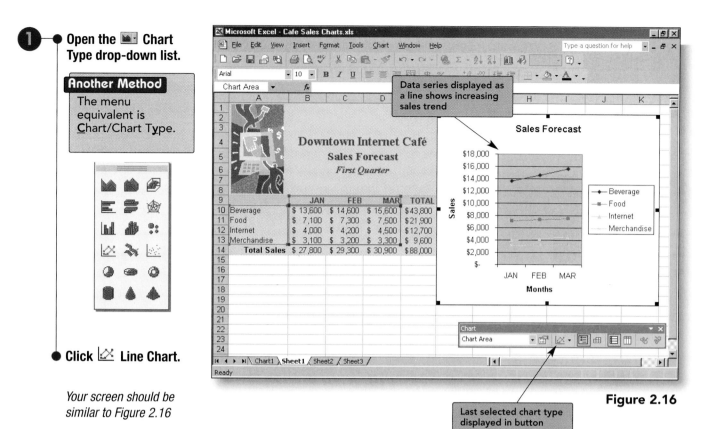

Figure 2.16

The line chart shows the increasing sales trend from month to month. Notice the ⬜ Chart Type button displays a line chart, reflecting the last-selected chart type. You still don't find this chart very interesting so you will change it to a 3-D bar chart next.

2 ● **Open the** ⬜ **Chart Type drop-down list.**

● **Click** ⬜ **3-D Bar Chart.**

Your screen should be similar to Figure 2.17

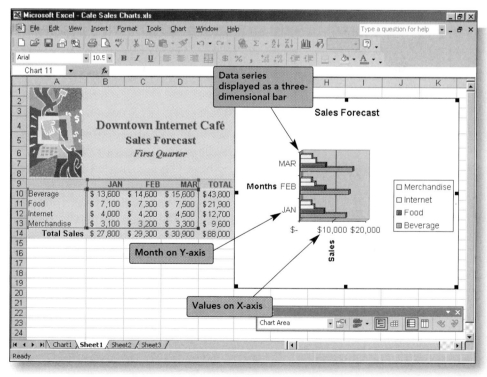

Figure 2.17

The 3-D bar chart reverses the X and Y axes and displays the data series as a three-dimensional bar.

As you can see, it is very easy to change the chart type and format once the data series are specified. The same data can be displayed in many different ways. Depending upon the emphasis you want the chart to make, a different chart style can be selected.

Although the 3-D bar chart shows the sales trends for the three months for the sales categories, again it does not look very interesting. You decide to look at several other chart types to see if you can improve the appearance.

First you would like to see the data represented as an area chart. An area chart represents data the same as a line chart but, in addition, it shades the area below each line to emphasize the degree of change.

3 ● Open the  Chart Type drop-down list.

● Click ▨ Area Chart.

Your screen should be similar to Figure 2.18

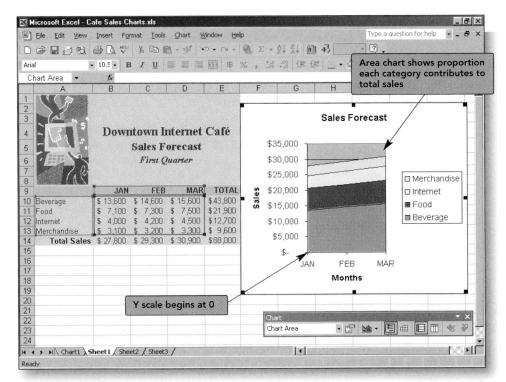

Figure 2.18

The Y-axis scale has changed to reflect the new range of data. The new Y-axis range is the sum of the four categories, or the same as the total number in the worksheet. Using this chart type, you can see the magnitude of change each category contributes to the total sales in each month.

Again you decide this is not the emphasis you want to show and will continue looking at other types of charts. Because not all chart types are available from the Chart Type drop-down list, you will use the Chart Type menu option in the Chart menu instead.

4 • Choose **C**hart/Chart Type.

Your screen should be similar to Figure 2.19

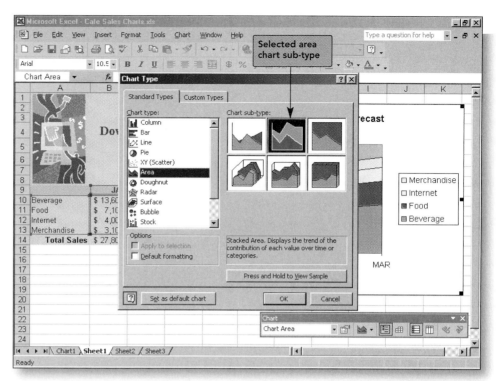

Figure 2.19

The Chart Type dialog box contains the same options as the Chart Wizard—Step 1 dialog box. The current chart type, Area, is the selected option. You want to see how this data will look as a stacked column chart.

5 • Select **⊞** Column.

• Select **⊞** Stacked column with a 3-D visual effect.

• Click and hold

Press and Hold to View Sample .

Your screen should be similar to Figure 2.20

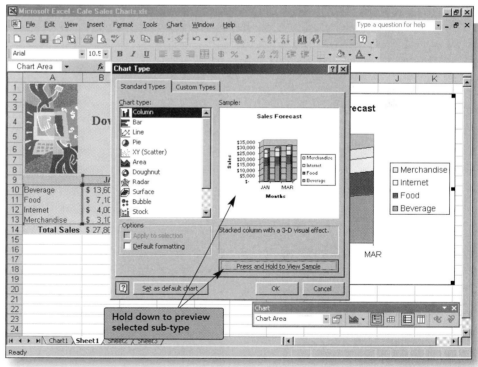

Figure 2.20

The sample chart is redrawn showing the data as a stacked-column chart. This type of chart also shows the proportion of each sales category to the total sales. To see what other types of charts are available,

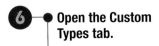

6 ● **Open the Custom Types tab.**

● **Click 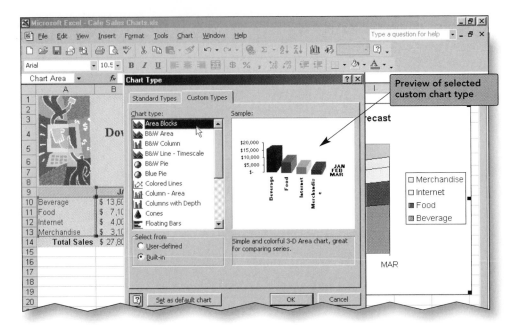 Area Blocks.**

Your screen should be similar to Figure 2.21

Figure 2.21

The Sample area shows how the data you selected for the chart will appear in this style. Custom charts are based upon standard types that are enhanced with additional display settings and custom formatting. Although this is interesting, you feel the data is difficult to read.

7 ● **Select several other custom chart types to see how the data appears in the Sample area.**

● **Select 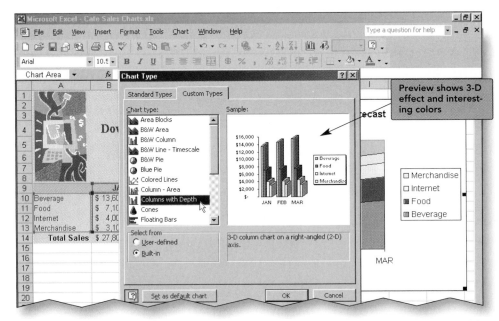 Columns with Depth.**

Your screen should be similar to Figure 2.22

Figure 2.22

This chart shows the sales for each category for each month with more interesting colors and three-dimensional depth.

8 ● **Click** [OK] .

*Your screen should be
similar to Figure 2.23*

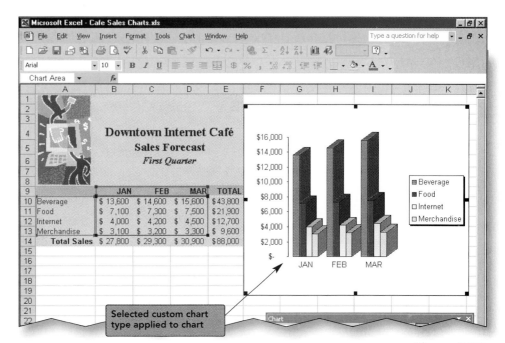

> Selected custom chart
> type applied to chart

Figure 2.23

Adding Chart Titles

Unfortunately, when applying a custom chart type, the chart titles are deleted and you need to add them again.

1 ● **Choose Chart/Chart
Options.**

● **In the Titles tab, enter
the following titles:**

Title	Entry
Chart	**Sales Forecast**
Category	**Months**
Value	**Sales**

*Your screen should be
similar to Figure 2.24*

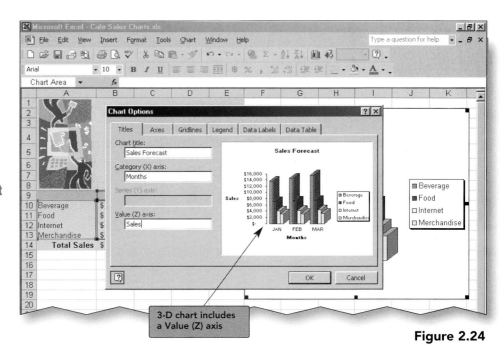

> 3-D chart includes
> a Value (Z) axis

Figure 2.24

Notice that this time instead of entering the Value axis data in the Y axis, you entered it in the Z axis. This is because the Y axis is used as a Series axis on a three-dimensional chart. This three-dimensional chart only has one series of data so the Y axis is not used.

Moving the Legend

While looking at the preview chart, you decide to move the legend below the X axis.

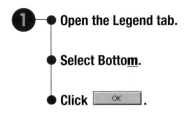

- **Open the Legend tab.**

- **Select Bottom.**

- **Click** OK **.**

Your screen should be similar to Figure 2.25

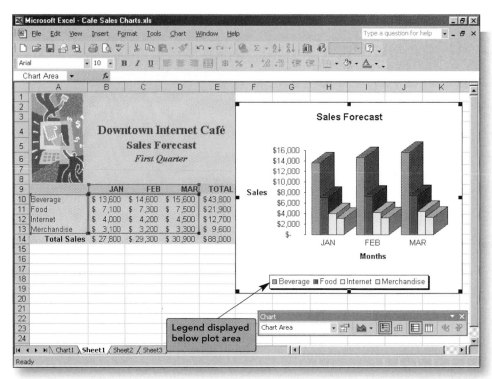

Figure 2.25

The legend is centered below the plot area of the chart and resized to fit the space.

Formatting Chart Elements

Next you want to improve the appearance of the chart by applying formatting to the different chart parts. All the different parts of a chart are separate objects. Because a chart consists of many separate objects, it is a group.

4   A **group** is two or more objects that behave as a single object when moved or sized. A chart consists of many separate objects. For example, the chart title is a single object within the chart object. Some of the objects in a chart are also groups that consist of other objects. For example, the legend is a group object consisting of separate items, each identifying a different data series.

Other objects in a chart are the axis lines, a data series, a data marker, the entire plot area, or the entire chart.

The first formatting change you want to make is to improve the appearance of the chart title. An entire group or each object in a group can be individually selected and then formatted or edited. By selecting the entire group, you can format all objects within the group at once. Alternatively, you can select an object within a group and format it individually.

1 ● **Click on the chart title to select it.**

Your screen should be similar to Figure 2.26

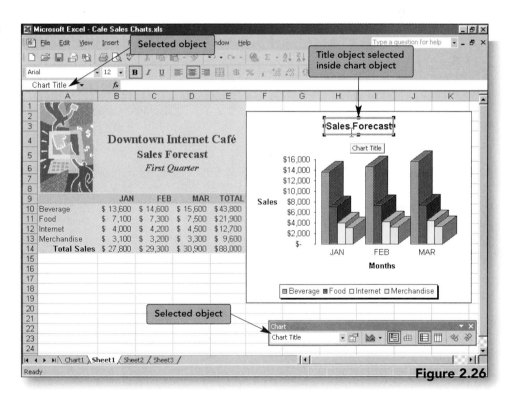

Figure 2.26

The title object is surrounded by a dotted border indicating it is a selected object and that the text inside it can be modified. In addition, the Name box and Chart Objects button display Chart Title as the selected chart object.

As different objects in the chart are selected, the commands on the Format menu change to commands that can be used on the selected object. In addition, the ▣ Format Object button on the Chart toolbar can be used to format the selected object.

2 ● **Click 🗗 Format Chart Title.**

Another Method

The menu equivalent is Format/Selected Chart Title and the shortcut is Ctrl + 1.

● **Open the Font tab.**

Your screen should be similar to Figure 2.27

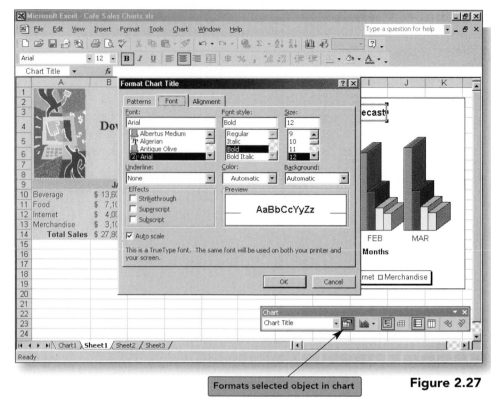

Formats selected object in chart

Figure 2.27

The Format Chart Title dialog box is used to change the patterns, font, and placement of the title.

3 ● **Scroll the Font list and select Tahoma.**

● **Scroll the Size list and select 14.**

● **Open the Color list and select Indigo (1st row, 7th column).**

● **Click OK.**

Your screen should be similar to Figure 2.28

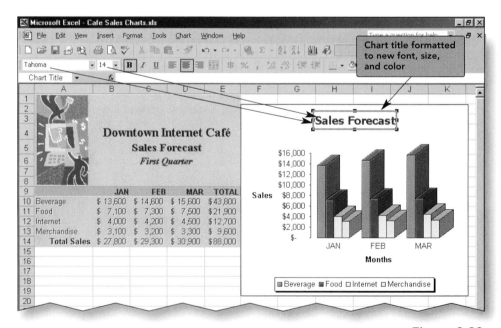

Chart title formatted to new font, size, and color

Figure 2.28

Next you want to change the color of the axis titles. A quicker way to make many formatting changes is to use the Formatting toolbar buttons.

4 ● Click the category-
axis title Months.

● Open the ▲ · Font
Color palette and
change the color to
Indigo.

● Change the color of
the Sales title to
Indigo in the same
manner.

● Click outside the title
to deselect it.

*Your screen should be
similar to Figure 2.29*

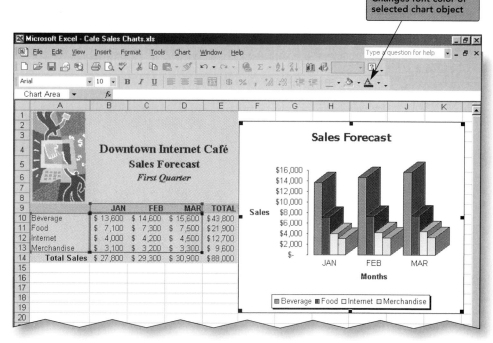

Figure 2.29

Changing Orientation

You also want to change the orientation of the Sales title along the axis so
that it is parallel with the axis line. To do this, you will rotate the label 90
degrees. You can quickly select a chart object and open the related Format
dialog box by double-clicking the object.

1 ● Double-click the Sales
title to open the
Format Axis Title dia-
log box.

● Open the Alignment
tab.

● Drag the Orientation
indicator line upward
to rotate the text 90
degrees.

Additional Information

You can use 🈚 Angle Text
Downward or 🈯 Angle Text
Upward on the Chart toolbar
to quickly change the angle
of a label to 45 degrees.

*Your screen should be
similar to Figure 2.30*

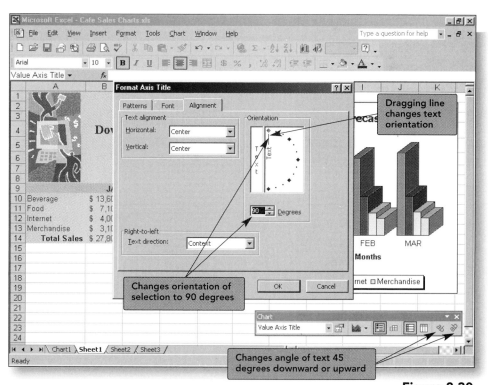

Figure 2.30

You could also enter a positive number in the Degrees box to rotate the selection from lower left to upper right or a negative number to rotate text in the opposite direction. Alternatively, you can use the Degrees scroll buttons to increase and decrease the degrees.

 **Click** OK .

Your screen should be similar to Figure 2.31

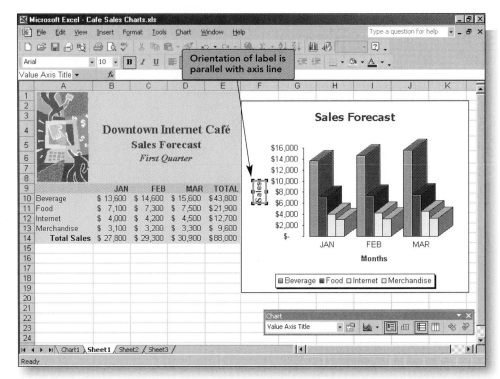

Figure 2.31

The Sales label is now displayed parallel with the Y-axis line.

Finally, you want to add a second line to the chart title. You want the subtitle to be in a smaller font size and italicized. You can select individual sections of text in an object and apply formatting to them just as you would format any other text entry.

3

- Select the chart title.

- Click at the end of the title to place the insertion point.

- Press ←Enter.

- Type **First Quarter**.

- Drag to select the words First Quarter.

- Click _I_ Italic.

- Choose 12 from the `14 ▾` Font Size dropdown list.

- Click in the title to deselect it.

- Save the workbook using the same file name.

Your screen should be similar to Figure 2.32

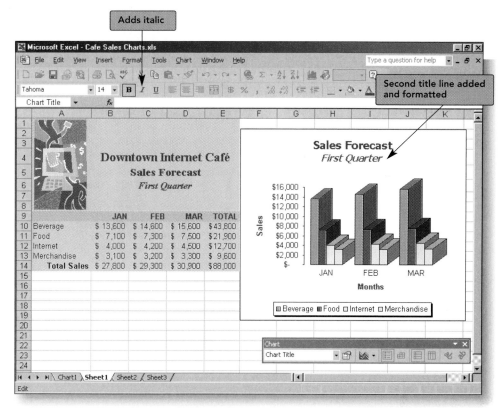

Figure 2.32

Creating a New Chart from an Existing Chart

Now you want to create another chart that will emphasize the sales trend for the Internet connection data series. This chart will use the same data series and titles as the current chart. Rather than recreate much of the same chart for the new chart, you will create a copy of the column chart and then modify it. The original chart remains in the workbook unchanged.

Copying a Chart

Copying a chart object is the same as copying any other Excel data or objects.

1 ● Select the entire chart.

● Click 📋 Copy.

● Move to A16.

● Click 📋 Paste.

Your screen should be similar to Figure 2.33

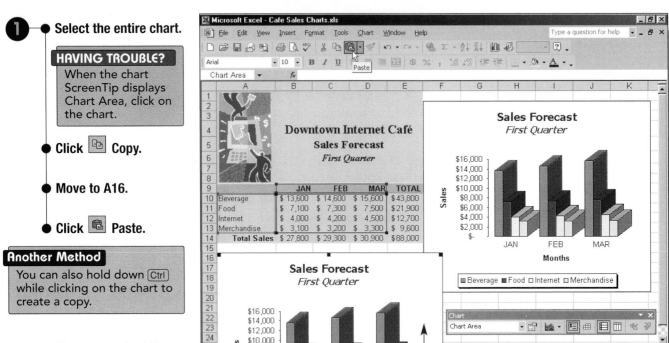

Figure 2.33

Copy of chart

2 ● Change the location of the new chart to a new chart sheet (Chart2).

● Move to Sheet1.

Creating a Combination Chart

To emphasize the Internet data, you want to display the data series as a line and all other data series as columns. This type of chart is called a **combination chart**. It uses two or more chart types to emphasize different information. Because you cannot mix a three-dimensional chart type with a one-dimensional chart type, you first need to change the chart type for the entire chart to a standard one-dimensional column chart. Then you can change the Internet data series to a line.

1 ● Select the chart and change the chart type to Column Chart.

● Click on one of the yellow columns to select the Internet data series.

HAVING TROUBLE?

Sometimes when there are many objects close together, it is easier to select the object from the Chart Objects drop-down list.

● From the 📊▾ Chart Type drop-down menu, select 📈 Line.

Your screen should be similar to Figure 2.34

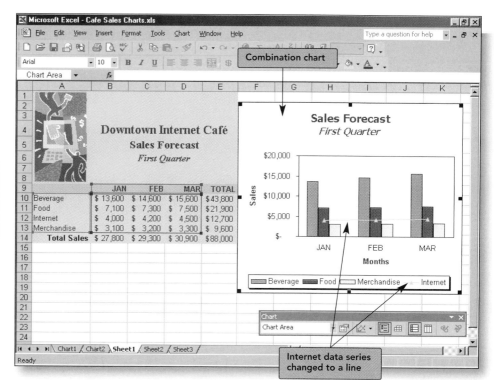

Figure 2.34

A combination chart makes it easy to see comparisons between groups of data or to show different types of data in a single chart. In this case, you can now easily pick out the Internet sales from the other sales categories.

Adding Data Labels

You would like to display data labels containing the actual numbers plotted for the Internet sales on the combination chart.

concept 5

Data Labels

5 **Data labels** provide additional information about a data marker. They can consist of the value of the marker, the name of the data series or category, a percent value, or a bubble size. The different types of data labels that are available depend on the type of chart and the data that is plotted.

Value data labels are helpful when the values are large and you want to know the exact value for one data series. Data labels that display a name are helpful when the size of the chart is large and it is hard to tell what value the data point is over. The percent data label is used when you want to display the percent of each series on charts that show parts of the whole. Bubble size is used on bubble charts to help the reader quickly see how the different bubbles vary in size.

1 ● Double-click the
Internet data series.

● Open the Data Labels
tab.

Another Method
The menu equivalent is
Format/Selected Data
Series/Data Labels.

*Your screen should be
similar to Figure 2.35*

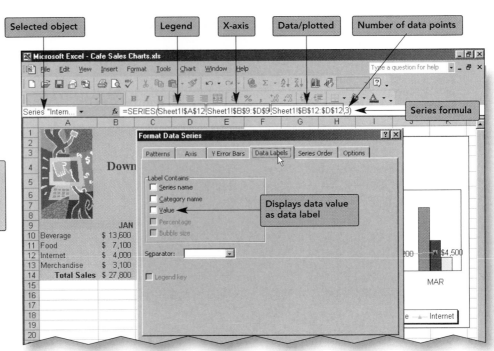

Figure 2.35

Notice that the formula bar displays a **series formula**. This formula links
the chart object to the source worksheet, Sheet1. The formula contains four
arguments: a reference to the cell that includes the data series name (used
in the legend), references to the cells that contain the categories (X-axis
numbers), references to the numbers plotted, and an integer that specifies
the number of data series plotted.

2 ● Select **Value**.

● Click 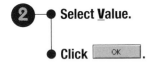 .

*Your screen should be
similar to Figure 2.36*

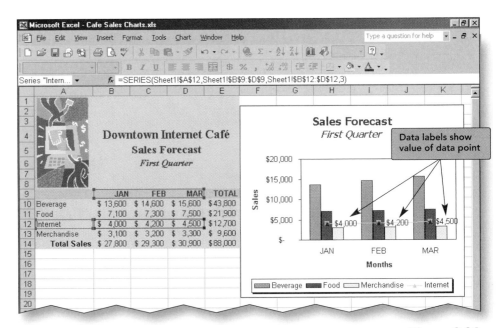

Figure 2.36

Data labels containing the actual values for Internet sales are displayed
next to the data points on the line in the chart.

Changing Data Series Fill Colors

To enhance the appearance of a chart, you can change the format of the data series from the default colors to colors of your choice. As the yellow line is difficult to see on a white background, you want to change the color of the line to make it more visible.

1 ● **Double-click the Internet data series line to open the Format Data Series dialog box.**

● **Open the Patterns tab.**

Your screen should be similar to Figure 2.37

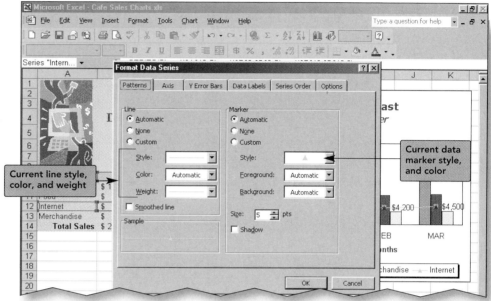

Figure 2.37

The current line and data marker settings are displayed in the Patterns tab. The Sample area shows how your selections will appear.

2 ● **Open the Line Color palette and change the color to blue.**

● **Open the Line Weight drop-down list and increase the line weight setting by one.**

● **Change the Foreground and Background marker color to blue.**

● **Click** OK **.**

Your screen should be similar to Figure 2.38

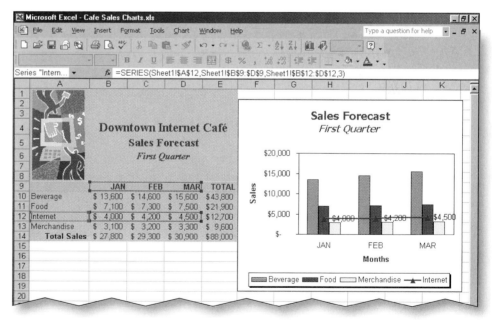

Figure 2.38

Changing Plot Area Colors

Although changing the line color increased its visibility, you think that changing the color of the plot area would also help. You could use the Format Plot Area dialog box to change the color or the ⬛ Fill Color button on the Formatting toolbar.

1 ● Select the plot area.

● Open the [icon] Fill Color drop-down list.

● Choose tan.

Your screen should be similar to Figure 2.39

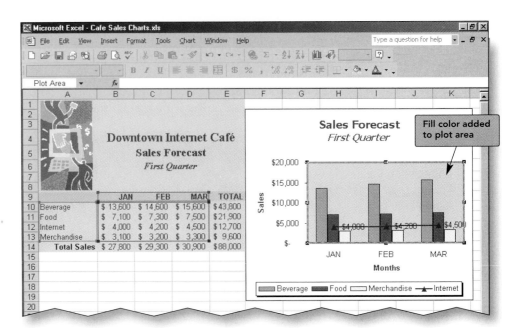

Figure 2.39

Changing Worksheet Data

After checking the worksheet and reconsidering the amounts you have budgeted for the different categories, you now feel that you have underestimated the increase in Internet sales. You are planning to heavily promote the Internet aspect of the Café and anticipate that Internet usage will increase dramatically in February and March and then level off in the following months. You want to change the worksheet to reflect this increase.

1 ● Change the February Internet sales value to **6000**.

● Change the March Internet sales value to **12000**.

Your screen should be similar to Figure 2.40

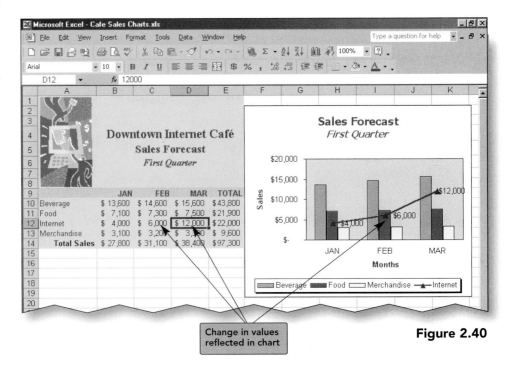

Figure 2.40

The worksheet has been recalculated and all charts that reference those worksheet cells have been redrawn to reflect the change in the data for the Internet sales. Since the chart document is linked to the source data, changes to the source data are automatically reflected in the chart.

2 ● **Look at the charts in the Chart1 and Chart2 sheets to see how they have changed to reflect the change in data.**

Your screen should be similar to Figure 2.41

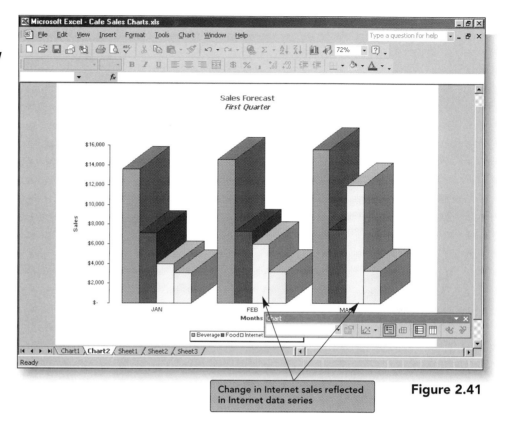

Change in Internet sales reflected in Internet data series

Figure 2.41

The Internet Sales column reflects the change in data in both charts.

Adding a Text Box

Sometimes the information you want to convey in a chart is complicated and may need clarification. In this case, although the chart reflects the Internet sales changes you made in the worksheet, it does not identify the reason for the increase. This information can be entered in a text box.

concept 6

Text Box

6 A **text box** is a rectangular object in which you type text. Text boxes can be added to a sheet or a chart object. To add it to a chart, the chart object must be selected first, otherwise the text box is added to the worksheet. A text box that is part of a chart object can only be sized and moved within the chart object. If you move the chart object, the text box moves with it because it is part of the group. If you do not add it to the chart, it will not move as part of the chart if you move the chart to another location.

Text that is entered in a text box wraps to fit within the boundaries of the text box. This feature is called **word wrap** and eliminates the need to press [Enter] to end a line. If you change the size and shape of the text box, the text automatically rewraps on the line to adjust to the new size.

You will add a text box containing the text Internet Promotion to draw attention to the increase in Internet sales. A text box is created using the  Text Box button on the Drawing toolbar.

1
● **Switch to Sheet1.**

● **Select the chart.**

● **Click** 🖉 **Drawing (on the Standard toolbar).**

● **Click** 🔲 **Text Box (on the Drawing toolbar).**

● **Move the mouse pointer to the space above the February columns of data and drag to create a text box that is approximately 1 1/2 inch by 1/2 inch (see Figure 2.42).**

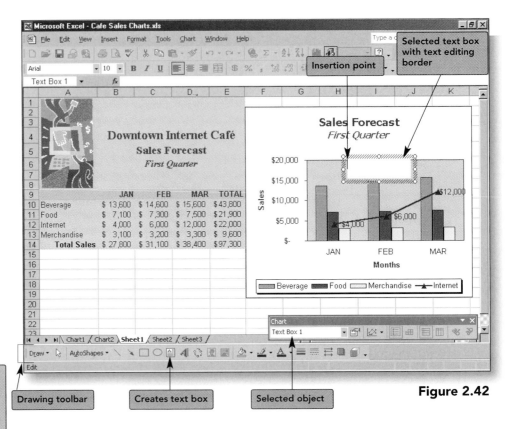

Figure 2.42

Additional Information
The mouse pointer appears as ↓, indicating a text box will be created as you drag the mouse.

Your screen should be similar to Figure 2.42

Additional Information
A dotted border around a selected object indicates that you can format the box itself. Clicking the hatched border changes it to dotted border.

The text box is a selected object and is surrounded with a hatched border that indicates you can enter, delete, select, and format the text inside the box. It also displays an insertion point indicating that it is waiting for you to enter the text. As you type the text in the text box, do not be concerned if all the text is not visible within the text box. You will resize the box if needed to display the entire entry.

② ● Type **Effects of Internet Promotion.**

● If necessary, adjust the size of the text box by dragging the sizing handles until it is just large enough to fully display the text on two lines.

● Click outside the text box to deselect it.

Your screen should be similar to Figure 2.43

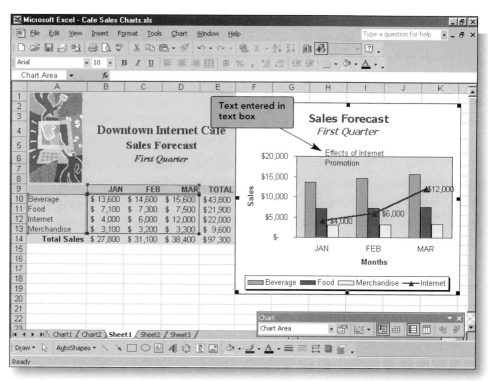

Figure 2.43

The text in the text box is difficult to read because it overlaps the plot area and the box does not include a border line or fill color. To make it stand out better, you will add a fill color to the text box.

③ ● Select the text box.

● Click the hatched text box border to turn off text editing (the insertion point disappears).

Additional Information

The text box border is dotted and the insertion point is not displayed, indicating you can edit the text box.

● Open the 🖌️▾ Fill Color drop-down list and select Indigo.

Additional Information

You can use the 🖌️▾ and A▾ buttons on either the Formatting or Drawing toolbars.

● From the A▾ Font Color list, select White.

● Readjust the size of the text box and move it to the position displayed in Figure 2.44.

Your screen should be similar to Figure 2.44

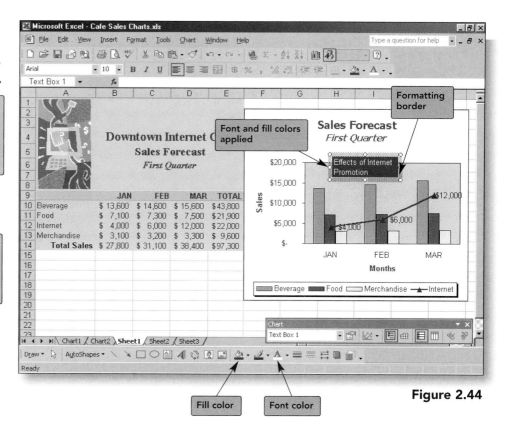

Figure 2.44

Adding Arrows

Next you want to draw an arrow from the text box to the Internet data series line. Like a text box, an arrow is a separate object that can be added to a worksheet or a chart.

1 ● Click  Arrow (on the Drawing toolbar).

Additional Information

The mouse pointer appears as a ✛.

● To draw the arrow, click on the lower-right corner of the text box and drag to the Internet line. (See Figure 2.45)

Additional Information

If you hold down ⬆Shift while dragging, a straight horizontal line is drawn.

Your screen should be similar to Figure 2.45

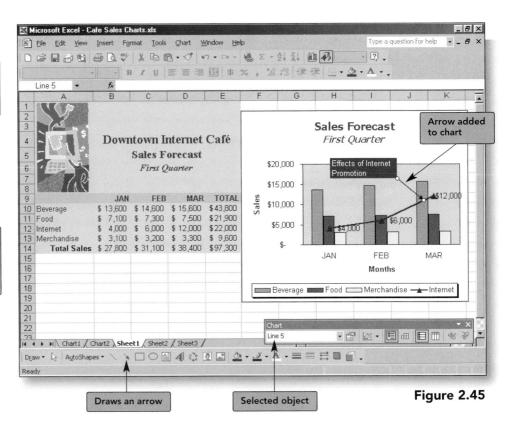

Draws an arrow

Selected object

Figure 2.45

A line with an arrowhead at the end is displayed. The arrow is automatically a selected object. The handles at both ends of the arrow let you adjust its size and location. You can also change the color and weight of the line to make it stand out more.

2
- If necessary, move and size the arrow to adjust its position as in Figure 2.46.

- Click [icon] Line Color and select Indigo.

- Click [icon] Line Style and increase the line weight to 1 1/2 point.

- Deselect the arrow.

- Click [icon] Save.

Your screen should be similar to Figure 2.46

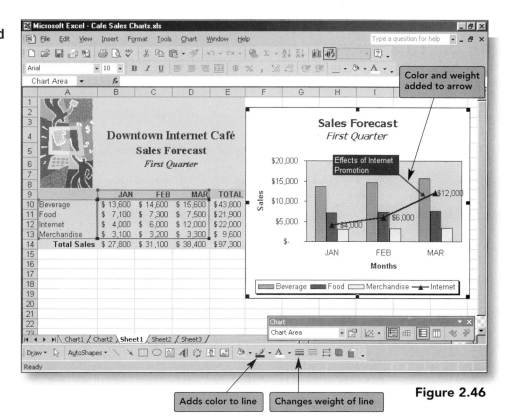

Figure 2.46

Color and weight added to arrow

Adds color to line

Changes weight of line

Creating and Formatting a Pie Chart

The last chart you will make will use the Total worksheet data in column E. You want to see what proportion each type of sales are of all sales for the quarter. The best chart for this purpose is a pie chart.

A pie chart compares parts to the whole in a similar manner to a stacked-column chart. However, in pie charts, there are no axes. Instead, the worksheet data that is charted is displayed as slices in a circle or pie. Each slice is displayed as a percentage of the total.

Selecting the Pie Chart Data

The use of X (category) and data series settings in a pie chart is different from their use in a column or line chart. The X series labels the slices of the pie rather than the X axis. The data series is used to create the slices in the pie. Only one data series can be specified in a pie chart.

The row labels in column A will label the slices and the total values in column E will be used as the data series.

In addition to creating a chart using the Wizard, you can create a chart by selecting the chart type from the Chart Type toolbar button after the data series has been selected.

Additional Information

You can also create a chart using the default chart type (column) in a new chart sheet by selecting the data range and pressing F11.

1 ● **Select A10 through A13 and E10 through E13.**

HAVING TROUBLE?
Hold down Ctrl while selecting nonadjacent ranges.

● **If necessary, display the Chart toolbar.**

● **Open the [⬚]▾ Chart Type drop-down menu and choose [⬚] 3-D Pie Chart.**

Your screen should be similar to Figure 2.47

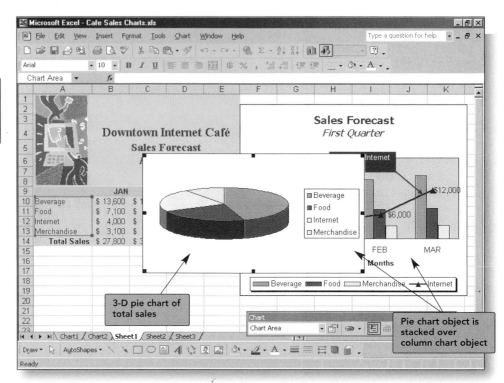

Figure 2.47

A three-dimensional pie chart is drawn in the worksheet. Each value in the data series is displayed as a slice of the pie chart. The size of the slice represents the proportion each sales category is of total sales.

As objects are added to the worksheet, they automatically **stack** in individual layers. The stacking order is apparent when objects overlap. Stacking allows you to create different effects by overlapping objects. Because you can rearrange the stacking order, you do not have to add or create the objects in the order in which you want them to appear.

2 ● **Move the combination chart to top-align with cell A16 below the worksheet data.**

● **Move and size the pie chart to be displayed over cells F1 through K14.**

Additional Information
Hold down Alt while moving to snap the chart to the cells.

Your screen should be similar to Figure 2.48

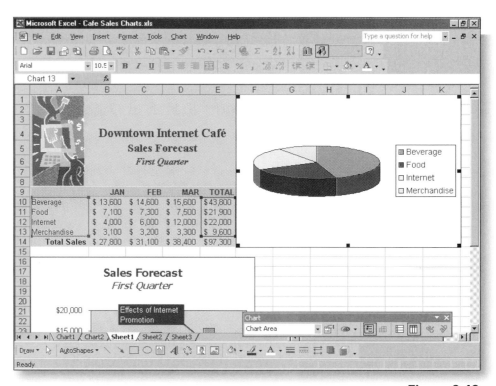

Figure 2.48

Formatting the Pie Chart

To clarify the meaning of the chart, you need to add a chart title. In addition, you want to turn off the legend and display data labels instead to label the slices of the pie.

1 ● **Choose Chart/Chart Options.**

● **Open the Titles tab.**

● **In the Chart Title text box, enter Total Sales by Category.**

● **Open the Legend tab and clear the Show Legend option.**

Another Method

You can also click
🔳 Legend to turn
on/off the display of
the legend.

● **Open the Data Labels tab and select the Category name and Percentage options.**

● Click ⬜ OK ⬜.

Your screen should be similar to Figure 2.49

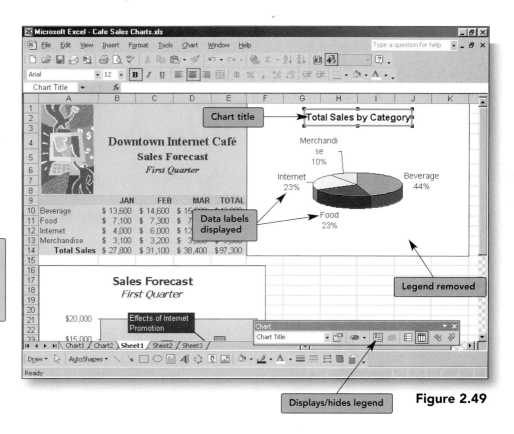

Figure 2.49

The pie chart is redrawn to show the data labels and percents. The data label text box size is based on the size of the chart and the text is appropriately sized to fit in the box. Because the default size of data labels is a little too large, the entire Merchandise label does not appear on one line. To fix this, you will change the font of the data label text. You also want to enhance the appearance of the data labels and title.

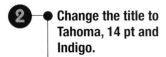

2 ● Change the title to Tahoma, 14 pt and Indigo.

● Select the data labels.

● Change the font to Arial Narrow.

● Change the font color to Indigo.

Your screen should be similar to Figure 2.50

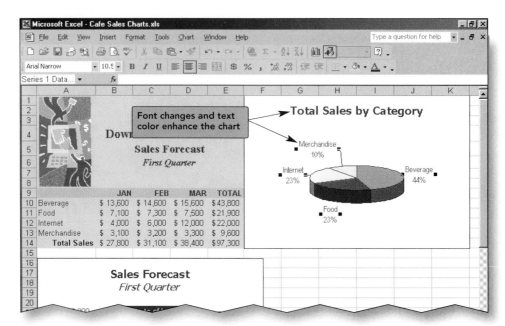

Figure 2.50

Exploding and Rotating the Pie

Next, you want to separate slightly or **explode** the Internet slice of the pie to emphasize the data in that category.

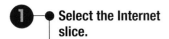

1 ● Select the Internet slice.

HAVING TROUBLE?

To select an object within a group, select the group first and then select the object within the group. Selection handles surround the selected object.

● Drag the selected slice away from the pie.

Additional Information

If all slices on the pie are selected, dragging one slice explodes all slices at the same time.

Your screen should be similar to Figure 2.51

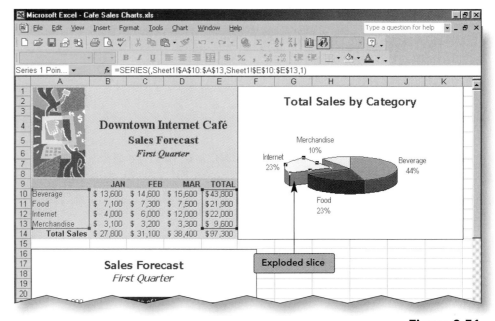

Figure 2.51

The slice is separated from the rest of the pie chart. You also want to change the position of the Internet slice so that it is toward the front of the pie. When a pie chart is created, the first data point is placed to the right of the middle at the top of the chart. The rest of the data points are placed in order to the right until the circle is complete. To change the order in which the slices are displayed, you can rotate the pie chart.

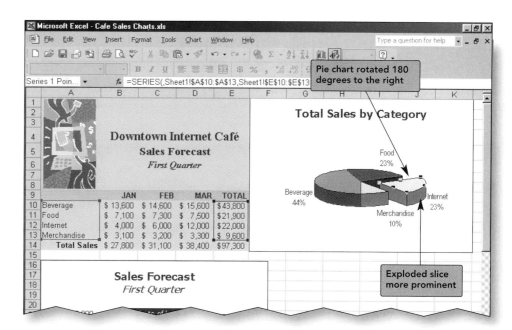

2 ● **Double-click the Internet data series slice.**

● **Open the Options tab.**

● **Change the Angle of first slice setting to 180 degrees.**

● **Click [OK].**

Your screen should be similar to Figure 2.52

Figure 2.52

The entire pie chart has rotated 180 degrees to the right and now the Internet data slice appears toward the front of the chart.

Applying Patterns and Color

The last change you would like to make is to add patterns to the pie chart data points. As you have seen, when Excel creates a chart each data series (or data point in the case of a pie chart) is automatically displayed in a different color. Although the data series are easy to distinguish from one another onscreen, if you do not have a color printer the colors are printed as shades of gray and may be difficult to distinguish. To make the data series more distinguishable on a black-and-white printer, you can apply a different pattern to each data series object.

1 ● **Double-click the Beverage data series slice.**

● **Open the Patterns tab.**

Your screen should be similar to Figure 2.53

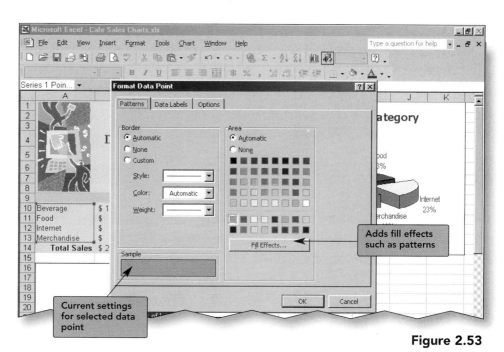

Figure 2.53

The options available in the Pattern tab vary depending upon the type of data point that is selected. In this case, because the selected data point is a pie slice, the options let you change the border and the background area. The current setting for the selected data point is displayed in the sample area. This consists of a black border with a fill color of periwinkle blue. You will add a pattern.

2 • Click .

• Open the Pattern tab.

Your screen should be similar to Figure 2.54

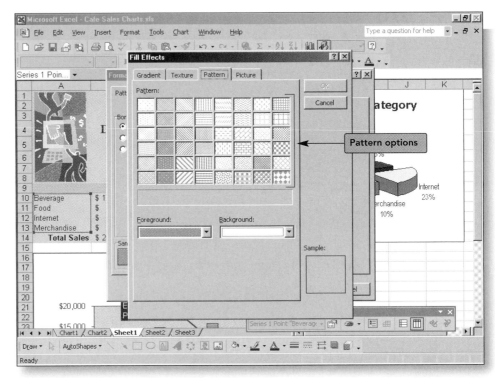

Figure 2.54

From the Fill Effects dialog box, you can change options for gradients, textures, patterns, and pictures used in formatting the selected object. You will add a pattern to the existing fill.

3 • From the Pattern palette, select a pattern of your choice.

• Click 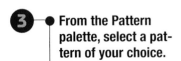 (twice) to close both dialog boxes.

Your screen should be similar to Figure 2.55

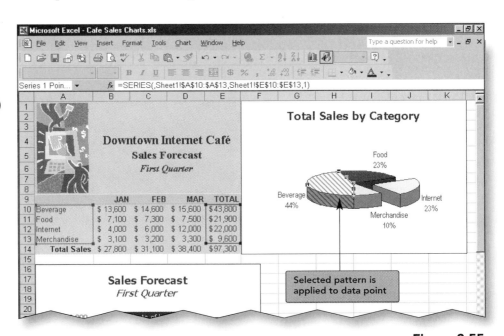

Figure 2.55

The pattern is applied to the selected data point. Next you will add a pattern to the Internet data series slice.

4
- Double-click the Internet data series slice.
- Click `Fill Effects...`.
- Open the Pattern tab.

Your screen should be similar to Figure 2.56

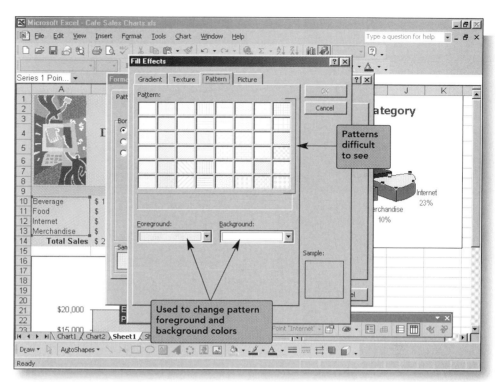

Figure 2.56

Because yellow is a light color, it is difficult to see the patterns in the Fill Effects dialog box. A pattern consists of a foreground color and a background color. The default foreground color is the same as the fill color and the background color is white. To increase the contrast, you can change the color selection of either.

5
- From the Foreground color drop-down list, select a darker color of your choice.
- Select a different pattern.
- Click `OK` (twice).

Your screen should be similar to Figure 2.57

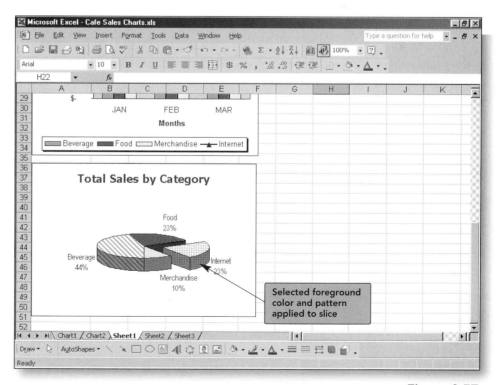

Figure 2.57

You will leave the other two data points without patterns. Finally you want to make the pie chart plot area larger.

6

- Select the plot area.

- Drag the sizing handle outward to increase the pie chart size slightly as in Figure 2.58.

- Select the pie chart and move it below the combination chart to top-align with cell A36.

- Deselect the chart.

- Close the Chart toolbar.

- Save the workbook.

Your screen should be similar to Figure 2.58

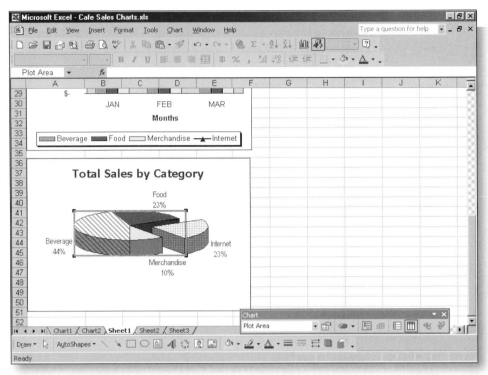

Figure 2.58

Documenting a Workbook

Now you are ready to preview and print the worksheet and charts. Before doing this, however, you will add documentation to the workbook. Each workbook includes summary information that is associated with the file.

1

- Choose File/Properties.

- Select each tab in the Properties dialog box and look at the recorded information.

- Open the Summary tab.

Your screen should be similar to Figure 2.59

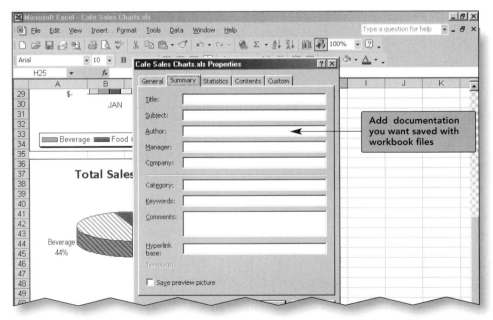

Add documentation you want saved with workbook files

Figure 2.59

The Summary tab is used to specify information you want associated with the file such as a title, subject, author, keywords, and comments about the workbook file. Additionally, you can specify to save a picture of the first page of the file for previewing in the Open dialog box. This information helps you locate the workbook file you want to use as well as indicate the objectives and use of the workbook.

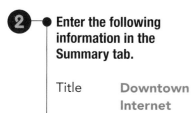

2 ● Enter the following information in the Summary tab.

Title   **Downtown Internet Cafe**

Subject   **Sales Forecast**

Author   **your name**

● Select the Save preview picture option.

● Click   OK .

Your chart should be similar to Figure 2.60

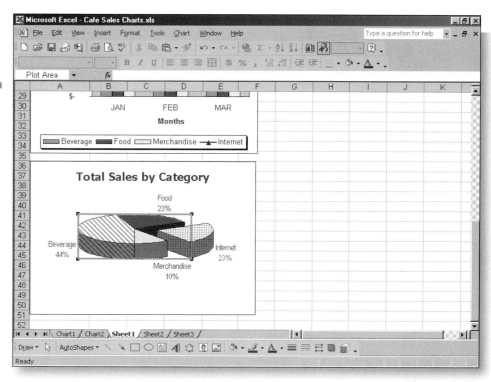

Figure 2.60

Preparing the Workbook for Printing

It is very important before printing charts to preview how they will appear when printed. Formats that look good onscreen may not produce good printed results.

Before printing, you can change the layout of the worksheet and charts to improve the appearance of the printed output. The size and alignment of the worksheet can be changed to make it more attractive on the paper. Additionally, you can include information in a header on each page.

Previewing the Workbook

Your workbook file includes two new chart sheets and a worksheet. You decide the worksheet would look better with more space between the data and charts. You will adjust the placement of the charts and then preview the entire workbook. To preview them all at once, you need to change the print setting to print the entire workbook first.

1 ● Move the combination chart to top-align with cell A18.

● Move the pie chart to top-align with cell A40.

Your screen should be similar to Figure 2.61

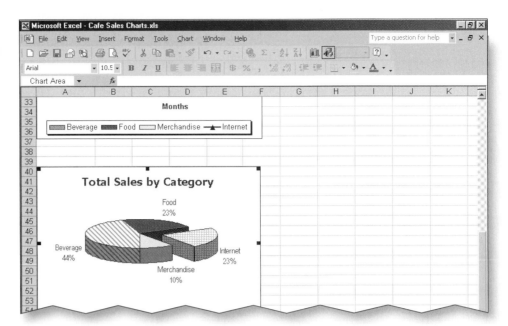

Figure 2.61

2 ● Deselect the chart object.

● Choose **File/Print/Entire workbook.**

● Click Preview.

● If necessary, reduce the zoom to see the full page.

Your screen should be similar to Figure 2.62

Changes settings associated with sheet you are previewing

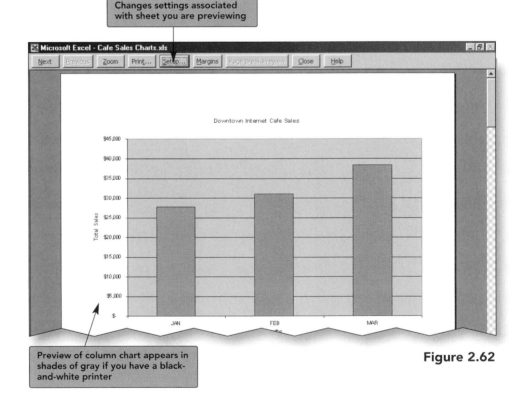

Preview of column chart appears in shades of gray if you have a black-and-white printer

Figure 2.62

Because the column chart is on a separate chart sheet, it is displayed on a page by itself. In addition, if you are not using a color printer, the preview displays the chart colors in shades of gray as it will appear when printed on a black-and-white printer. You will change the print setting associated with this chart sheet to fix this problem. The Print Preview toolbar buttons are used to access many print and page layout changes while you are previewing a document.

3

● Click [Setup...].

● **Open the Chart tab.**

Your screen should be similar to Figure 2.63

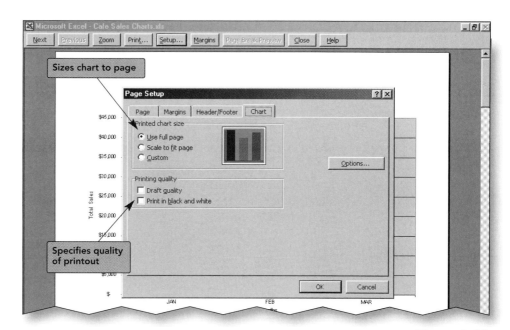

Figure 2.63

Additional Information

You can print an embedded chart without the worksheet by selecting it before using the command to print.

Because chart sheets print only one chart on a page, the default setting is to size the chart to fill the entire page. The Draft Quality setting suppresses the printing of graphics and gridlines, thereby reducing printing time. The black-and-white option applies patterns to data series in place of colors while leaving other areas in shades of gray. If there is a single data series, it is changed to solid black. On a color printer, all other areas are still printed in color when this option is selected.

4

● **Select Print in black and white.**

● **Click [OK].**

Your screen should be similar to Figure 2.64

Another Method

The menu equivalent is File/Page Setup/Chart/Print in black and white.

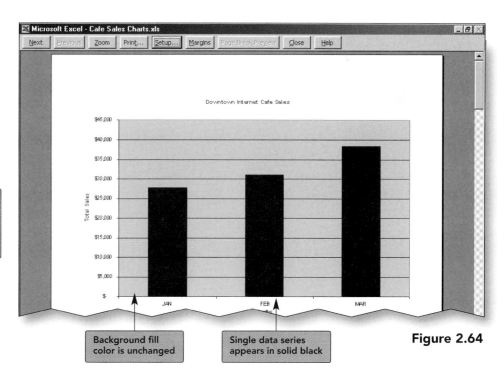

Figure 2.64

The data series changes to black and the background fill has not changed.

5 ● Click `Next` to see the chart in the next Chart sheet.

Your screen should be similar to Figure 2.65

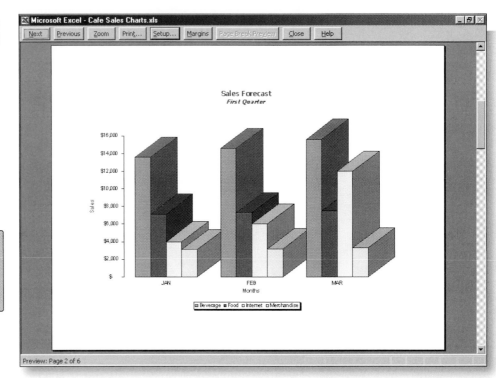

Figure 2.65

Chart 2 looks as if it will print satisfactorily using the default print settings.

6 ● Click `Next` to see the worksheet and charts in Sheet 1.

Your screen should be similar to Figure 2.66

Not centered on page

Bottom of pie chart is cut off

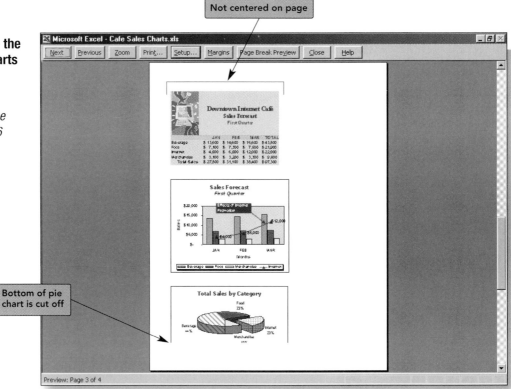

Figure 2.66

You can now see that the bottom of the pie chart exceeds the page margins and will not print on the page. You can also see that the printout will not appear balanced between the page margins. You will make several changes to the layout of the page to correct these problems.

Sizing the Worksheet

First you will reduce the worksheet and chart sizes so that they will fit on one page. Although you could resize the charts in the worksheet, a quicker way is to use the scaling feature to reduce or enlarge the worksheet contents by a percentage or to fit it to a specific number of pages. You want to have the program scale the worksheet to fit on one page.

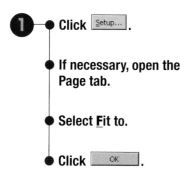

● Click Setup... .

● If necessary, open the Page tab.

● Select Fit to.

● Click OK .

Your screen should be similar to Figure 2.67

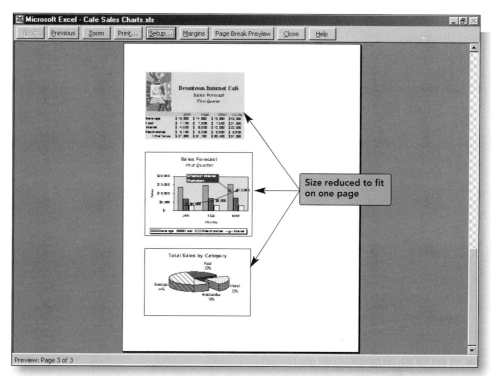

Figure 2.67

The size of the worksheet and charts has been reduced and they now fit on a single page.

Aligning a Sheet on a Page

You would also like to center the worksheet horizontally on the page. The default worksheet margin settings include 1-inch top and bottom margins and .75-inch right and left margins. The **margins** are the blank space outside the printing area around the edges of the paper. The worksheet contents appear in the printable area inside the margins. You want to center the worksheet data horizontally within the existing margins.

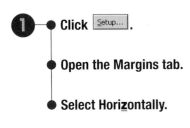

1 ● Click [Setup...].

● Open the Margins tab.

● Select Hori<u>z</u>ontally.

Your screen should be similar to Figure 2.68

Another Method

The menu equivalent is <u>F</u>ile/Page Set<u>u</u>p/Margins/ Hori<u>z</u>ontally.

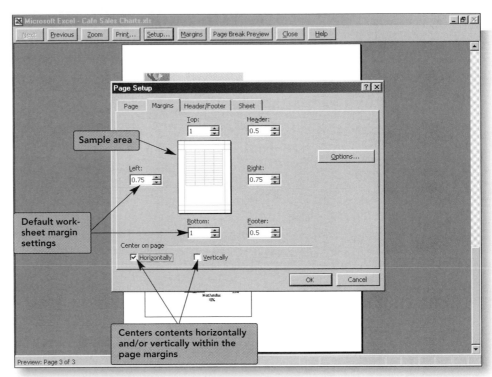

Figure 2.68

The sample area shows the effect of this change on the page layout.

Adding Predefined Headers and Footers

Finally, you want to include your name and the date in a header.

---

concept 7

Header and Footer

7 A **header** is a line or several lines of text that appears at the top of a page just above the top margin line. A **footer** is a line or several lines of text that appears at the bottom of a page just below the bottom margin line. Information that is commonly placed in a header or footer includes the date and page number.

You can select from predefined header and footer text or enter your own custom text. The information contained in the predefined header and footer text is obtained from the document properties associated with the workbook and from the program and system settings.

Header and footer text can be formatted like any other text. In addition, you can control the placement of the header and footer text by specifying where it should appear: left-aligned, centered, or right-aligned in the header or footer space.

You will add a predefined header to the worksheet that displays your name, the date and page number.

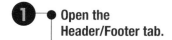

1 ● Open the Header/Footer tab.

● Open the Header drop-down list box and select the Prepared By [your name] [date], Page 3 option.

Another Method

The menu equivalent is <u>F</u>ile/ Page Set<u>u</u>p/Header/Footer.

Your screen should be similar to Figure 2.69

Additional Information

Predefined footers can be added by selecting the footer option from the Footer drop-down list.

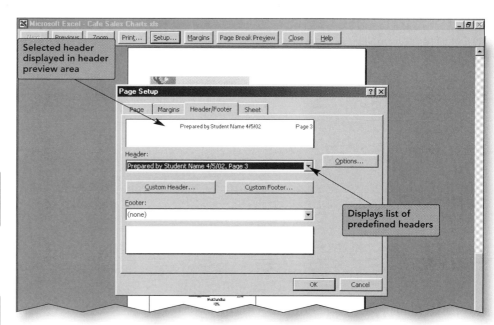

Figure 2.69

The selected header is displayed in the header area of the dialog box. It could then be edited or formatted to meet your needs.

2 ● Click [OK].

Your screen should be similar to Figure 2.70

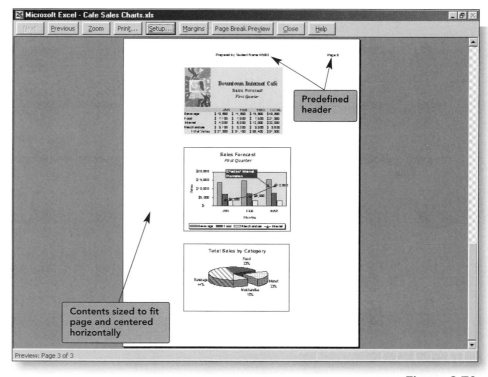

Figure 2.70

The preview window displays the worksheet centered horizontally between the right and left margins. The header you selected is displayed above the top margin line. It now appears the way you want it to look when printed.

● Add a predefined
footer to each of the
chart sheets that dis-
plays your name, page
number, and date.

HAVING TROUBLE?

Click Previous to
display previous
sheets.

*Your screen should be
similar to Figure 2.71*

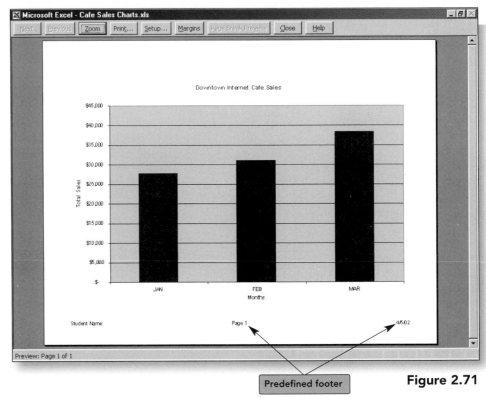

Predefined footer

Figure 2.71

Printing the Workbook

Printing a worksheet that includes charts requires a printer with graphics
capability. However, the actual procedure to print is the same as printing a
worksheet that does not include charts.

1 ● Click Print....

● Move to cell A9 of Sheet1.

● If necessary, close the Chart and Drawing toolbars.

● Exit Excel, saving the workbook again.

The workbook documentation and page layout settings you specified have
been saved with the workbook file.

Your printed output should be similar to that shown here.

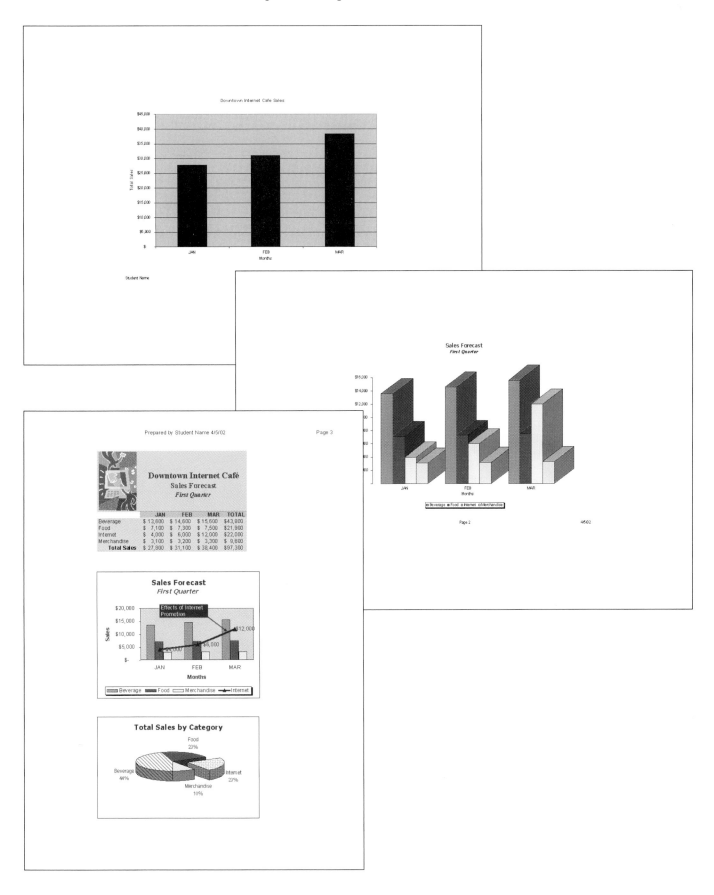

LAB 2

Organizing Your Work

Chart (EX2.5)

A **chart** is visual representation of data that is used to convey information in an easy-to-understand and attractive manner. Different types of charts are used to represent data in different ways.

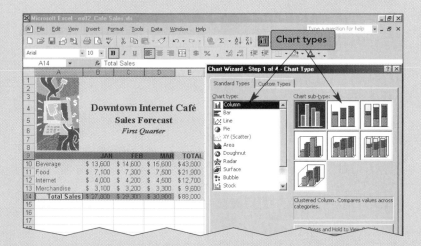

Chart Elements (EX2.6)

Chart elements consist of a number of parts that are used to graphically display the worksheet data.

Chart Objects (EX2.12)

A **chart object** is a graphic object that is created using charting features included in Excel. A chart object can be inserted into a worksheet or into a special chart sheet.

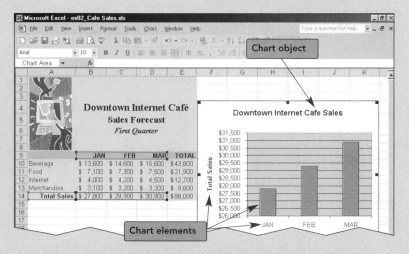

Group (EX2.25)

Because it consists of many separate objects, a chart object is a group. A **group** is two or more objects that behave as a single object when moved or sized.

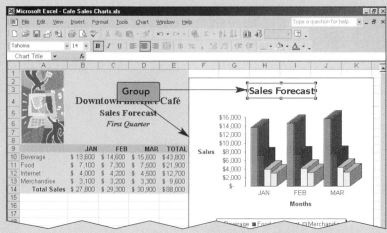

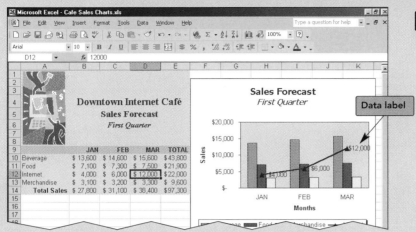

Data Label (EX2.31)

Data labels provide additional information about a data marker.

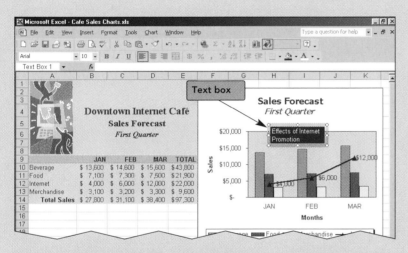

Text Box (EX2.35)

A **text box** is a rectangular object in which you type text. Text boxes can be added to a sheet or to a chart object.

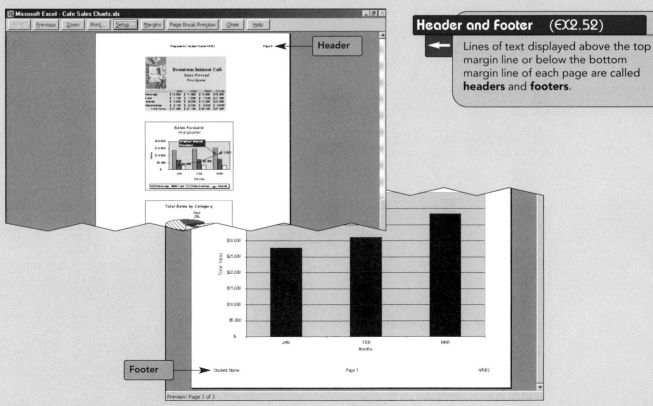

Header and Footer (EX2.52)

Lines of text displayed above the top margin line or below the bottom margin line of each page are called **headers** and **footers**.

key terms

category-axis EX2.6	data series EX2.6	stack EX2.40
category-axis title EX2.6	embedded chart EX2.12	text box EX2.35
category name EX2.6	explode EX2.42	value axis EX2.6
chart EX2.5	footer EX2.52	value-axis title EX2.6
chart gridlines EX2.6	group EX2.25	word wrap EX2.35
chart object EX2.12	header EX2.52	X axis EX2.6
chart title EX2.6	legend EX2.6	Y axis EX2.6
combination chart EX2.30	margins EX2.51	Z axis EX2.6
data label EX2.31	plot area EX2.6	
data marker EX2.6	series formula EX2.32	

mous skills

The Microsoft Office User Specialist (MOUS) certification program is designed to measure your proficiency in performing basic tasks using the Office XP applications. Getting certified demonstrates that you have the skills and provides a valuable industry credential for employment. After completing this lab, you have learned the following Microsoft Office User Specialist skills:

Skill	Description	Page
Formatting and Printing Worksheets	Modify Page Setup options for worksheets	EX2.51
Creating and Modifying Graphics	Create, modify, and position and print charts	EX2.49

command summary

Command	Shortcut Keys	Button	Action
File/Print/Entire Workbook			Prints all the sheets in a workbook
File/Properties/Summary			Specify information to document file
File/Page Setup/Header/Footer			Adds header and/or footer
File/Page Setup/Chart/ Print in black and white			Prints chart in black and white
File/Page Setup/Margins/ Horizontally			Horizontally centers contents between margins
File/Page Setup/Page/Fit to			Sizes print area to fit on a specified number of pages
Insert/Chart		📊	Starts the Chart Wizard
Format/Selected Data Series/ Data Labels			Adds data labels to data points
Format/Selected Legend	Ctrl + 1		Changes format of legend
Format/Selected Chart Title	Ctrl + 1	🔲	Changes format of selected chart title
Format/Selected Data Series	Ctrl + 1	🔲	Changes format of selected data series
Chart/Chart Type		📊▾	Changes type of chart
Chart/Chart Options/Legend/ Show Legend		🔲	Displays/Hides legend
Chart/Location			Places chart in selected worksheet or chart sheet

Terminology

screen identification

In the following worksheet and chart, letters identify important elements. Enter the correct term for each screen element in the space provided.

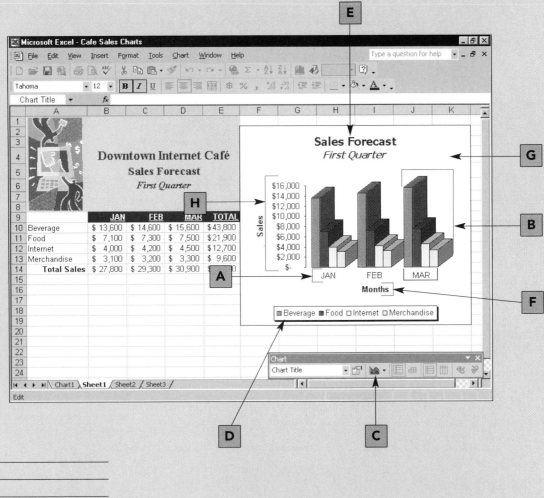

A. _____

B. _____

C. _____

D. _____

E. _____

F. _____

G. _____

H. _____

matching

Match the lettered item on the right with the numbered item on the left.

1. [icon] _____   a. numbered scale along left boundary line of the chart

2. data marker _____   b. bottom boundary line of the chart

3. [icon] _____   c. identifies each number represented in a data series

4. X-axis _____   d. area of chart bounded by X- and Y-axes

5. explode _____   e. changes the type of chart

6. plot area _____   f. identifies the chart data series names and data markers

7. column chart _____   g. a chart that displays data as vertical columns

8. Value axis _____   h. starts the Chart Wizard

9. legend _____   i. to separate wedge slightly from other wedges of pie

10. combination chart _____   j. includes mixed data markers

multiple choice

Circle the correct response to the questions below.

1. A(n) _____ links a chart object to the source worksheet.
   a. embedded chart
   b. stack
   c. series formula
   d. data marker

2. The _____ names displayed along the X-axis correspond to the headings for the worksheet data that is plotted along the X-axis.
   a. variable
   b. category
   c. value
   d. option

3. A _____ identifies the chart data series names and data markers that correspond to each data series.
   a. category
   b. value axis
   c. legend
   d. data label

4. Charts that are inserted into a worksheet are called:
   a. embedded objects
   b. attached objects
   c. inserted objects
   d. active objects

5. A(n) _____ represents data like a line chart and shades the area below each line to emphasize the degree of change.
   a. combination chart
   b. area chart
   c. surface chart
   d. doughnut chart

6. _____ can consist of the value of the marker, the name of the data series or category, a percent value, or a bubble size.
   a. legends
   b. X axis
   c. Y axis
   d. data labels

7. A(n) _____ is a rectangular object in which you type text.
   a. text box
   b. label
   c. input box
   d. embedded object

8. A _____ displays the data values as columns stacked upon each other.
   a. line chart
   b. bar chart
   c. stacked-column chart
   d. combination chart

9. Charts that display data as slices of a circle and show the relationship of each value in a data series to the series as a whole are called:
   a. area charts
   b. value charts
   c. pie charts
   d. bar charts

10. A chart that uses two or more chart types to emphasize different information is called a(n):
    a. area chart
    b. pie chart
    c. bar chart
    d. combination chart

true/false

Circle the correct answer to the following questions.

1.	The plot area is visually displayed within the X- and Y-axis boundaries.	True	False
2.	A bar chart displays data as a line and is commonly used to show trends over time.	True	False
3.	The Y-axis title line is called the category-axis title.	True	False
4.	An entire group or each object in a group can be individually selected and then formatted or edited.	True	False
5.	A series formula links the chart object to the source worksheet.	True	False
6.	Value data labels are helpful when the values are large and you want to know the exact value for one data series.	True	False
7.	Text that is entered in a text box wraps to fit within the boundaries of the text box.	True	False
8.	Separating slightly or exploding a slice of a pie chart emphasizes the data.	True	False
9.	Patterns can be added to slices of a pie chart to make it easier to read.	True	False
10.	A header is a line or several lines of text that appears at the bottom of each page just below the top margin.	True	False

Concepts

fill-in questions

Complete the following statements by filling in the blanks with the correct terms.

1. A visual representation of data in an easy-to-understand and attractive manner is called a(n) _____.

2. A(n) _____ describes the symbols used within the chart to identify different data series.

3. The bottom boundary of a chart is the _____ and the left boundary is the _____.

4. A chart that is inserted into a worksheet is a(n) _____ object.

5. A(n) _____ is a line or several lines of text that appears at the top of each page just below the top margin.

6. A(n) _____ is two or more objects that behave as a single object.

7. _____ provide additional information about a data marker.

8. A(n) _____ identifies the chart data series names and data markers that correspond to each data series.

9. The _____ is a numbered scale whose numbers are determined by the data used in the chart.

10. A chart that is inserted into a separate chart sheet is also saved with the _____ file.

discussion questions

1. Define each of the following terms and discuss how they are related to one another: chart type, chart element, and chart object.

2. Discuss how column and bar charts represent data. How do they differ from pie charts?

3. What type of information would best be represented by a line chart?

4. Describe how a 3-D column chart differs from a 2-D column chart.

Hands-on Exercises

rating system

★ Easy

★★ Moderate

★★★ Difficult

step-by-step

Charting U.S. Home Values

★ **1.** Kevin Young works for a real estate company and has been collecting information on sales prices for existing homes across the country. Kevin wants to graph some of the data in the worksheet for his upcoming presentation on home prices in the Midwest. The completed worksheet with charts is shown here.

a. Open the workbook file ex02_Real Estate Prices.

b. Create a line chart on a separate sheet showing the housing prices for the four years for the Midwest only. Title the chart appropriately. Remove the legend.

c. Make the line heavier and change the line and data marker color. Change the fill of the plot area to a gradient effect with two colors of your choice.

d. Add data labels that display the values. Increase the size of the data labels and position them below the line.

e. Increase the size of the chart title and axis labels and add a text color of your choice. Save the workbook as Real Estate Charts.

f. Create a column chart in the worksheet showing housing prices for the four regions for the four years. The X axis will display the years and the regions will be the legend. Title the chart appropriately. Move the legend to the bottom of the chart.

g. Position the chart below the worksheet data and size it appropriately. Increase the size of the chart title and add color. Turn off the plot area fill color.

h. Document the workbook file by adding your name as author and include a preview picture.

i. Preview the workbook. Add a predefined header to the worksheet and chart sheet that displays your name, page number, and date. Center the worksheet horizontally on the page. Print the worksheet. Print the chart sheet

j. Save the workbook again.

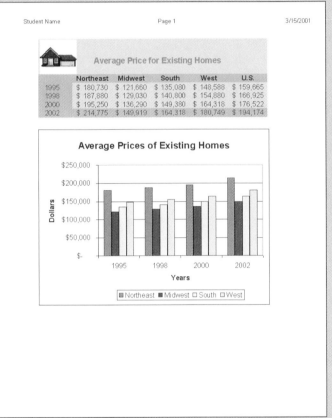

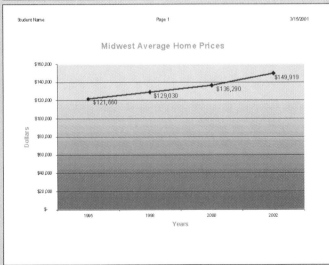

Bengal Tiger Populations

★★ **2.** Jennifer's environmental studies paper is on the endangered Bengal tiger. She has some data saved in a worksheet on the estimated number of tigers in 1997. She has asked you to help her chart the data and make the worksheet look more attractive. The completed worksheet with charts is shown here.

a. Open the workbook ex02_Tiger Data.

b. Use ChartWizard to create a stacked column with 3-D effect chart of the data in cells B6 through D11. Plot the data series from the rows. Enter the chart title **Tiger Population Estimates**. Enter the Value (Z) axis title of **Number of Tigers**. Embed the chart in the worksheet.

c. Size the chart over cells A13 through E30.

d. Rotate the Z-axis title 90 degrees. Change the chart and axis title color to green. Change the color for the China data series to green.

e. Save the workbook as Tiger Charts.

f. Create a 3-D pie chart in the worksheet showing the maximum tiger population estimates. Include the title **Maximum Estimated Tiger Population** and display the category name and percents as data labels. Do not include a legend.

g. Move the pie chart below the column chart and size it over cells A32 through E48.

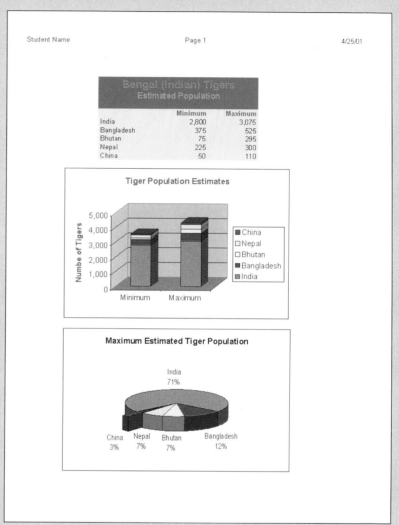

h. Change the data label font to Arial Narrow. Rotate the chart 230 degrees. Explode the China slice. Change the color of the China slice to green.

i. Change the maximum estimated tiger population for China to 110.

j. Document the workbook file by adding your name as author.

k. Preview the worksheet. Add a predefined header to the worksheet that displays your name, page number, and date. Center the worksheet horizontally on the page.

l. Print the worksheet on one page.

m. Save the workbook again.

acking Winter Bird Populations

★★ **3.** Richard Johnson volunteers for the Downtown City Park Bird Observation Society. He has compiled a worksheet of the number of bird observations in the park for the last year. He would like a chart that shows the society how the winter bird population differs by month and a chart that shows the total number of bird sightings this year. The completed worksheet with charts is shown here.

   a. Open the file ex02_Birds.

   b. Chart the monthly data for the 3 types of birds as a line chart. Set the series to be displayed in Rows.

   c. Enter the Chart title **Bird Observations by Month**, and the Value (Y) axis as **Number of Birds**. Display the legend below the chart.

   d. Position the chart over cells A11 through N27.

   e. Add color and font refinements to the chart titles as you like. Change the plot area color to blue. Change the Fox Sparrow data series color to red.

   f. Save the workbook as Bird Observations.

   g. Create another chart of the data in columns A and N as a 3-D Pie Chart. Title the chart **Total Bird Observations**. Turn off the legend and use the category name and percentage to label the data labels.

   h. Position the chart over cells A29 through N45. Add color and font refinements to the chart title as you like. Rotate the chart 120 degrees so the Pied-billed Grebe slice is at the front of the chart. Increase the size of the plot area. Change the data label point size to 12. Explode the Pied-billed Grebe slice.

   i. Document the workbook file by adding your name as author. Save the workbook with a picture preview.

   j. Preview the worksheet. Add a predefined header to the worksheet that displays your name, page number, and date. Center the worksheet horizontally on the page. Print the worksheet.

   k. Save the workbook file again.

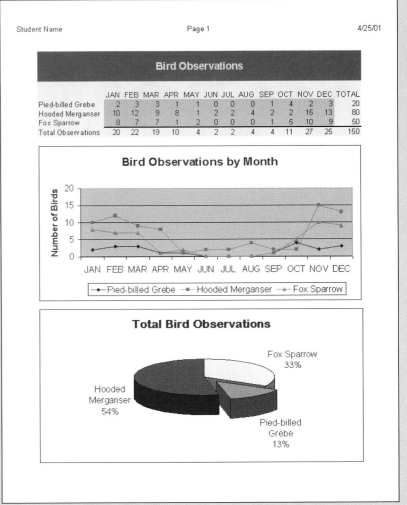

Children's Athletic Programs

★ ★ ★ **4.** Carol Hayes is the program coordinator for Fitness Lifestyles, a physical conditioning and health center. She is proposing to management that they increase their emphasis on child fitness. To reinforce the need for this type of investment, she has found some recent data about growth in the number of children (in millions) participating in sports. She wants to create several charts of this data to emphasize the demand.

a. Create a worksheet of the following data.

	1992	1995	2000
Baseball	3320	3421	3694
Basketball	6125	6200	7420
In-line Skating	1893	7110	8176
Running/Jogging	3510	3429	3257
Slow-pitch Softball	3652	3946	4261
Soccer	2585	2674	3510
Touch Football	4500	4040	4363
Volleyball	3620	3941	4295

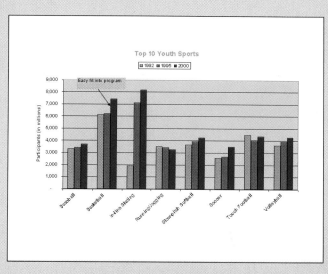

b. Add an appropriate title over the data and format the numbers to show commas with no decimal places. Calculate the percent change from 1992 to 2000 in column E (2000 value – 1992 value)/1992 value). Add a column heading. Enhance the worksheet as you like to improve its appearance. Save the workbook as Youth Sports Charts.

c. Create a clustered column chart of the worksheet data in columns A through D as a new sheet. Enter a chart title and Y axis title. Include a text box and arrow pointing to the increase in basketball and indicate that this would be an easy fit into the existing program. Enhance the chart using features presented in the lab.

d. Create an embedded column chart in the worksheet showing the Gain/Loss data for the sports. Include the title Percent Change in Participation 1992–2000. Remove the legend and format the Y-axis to a font size of 12 and no decimal places. Format the X-axis to a font size of 12 and display the labels at a 45-degree angle.

e. Move the chart below the worksheet and re-size.

f. Enhance the chart using features presented in the lab.

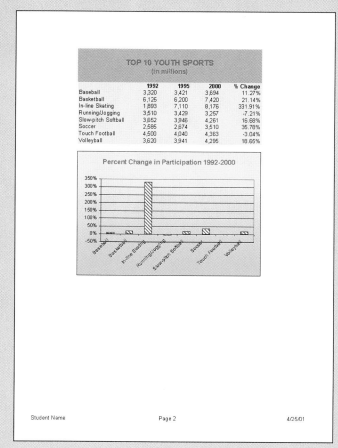

g. Document the workbook by adding your name as author. Save the workbook with a picture preview.

h. Preview the worksheet. Add a predefined footer to the worksheet that displays your name, page number, and date to both sheets. Center the worksheet horizontally on the page. Print the worksheet and the area chart.

i. Save the workbook again.

Salaries in Higher Education

★ ★
★ 5. Wendy Murray's class is studying career opportunities. Part of her class is interested in pursuing careers in higher education. She has done some research and found data that she entered into a worksheet. She would like to chart the data to make an impression on her students.

a. Open the workbook ex02_Higher Education.

b. Format the worksheet using the features you have learned.

c. Create an embedded column chart for the six levels for the four school categories and Average. Move the legend to the bottom of the chart.

d. Display the chart below the worksheet. Change the Average data to a line. Display the average values as data labels. Format the chart to your liking.

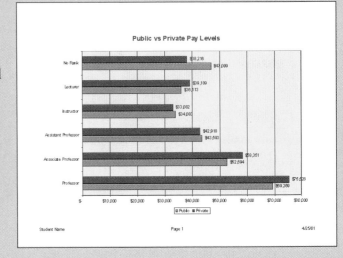

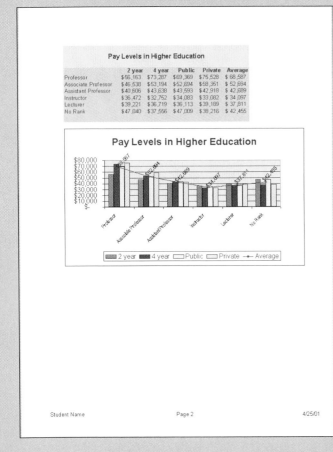

e. Create a bar chart of the Public and Private data as a new sheet. Display the values as data labels. Format the chart similar to your previous chart.

f. Document the workbook file by adding your name as author. Save the workbook with a preview picture.

g. Preview the worksheet. Add a predefined footer to the worksheet and chart sheets that displays your name, page number, and date. Center the worksheet horizontally on the page. Print the worksheet and the charts.

h. Save the workbook file as Higher Education Charts.

Market Seminar

★ 1. Tom Duggan is preparing for an upcoming job market seminar he is presenting. He has collected data comparing the average hourly pay rate for several professional jobs in the state to the U.S. average rates. He thinks the information would be much more meaningful and have greater impact if it was presented in a chart. Using the data in the workbook ex02_ Job Market, create an appropriate chart of the data for Physicians and Surgeons, Podiatrists, Dentists, and Lawyers on a separate chart sheet. Include appropriate chart titles. Add a pattern to the data series and change the plot area fill color. Enhance the chart in other ways using different font sizes and font colors. Position the legend at the bottom of the chart. Document the workbook by adding your name as author. Add a predefined header to the chart sheet that displays your name, page number, and date. Save the workbook as Seminar and print the chart.

Grade Tracking

★ 2. Create a worksheet that tracks your grades. It can be a record of the test scores you received this semester, or it can be a record of your GPA each semester. Create an embedded chart that best represents your grade trends. Use the formatting techniques you have learned to change the appearance of the worksheet and the chart. Save the workbook as Grades. Include a header or footer that displays your name and the current date in the worksheet. Print the worksheet with the chart.

Stock Market Workbook

★ ★ 3. You are interested in the stock market. Use Help to learn more about the Stock chart type. Pick four related stocks and create an embedded stock chart of the data. Save the worksheet with the chart as Stocks. Include a header or footer that displays your name and the current date in the worksheet. Print the worksheet and the chart.

Win/Loss Data

★ ★ ★ 4. Kevin Tillman has started a new job with Baseball Statistics, Inc. He would like some help creating a worksheet that contains team win/loss records for the last five years. He asks you to search the Web for records. Choose a MLB team of your choice and locate the win/loss record for the last five years. Enter the data into a worksheet. Enhance the worksheet using the features you have learned. Create an embedded chart that displays the information over the five years. Include a header or footer that displays your name and the current date in the worksheet. Save the workbook as Statistics. Print the worksheet with the chart.

Insurance Comparisons

★ ★ ★ 5. Robert Sanchez is thinking about purchasing a new SUV. However, he is concerned about the insurance rates for the vehicles he is considering. Before purchasing, he wants to find out the insurance rates on the vehicles he is evaluating. Select three different comparable SUVs and use the Web or visit several insurance agents to get the insurance premium cost information for the same amount of coverage from two different insurance companies. Use your own personal information as the basis for the insurance quotes. Create a worksheet that contains the SUV models, purchase price, and insurance premium quotes for each vehicle. Create an embedded chart of the data that shows the models and premiums. Enhance the chart appropriately. Include a header or footer that displays your name and the current date in the worksheet. Save the workbook as Insurance. Print the worksheet and chart.

Managing and Analyzing a Workbook

LAB 3

objectives

After completing this lab, you will know how to:

1.	Spell-check a sheet.
2.	Use Paste Function.
3.	Use absolute references.
4.	Copy, move, and name sheets.
5.	Use Autofill.
6.	Reference multiple sheets.
7.	Zoom the worksheet.
8.	Split windows and freeze panes.
9.	Use What-If analysis and Goal Seek.
10.	Change page orientation.
11.	Add custom headers and footers.
12.	Print selected sheets.

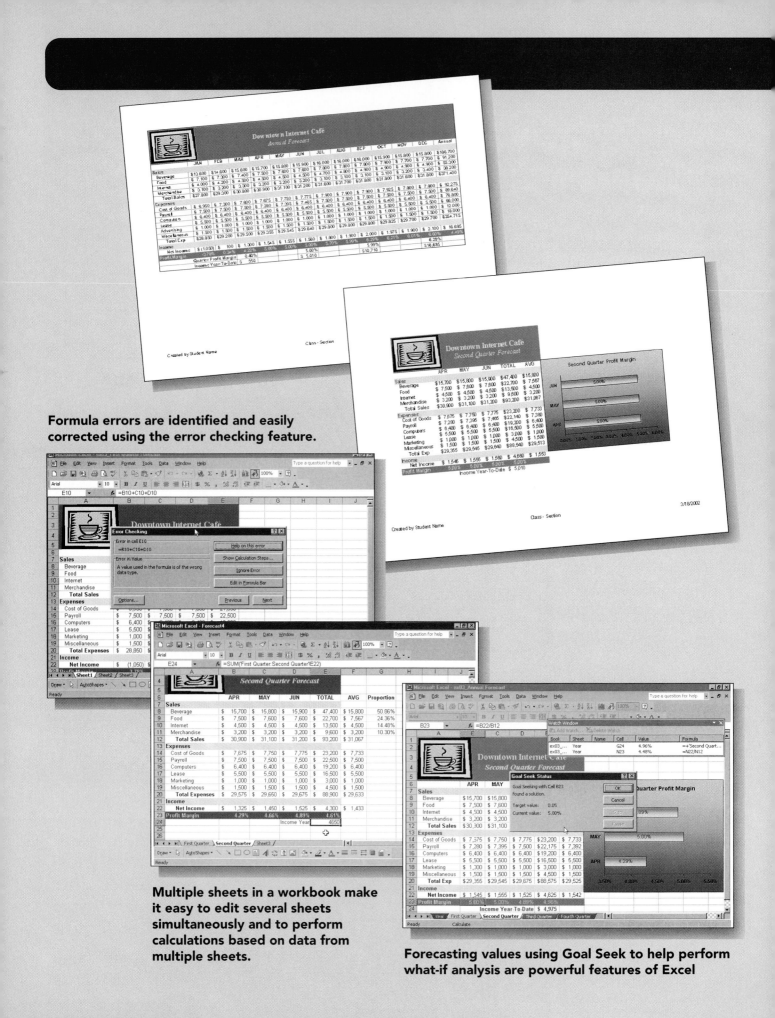

Formula errors are identified and easily corrected using the error checking feature.

Multiple sheets in a workbook make it easy to edit several sheets simultaneously and to perform calculations based on data from multiple sheets.

Forecasting values using Goal Seek to help perform what-if analysis are powerful features of Excel

Downtown Internet Café

You present your new, more optimistic, first quarter forecast for the Downtown Internet Café to Evan, who has made several formatting and design changes. In addition, he asks you to include an Average calculation and to extend the forecast for the next three quarters. Moreover, he wants to hold back on your idea of an aggressive Internet sales promotion. The Café's funds are low due to the cost of the recent renovations. Evan feels, therefore, that you should stick with a more conservative forecast of income derived from Internet sales.

After discussing the situation, you agree that the Café will likely lose money during the first month of operations. Then the Café should show increasing profitability. Evan stresses that the monthly profit margin should reach 5 per cent in the second quarter.

As you develop the Café's financial forecast, the worksheet grows in size and complexity. You will learn about features of Excel 2002 that help you manage a large workbook efficiently. You will also learn how you can manipulate the data in a worksheet to reach a goal using the what-if analysis capabilities of Excel. The completed annual forecast is shown here.

concept overview

The following concepts will be introduced in this lab:

1   **Spell Checking**   The spell-checking feature locates misspelled words, duplicate words, and capitalization irregularities in the active worksheet and proposes the correct spelling.

2   **Absolute References**   An absolute reference is a cell or range reference in a formula whose location does not change when the formula is copied.

3   **Sheet Names**   Each sheet in a workbook can be assigned a descriptive name to identify the contents of the sheet.

4   **Autofill**   The Autofill feature makes entering long or complicated headings easier by logically repeating and extending the series.

5   **Sheet and 3-D References**   A formula containing sheet and 3-D references to cells in different worksheets in a workbook allows you to use data from other worksheets and to calculate new values based on this data.

6   **Split Windows**   A sheet window can be split into sections called panes to make it easier to view different parts of the sheet at the same time.

7   **Freeze Panes**   Freezing panes prevents the data in the panes from scrolling as you move to different areas in the worksheet.

8   **What-If Analysis**   What-if analysis is a technique used to evaluate the effects of changing selected factors in a worksheet.

9   **Goal Seek**   Goal Seek is a tool that is used to find the value needed in one cell to attain a result you want in another cell.

Correcting Worksheet Errors

Excel 2002 includes several tools to help you find and correct errors in both text and formula entries. Text errors, such as spelling and typing errors, can be located quickly and corrected using the spelling checker. Potential problems in formulas are identified and can be corrected using the formula error checking features.

Checking Spelling

After talking with Evan, the owner of the Café, about the first quarter forecast, you are ready to begin making the changes he suggested. Evan returned the workbook file to you containing the changes he made to the format of the worksheet. To see the workbook file with these changes,

Start Excel 2002.

Open the workbook
ex03_First Quarter
Forecast.

*Your screen should be
similar to Figure 3.1*

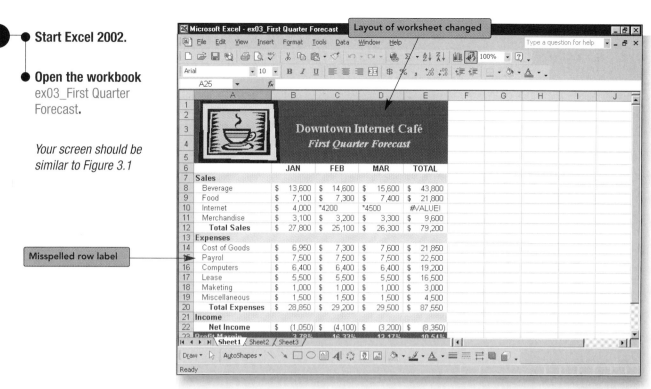

Layout of worksheet changed

Misspelled row label

Figure 3.1

As you can see, Evan made several formatting changes to the worksheet. He found a new graphic and changed the fill and text colors to coordinate with the picture. Additionally, he made several changes to the row labels. For example, the Salary label has been replaced with Payroll. However, the new label is misspelled. Just to make sure there are no other spelling errors, you will check the spelling of all text entries in this worksheet.

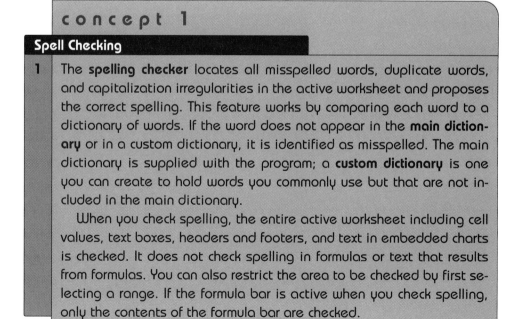

concept 1

Spell Checking

1   The **spelling checker** locates all misspelled words, duplicate words, and capitalization irregularities in the active worksheet and proposes the correct spelling. This feature works by comparing each word to a dictionary of words. If the word does not appear in the **main dictionary** or in a custom dictionary, it is identified as misspelled. The main dictionary is supplied with the program; a **custom dictionary** is one you can create to hold words you commonly use but that are not included in the main dictionary.

When you check spelling, the entire active worksheet including cell values, text boxes, headers and footers, and text in embedded charts is checked. It does not check spelling in formulas or text that results from formulas. You can also restrict the area to be checked by first selecting a range. If the formula bar is active when you check spelling, only the contents of the formula bar are checked.

Excel begins checking all worksheet entries from the active cell forward. To check the spelling in the worksheet,

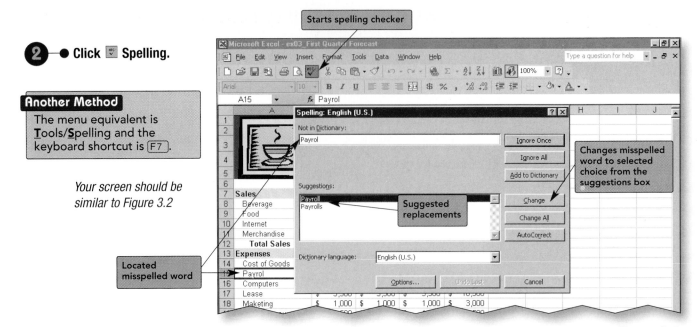

Figure 3.2

The spelling checker immediately begins checking the worksheet for words that it cannot locate in its main dictionary. The cell selector moves to the first cell containing a misspelled word, in this case Payrol, and the Spelling dialog box is displayed. The word it cannot locate in the dictionary is displayed in the Not in Dictionary text box. The Suggestions text box displays a list of possible replacements. If the selected replacement is not correct, you can select another choice from the suggestions list or type the correct word in the Not in Dictionary text box.

The option buttons shown in the table below have the following effects:

Option	Effect
Ignore Once	Leaves selected word unchanged
Ignore All	Leaves this word and all identical words in worksheet unchanged
Change	Changes selected word to word highlighted in Suggestions text box
Add to Dictionary	Adds selected word to a custom dictionary so Excel will not question this word during subsequent spell checks
Change All	Changes this word and all identical words in worksheet to word highlighted in Suggestions text box
AutoCorrect	Adds a word to the AutoCorrect list so the word will be corrected as you type

You want to accept the suggested replacement, Payroll.

3 ● Click [Change].

Your screen should be similar to Figure 3.3

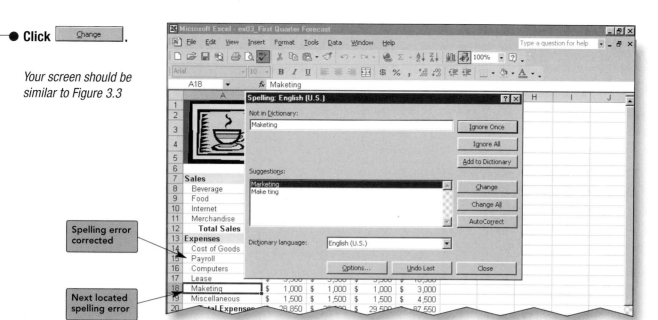

Spelling error corrected

Next located spelling error

Figure 3.3

The correction is made in the worksheet, and the program continues checking the worksheet and locates another error, Maketing.

4 ● **Change this word to Marketing.**

Your screen should be similar to Figure 3.4

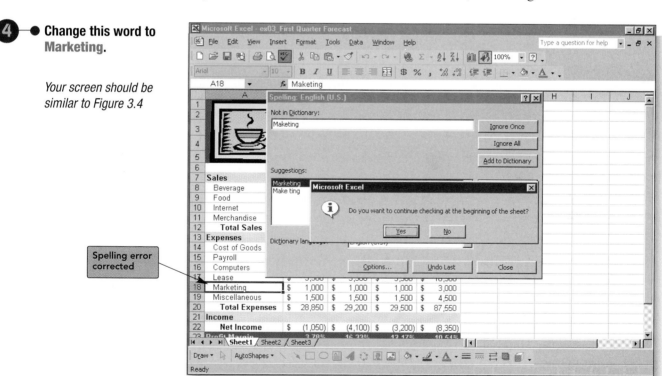

Spelling error corrected

Figure 3.4

The program continues checking the worksheet. When it reaches the end of the sheet, because the cell selector was not at the beginning of the sheet when checking started, the program asks if you want to continue checking at the beginning of the sheet. When no other errors are located, a dialog box is displayed, informing you that the entire worksheet has been checked.

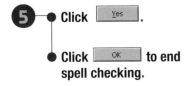

5 ● Click [Yes].

● Click [OK] to end spell checking.

Your screen should be similar to Figure 3.5

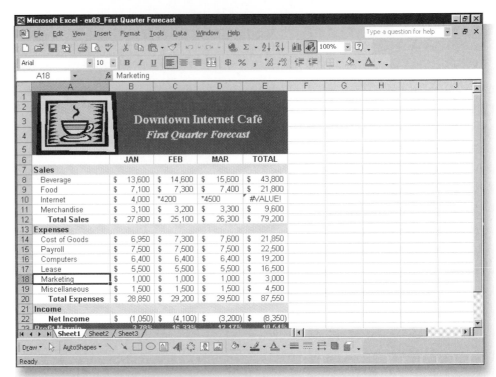

Figure 3.5

Correcting Formula Errors

As you continue to check over the worksheet, you notice a problem in cell E10. If a formula cannot properly calculate a result, an error value is displayed and a triangle appears in the top-left corner of the cell. Each type of error value has a different cause as described in the following table.

Error value	Cause
#####	Column not wide enough to display result or negative date or time is used
#VALUE!	Wrong type of argument or operand is used
#DIV/0!	Number is divided by zero
#NAME?	Text in formula not recognized
#N/A	Value not available
#REF!	Cell reference is not valid
#NUM!	Invalid number values
#NULL!	Intersection operator is not valid

You can correct each identified error individually or use the formula checker to check them all, one at a time. To correct them individually, select the cell and click ⬧ Error Options to display the menu of options that can be used to correct the problem. The formula checker is similar to the spelling checker in that it goes to each location in the worksheet containing a formula error, identifies the problem, and suggests corrections. You will use the formula checker to correct this error and check the entire worksheet for others.

1 Choose **T**ools/Error
Che**ck**ing.

If necessary, move the
dialog box to see the
located formula error.

*Your screen should be
similar to Figure 3.6*

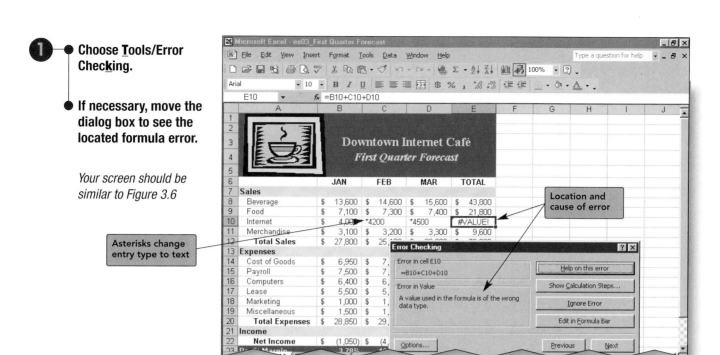

**Asterisks change
entry type to text**

**Location and
cause of error**

Figure 3.6

The Error Checking dialog box identifies the location and cause of the
error. In this case, when Evan changed the Internet sales values back to the
original estimates, he included an * in the cell entry to make sure you no-
ticed the change. Because Excel interprets this entry as a text entry, it cannot be used in this formula.. To correct the problem, you need to enter the
values correctly.

2 Move to cell C10 and
enter **4200**.

Enter **4500** in cell D10.

*Your screen should be
similar to Figure 3.7*

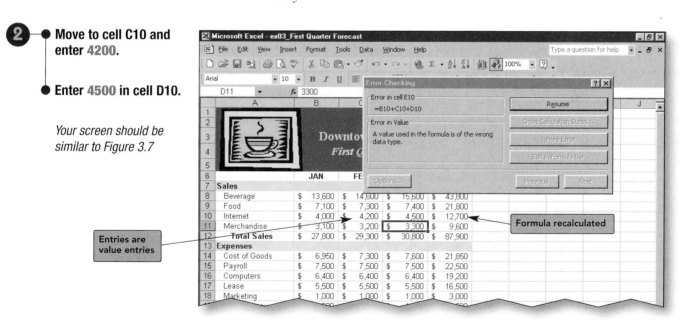

**Entries are
value entries**

Formula recalculated

Figure 3.7

Cell E10 now displays the correctly calculated result. The two values you
entered will need to be formatted again to Accounting. You will continue
checking the worksheet for formula errors and, when error checking is
complete, you will reformat the values.

3 ● Click 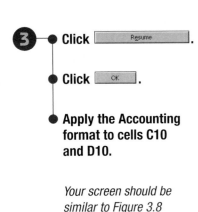 .

● Click OK .

● **Apply the Accounting format to cells C10 and D10.**

Your screen should be similar to Figure 3.8

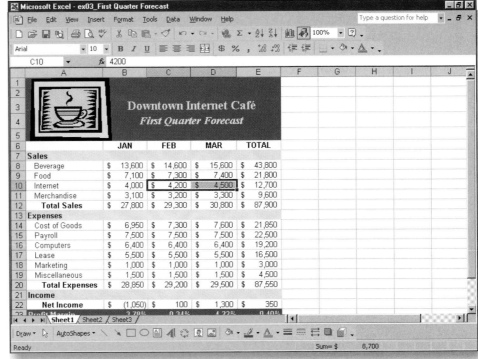

Figure 3.8

Now you are ready to make several of the changes requested by Evan. First you will add a column showing the average values for the first quarter.

4 ● **Enter the heading AVG in cell F6.**

● **Move to F8.**

Your screen should be similar to Figure 3.9

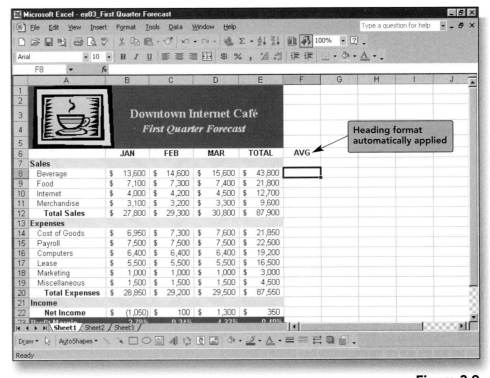

Figure 3.9

Notice the new heading is already appropriately formatted to bold and centered. This is because Excel automatically extends formats to new cells if the format of at least three of the last five preceding columns appears that way.

In addition to the SUM function, you can also use Σ AutoSum to enter several other commonly used functions. This includes functions to calculate an Average, Minimum, Maximum, and Count.

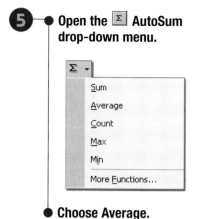

5 ● Open the Σ AutoSum drop-down menu.

● Choose Average.

Your screen should be similar to Figure 3.10

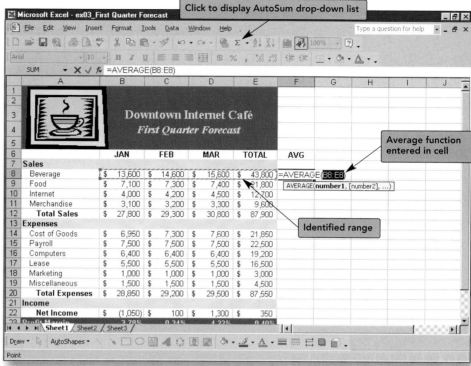

Figure 3.10

Excel identifies the range of cells B8 through E8 for the function argument. Because it incorrectly includes the total value in cell E8, you need to specify the correct range.

6 ● Drag to select cells B8 through D8.

● Press ⏎Enter.

Your screen should be similar to Figure 3.11

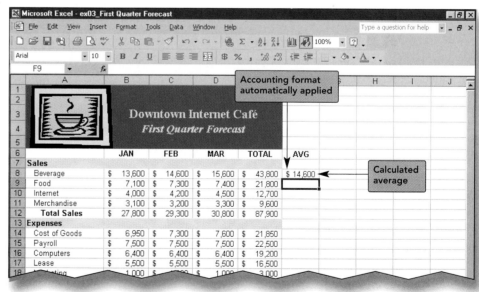

Figure 3.11

The average of the beverage sales for the quarter, 14,600, is calculated and displayed in cell F8. Notice that Excel again extended the format to the new cell, saving you the step of applying the Accounting format.

Next you need to copy the function down column F.

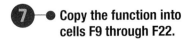

7 ● **Copy the function into cells F9 through F22.**

Your screen should be similar to Figure 3.12

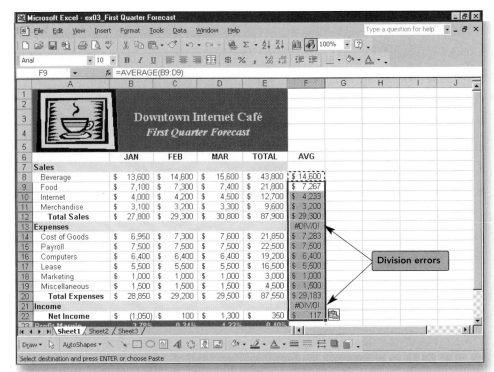

Figure 3.12

The average value has been correctly calculated for each row. Notice, however, that two cells display the error value #DIV/0! indicating the cells contains a formula error.

8 ● **Move to cell F13.**

● **Point to** ⬦ **Error Options.**

Your screen should be similar to Figure 3.13

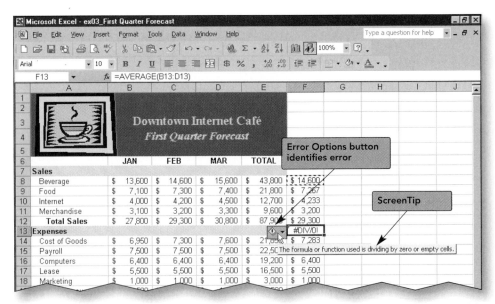

Figure 3.13

The Error Options button displays a ScreenTip identifying the cause of the error; in this case the formula is attempting to divide by zero or empty cells. This time you will individually correct the error.

9 ● Click  **Error Options.**

● **Choose Edit in Formula Bar.**

Your screen should be similar to Figure 3.14

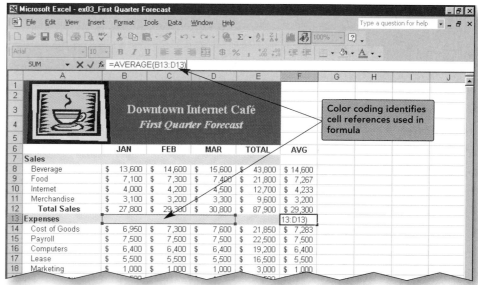

Figure 3.14

Notice that the cell references in the formula are color coded to match the borders Excel displays around the referenced worksheet cells. It is designed to provide visual cues to the relationships between the cells that provide values to the formulas or the cells that depend on the formulas. You can now easily see the error is caused by references to blank cells when the function was copied. Since you do not need this formula, you will delete it.

10 ● Press ⎙Esc⎙.

● Press ⎙Delete⎙.

Your screen should be similar to Figure 3.15

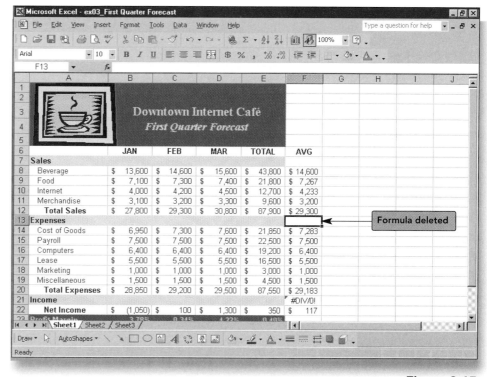

Figure 3.15

Likewise, you need to delete the function that was copied into cell F21. You will clear the entry in this cell using the fill handle.

11 ● Move to cell F21.

● Point to the fill handle and when the mouse pointer changes to **+**, drag upward until the cell is gray.

● Release the mouse button.

Your screen should be similar to Figure 3.16

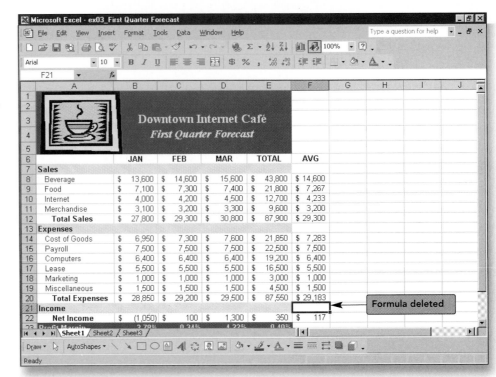

Figure 3.16

Using Absolute References

While looking at the sales data in the worksheet, you decide it may be interesting to find out what contribution each sales item makes to total sales. To find out, you will enter a formula to calculate the proportion of sales by each in column G. The formula to calculate the proportion for beverage sales is Total Beverage Sales/Total Sales.

1 ● Enter the heading **Proportion** in cell G6.

● Enter the formula **=E8/E12** in cell G8.

● If necessary, move to G8.

Your screen should be similar to Figure 3.17

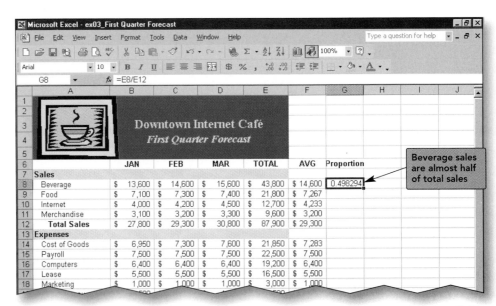

Figure 3.17

The value 0.498294 is displayed in cell G8. This shows that the beverage sales are approximately 50 percent of total sales.

Next, to calculate the proportion for Food Sales, you will copy the formula from G8 to G9. Another quick way to copy cell contents is to drag the cell border while holding down ⌃Ctrl. This method is most useful when the distance between cells is short and they are both visible in the window. It cannot be used if you are copying to a larger range than the source range.

2 ● Point to the border of cell G8 and when the mouse pointer shape is ↖, hold down ⌃Ctrl and drag the mouse pointer to cell G9.

Your screen should be similar to Figure 3.18

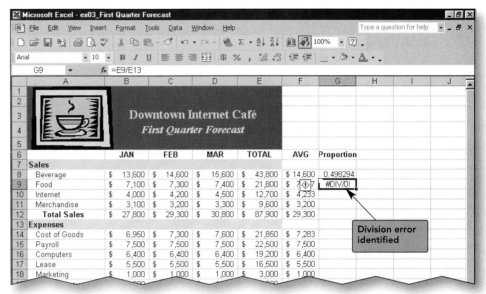

Figure 3.18

You see a #DIV/0! error value is displayed in cell G9 and want to check the formula in that cell.

3 ● If necessary, move to cell G9.

● Choose Edit in Formula Bar from the ⚠ Error Options drop-down menu.

Your screen should be similar to Figure 3.19

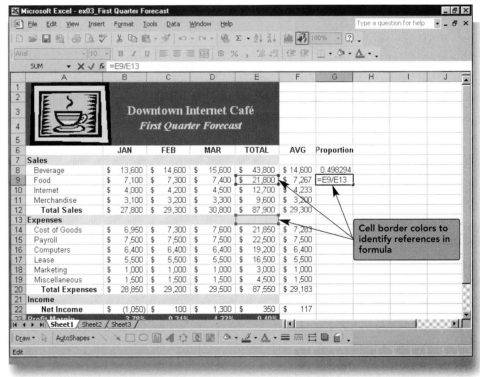

Figure 3.19

You can now see the error occurred because the relative reference to cell E12 adjusted correctly to the new location when the formula was copied and now references cell E13, a blank cell. The formula in G8 needs to be entered so that the reference to the Total Sales value in cell E12 does not change when the formula is copied. To do this, you need to make the cell reference absolute.

concept 2

Absolute References

2 An **absolute reference** is a cell or range reference in a formula whose location does not change when the formula is copied.

To stop the relative adjustment of cell references, enter a $ (dollar sign) character before the column letter and row number. This changes the cell reference to absolute. When a formula containing an absolute cell reference is copied to another row and column location in the worksheet, the cell reference does not change. It is an exact duplicate of the cell reference in the original formula.

A cell reference can also be a **mixed reference**. In this type of reference, either the column letter or the row number is preceded with the $. This makes only the row or column absolute. When a formula containing a mixed cell reference is copied to another location in the worksheet, only the part of the cell reference that is not absolute changes relative to its new location in the worksheet.

The table below shows examples of relative and absolute references and the results when a reference in cell G8 to cell E8 is copied to cell H9.

Cell Contents of G8	Copied to Cell H9	Type of Reference
E8	E8	Absolute reference
E$8	F$8	Mixed reference
$E8	$E9	Mixed reference
E8	F9	Relative reference

You will change the formula in cell G8 to include an absolute reference for cell E12. Then you will copy the formula to cells G9 through G11.

You can change a cell reference to absolute or mixed by typing in the dollar sign directly or by using the ABS (Absolute) key, F4. To use the ABS key, the program must be in the Edit mode and the cell reference that you want to change must be selected.

4

● **Move to G8.**

● **Click on the reference to E12 in the formula bar to enter Edit mode and select the reference.**

● **Press** F4 .

Your screen should be similar to Figure 3.20

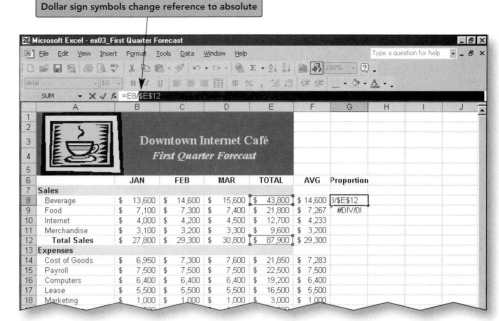

Dollar sign symbols change reference to absolute

Figure 3.20

The cell reference now displays $ characters before the column letter and row number, making this cell reference absolute. If you continue to press F4 , the cell reference will cycle through all possible combinations of cell reference types. Leaving the cell reference absolute, as it is now, will stop the relative adjustment of the cell reference when you copy it again.

5

● **Click** ☑ **Enter.**

● **Copy the revised formula to cells G9 through G11.**

● **Move to cell G9.**

Your screen should be similar to Figure 3.21

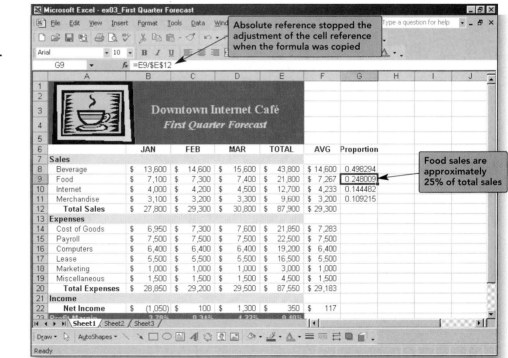

Absolute reference stopped the adjustment of the cell reference when the formula was copied

Food sales are approximately 25% of total sales

Figure 3.21

The formula when copied correctly adjusted the relative cell reference to Food sales in cell E9 and did not adjust the reference to E12 because it is an absolute reference.

The last change you need to make to the proportion data is to format it to the Percent style.

6

- Select G8 through G11.

- Click ▓ Percent Style.

- Click ▓ Increase Decimal (twice).

- Size column G to fit the contents.

- Move to cell A6 and save the workbook as Forecast4.

Your screen should be similar to Figure 3.22

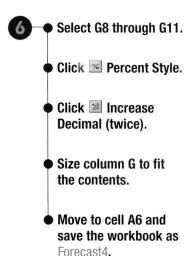

	A	B	C	D	E	F	G
6		JAN	FEB	MAR	TOTAL	AVG	Proportion
7	Sales						
8	Beverage	$ 13,600	$ 14,600	$ 15,600	$ 43,800	$ 14,600	49.83%
9	Food	$ 7,100	$ 7,300	$ 7,400	$ 21,800	$ 7,267	24.80%
10	Internet	$ 4,000	$ 4,200	$ 4,500	$ 12,700	$ 4,233	14.45%
11	Merchandise	$ 3,100	$ 3,200	$ 3,300	$ 9,600	$ 3,200	10.92%
12	Total Sales	$ 27,800	$ 29,300	$ 30,800	$ 87,900	$ 29,300	
13	Expenses						
14	Cost of Goods	$ 6,950	$ 7,300	$ 7,600	$ 21,850	$ 7,283	
15	Payroll	$ 7,500	$ 7,500	$ 7,500	$ 22,500	$ 7,500	
16	Computers	$ 6,400	$ 6,400	$ 6,400	$ 19,200	$ 6,400	
17	Lease	$ 5,500	$ 5,500	$ 5,500	$ 16,500	$ 5,500	
18	Marketing	$ 1,000	$ 1,000	$ 1,000	$ 3,000	$ 1,000	

Percent style applied to selection

Figure 3.22

The calculated proportion shows the same values that a pie chart of this data would show.

Working with Sheets

Next you want to add the second quarter forecast to the workbook. You want this data in a separate sheet in the same workbook file. To make it easier to enter the forecast for the next quarter, you will copy the contents of the first quarter forecast in Sheet1 into another sheet in the workbook. Then you will change the month headings, the title, and the number data for the second quarter. Finally, you want to include a formula to calculate a year-to-date total for the six months.

Copying Between Sheets

You want to copy the worksheet data from Sheet1 to Sheet2. Copying between sheets is the same as copying within a sheet, except that you switch to the new sheet to specify the destination.

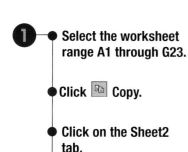

1 • Select the worksheet range A1 through G23.

• Click 🗐 Copy.

• Click on the Sheet2 tab.

• Click 🗐 Paste.

Your screen should be similar to Figure 3.23

Another Method

You can also use Edit/Move or Copy Sheet to move or copy a sheet into a new sheet in the workbook.

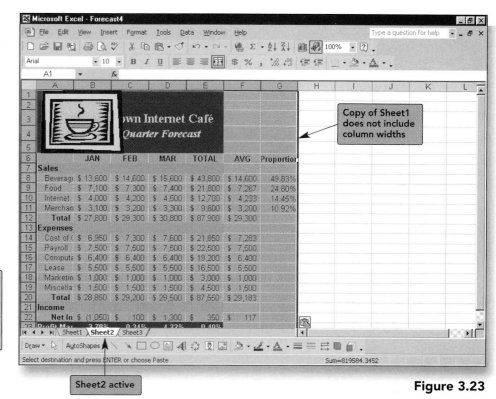

Figure 3.23

All the worksheet data and formatting, except for the column width settings, are copied into the existing Sheet2. You want to include the column width settings from the source.

2 • Click 🗐 Paste Options.

• Choose Keep Source Column Widths.

Your screen should be similar to Figure 3.24

Additional Information

If you select and copy the entire source sheet, all formatting including column widths is copied into the destination sheet.

Another Method

You can also create a copy of the active sheet in a new sheet by holding down Ctrl while dragging the active sheet tab to where you want the new sheet inserted.

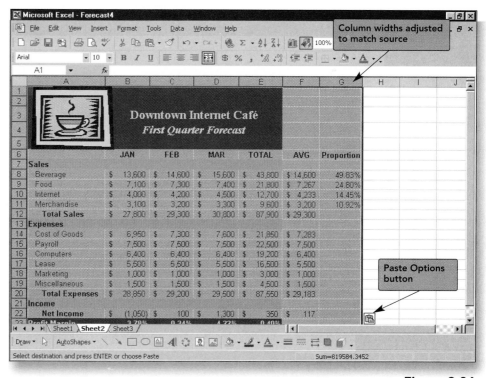

Figure 3.24

Sheet2 now contains a duplicate of the first quarter forecast in Sheet1.

Renaming Sheets and Coloring Sheet Tabs

As more sheets are added to a workbook, remembering what information is in each sheet becomes more difficult. To help clarify the contents of the sheets, you can rename the sheets.

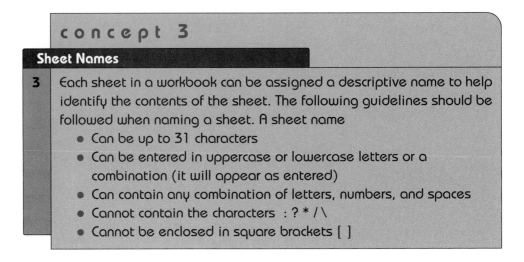

concept 3

Sheet Names

3 Each sheet in a workbook can be assigned a descriptive name to help identify the contents of the sheet. The following guidelines should be followed when naming a sheet. A sheet name

- Can be up to 31 characters
- Can be entered in uppercase or lowercase letters or a combination (it will appear as entered)
- Can contain any combination of letters, numbers, and spaces
- Cannot contain the characters : ? * / \
- Cannot be enclosed in square brackets [ ]

Double-clicking the sheet tab activates the tab and highlights the existing sheet name. The existing name is cleared as soon as you begin to type the new name. You will change the name of Sheet1 to First Quarter and Sheet2 to Second Quarter.

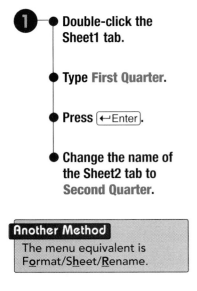

1 ● **Double-click the Sheet1 tab.**

● **Type First Quarter.**

● **Press ⏎Enter.**

● **Change the name of the Sheet2 tab to Second Quarter.**

Another Method

The menu equivalent is Format/Sheet/Rename.

Your screen should be similar to Figure 3.25

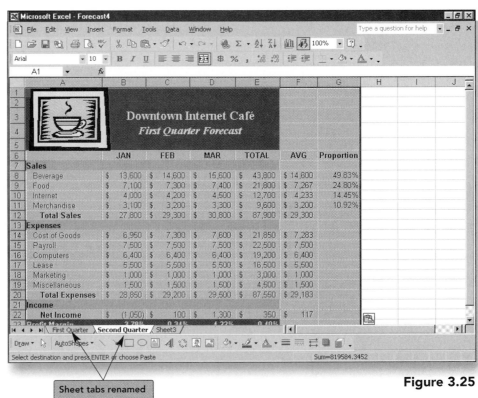

Sheet tabs renamed

Figure 3.25

To further differentiate the sheets, you can add color to the sheet tabs.

② ● **Right-click on the First Quarter tab.**

● **Choose Tab Color from the shortcut menu.**

● **Select yellow from the color pallet.**

● **Click** OK **.**

● **In the same manner, change the color of the Second Quarter sheet tab to green.**

Another Method

The menu equivalent is Format/Sheet/Tab Color.

Your screen should be similar to Figure 3.26

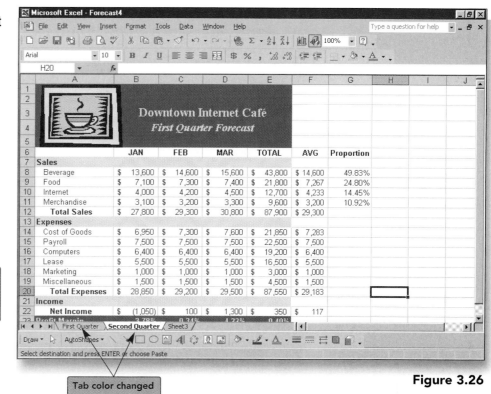

Tab color changed

Figure 3.26

Filling a Series

Now you can change the worksheet title and data in the second quarter sheet.

① ● **Change the title in cell B4 to Second Quarter Forecast.**

● **Change the month heading in cell B6 to APR.**

Your screen should be similar to Figure 3.27

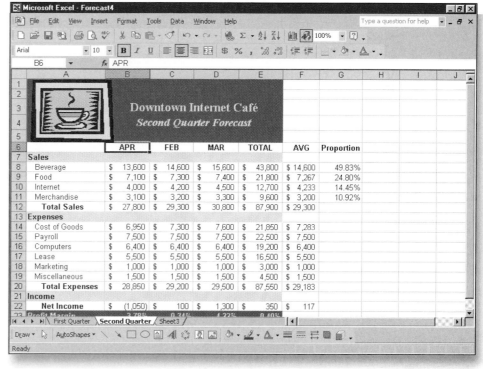

Figure 3.27

Now you need to change the remaining month headings to MAY and JUN. You will use the AutoFill feature to enter the month headings.

concept 4

AutoFill

4   The **AutoFill** feature makes entering a series of headings easier by logically repeating and extending the series. AutoFill recognizes trends and automatically extends data and alphanumeric headings as far as you specify.

Dragging the fill handle activates the AutoFill feature if Excel recognizes the entry in the cell as an entry that can be incremented. When AutoFill extends the entries, it uses the same style as the original entry. For example, if you enter the heading for July as JUL (abbreviated with all letters uppercase), all the extended entries in the series will be abbreviated and uppercase. Dragging down or right increments in increasing order, and up or left increments in decreasing order. A linear series increases or decreases values by a constant value, and a growth series multiplies values by a constant factor.

Initial Selection	Extended series
Qtr1	Qtr2, Qtr3, Qtr4
Mon	Tue Wed Thu
Jan, Apr	Jul, Oct, Jan

Additional Information

A starting value of a series may contain more than one item that can be incremented, such as JAN-02, in which both the month and year can increment. You can specify which value to increment by selecting the appropriate option from the AutoFill Options menu.

The entry in cell B6, APR, is the starting value of a series of months. You will drag the fill handle to the right to increment the months. The mouse pointer displays the entry that will appear in each cell as you drag.

2 ● Drag the fill handle of cell B6 to extend the range from cell B6 through cell D6.

Additional Information

If you do not want a series created when you drag the fill handle, hold down [Ctrl] as you drag and the entries will be copied, not incremented.

Your screen should be similar to Figure 3.28

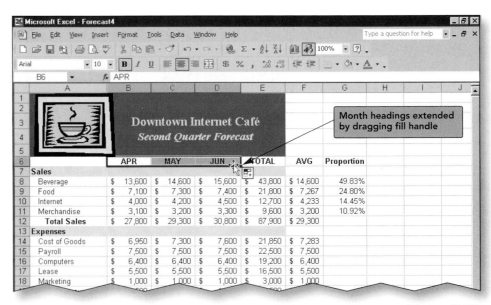

Figure 3.28

Referencing Multiple Sheets

Finally, you need to update the forecast for April through June beverage, food, Internet, and merchandise sales. Then you will enter a formula to calculate the year-to-date income total using data from both sheets.

1 ● Enter the following values in the specified cells.

Cell	Number
B8	15700
C8	15800
D8	15900
B9	7500
C9	7600
D9	7600
B10	4500
C10	4500
D10	4500
B11	3200
C11	3200
D11	3200

Your screen should be similar to Figure 3.29

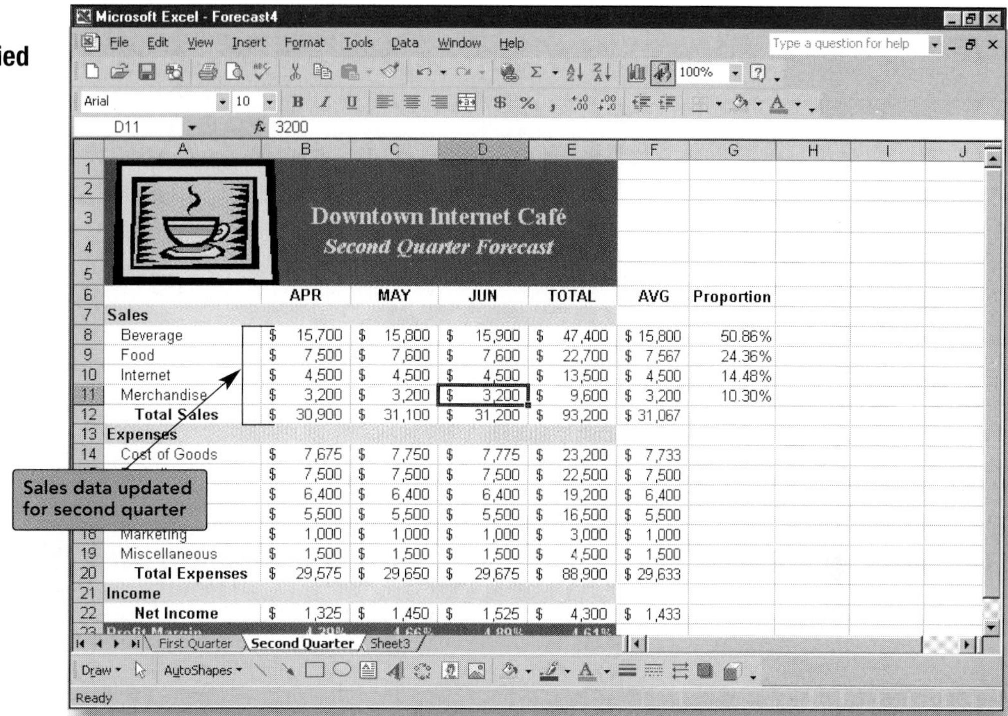

Figure 3.29

The worksheet has been recalculated and now contains the data for the second quarter.

Now you can enter the formula to calculate a year-to-date income total. The formula to make this calculation will sum the total income numbers from the First Quarter sheet in cell E22 and the Second Quarter sheet in cell E22. To reference data in another sheet in the same workbook, you enter a formula that references cells in other worksheets.

concept 5

Sheet and 3-D References

5 A formula that contains references to cells in other sheets of a workbook allows you to use data from multiple sheets and to calculate new values based on this data. The formula contains a **sheet reference** consisting of the name of the sheet, followed by an exclamation point and the cell or range reference. If the sheet name contains non-alphabetic characters, such as a space, the sheet name (or path) must be enclosed in single quotation marks.

If you want to use the same cell or range of cells on multiple sheets, you can use a **3-D reference**. A 3-D reference consists of the names of the beginning and ending sheets enclosed in quotes and separated by a colon. This is followed by an exclamation point and the cell or range reference. The cell or range reference is the same on each sheet in the specified sheet range. If a sheet is inserted or deleted, the range is automatically updated. 3-D references make it easy to analyze data in the same cell or range of cells on multiple worksheets.

Reference	Description
=Sheet2!B17	Displays the entry in cell B17 of Sheet2 in the active cell of the current sheet
=Sheet1!A1+Sheet2!B2.	Sums the values in cell A1 of Sheet1 and B2 of Sheet2
=SUM(Sheet1:Sheet4!H6:K6)	Sums the values in cells H6 through K6 in Sheets 1, 2, 3, and 4
=SUM(Sheet1!H6:K6)	Sums the values in cells H6 through K6 in Sheet1
=SUM(Sheet1:Sheet4!H6)	Sums the values in cell H6 of Sheets 1, 2, 3, and 4

Just like a formula that references cells within a sheet, a formula that references cells in multiple sheets is automatically recalculated when data in a referenced cell changes.

You will enter a descriptive text entry in cell D24 and then use a 3-D reference in a SUM function to calculate the year-to-date total in cell E24.

The SUM function argument will consist of a 3-D reference to cell E22 in the First and Second Quarter sheets. Although a 3-D reference can be entered by typing it using the proper syntax, it is much easier to enter it by pointing to the cells on the sheets. To enter a 3-D reference, select the cell or range in the beginning sheet and then hold down ⇧Shift and click on the sheet tab of the last sheet in the range. This will include the indicated cell range on all sheets between and including the first and last sheet specified.

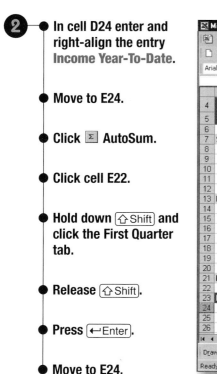

2 ● **In cell D24 enter and right-align the entry Income Year-To-Date.**

● **Move to E24.**

● **Click Σ AutoSum.**

● **Click cell E22.**

● **Hold down ⇧Shift and click the First Quarter tab.**

● **Release ⇧Shift.**

● **Press ↵Enter.**

● **Move to E24.**

Your screen should be similar to Figure 3.30

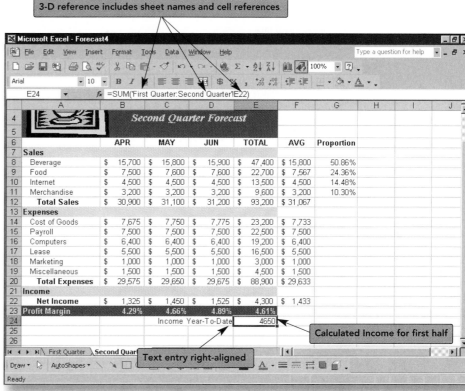

Figure 3.30

The calculated number 4650 appears in cell E24 and the function containing a 3-D reference appears in the formula bar.

You have now completed the forecast for the first half of the year.

3 • Change the format of cell E24 to Accounting with zero decimal places.

• Enter your name in the workbook file properties as the author.

• Add a predefined header containing your name, page number, and the date to both sheets.

• Preview the entire workbook. Print both worksheets.

• Close and save the workbook file.

Your printed output of the second quarter sheet should be similar to that shown here.

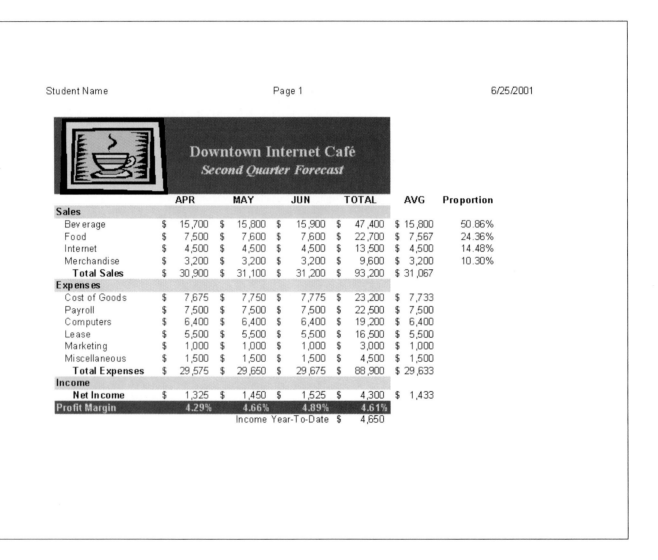

Note: If you are running short on lab time, this is an appropriate place to end this session and begin again at a later time.

Deleting and Moving Sheets

You presented the completed first and second quarterly forecasts to Evan. He is very pleased with the results and now wants you to create worksheets for the third and fourth quarters and a combined annual forecast. Additionally, Evan has asked you to include a column chart of the data for each quarter. Finally, after looking at the forecast, Evan wants the forecast to show a profit margin of 5 percent for each month in the second quarter.

You have already made several of the changes requested and saved them as a workbook file. To see the revised and expanded forecast,

Open the workbook file ex03_Annual Forecast.

Your screen should be similar to Figure 3.31

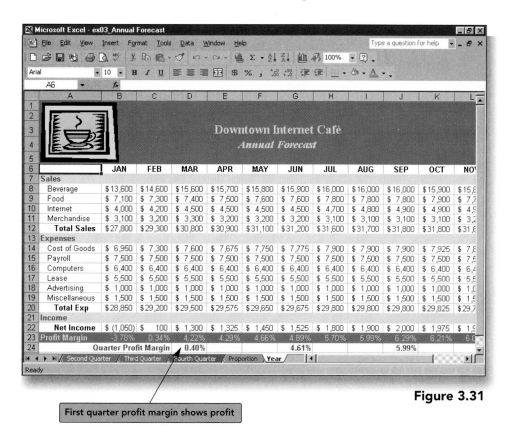

First quarter profit margin shows profit

Figure 3.31

The workbook file now contains six sheets: First Quarter, Second Quarter, Third Quarter, Fourth Quarter, Proportion, and Year. The Proportion sheet contains the proportion of sales values from the first and second quarters. The Year sheet contains the forecast data for the entire 12 months. Each quarter sheet also includes a chart of the profit margin for that quarter. As you can now easily see, the profit margin by the end of the first quarter is showing a profit.

2 ● **Click on each of the Quarter sheet tabs to view the quarterly data and profit margin chart.**

● **Display the Proportion sheet.**

Your screen should be similar to Figure 3.32

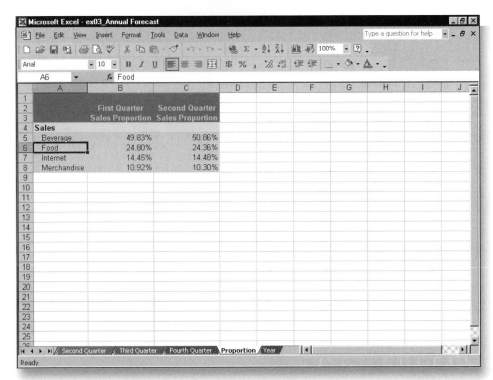

Figure 3.32

You decide this data, although interesting, is not needed in the forecast workbook and want to delete the entire sheet.

3 ● **Choose Edit/Delete Sheet.**

● **Click** `Delete` **to confirm that you want to permanently remove the sheet.**

Your screen should be similar to Figure 3.33

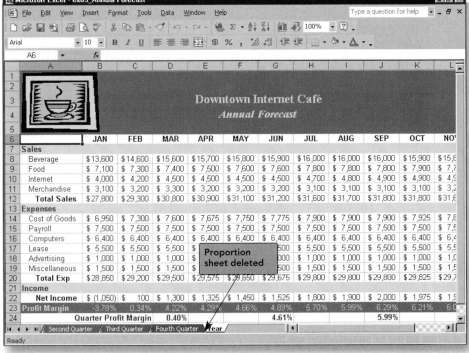

Figure 3.33

Additional Information
You can insert a blank new sheet using Insert/Worksheet. It is inserted to the left of the active sheet.

The entire sheet is deleted, and the Year sheet is now the active sheet. Next you want to move the Year sheet from the last position in the workbook to the first. You can quickly rearrange sheets in a workbook by dragging the sheet tab to the new location. The symbol ▼ indicates where the sheet will appear.

4 ● Drag the Year tab to the left end of the First Quarter tab.

Another Method

You can also use <u>E</u>dit/<u>M</u>ove or Copy Sheet to move a sheet to another location in the workbook.

Your screen should be similar to Figure 3.34

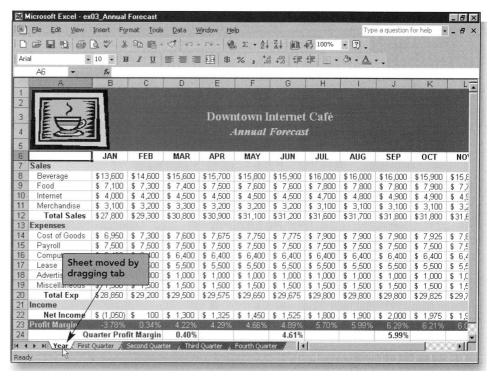

Figure 3.34

Managing Large Sheets

Now that the workbook is much larger you are finding that it takes a lot of time to scroll to different areas within and between sheets. To make managing large sheets easier, you can zoom a sheet, split the workbook window, and freeze panes.

Zooming the Worksheet

Additional Information

The Zoom feature is common in all Office XP programs.

The Year sheet displays all of the quarterly data. The entire sheet, however, is not visible in the window. You can change how much information is displayed in the window to make it easier to navigate, view, and select worksheet data by adjusting the zoom percentage. The default zoom setting is 100 percent. This setting displays data onscreen the same size that it will appear on the printed page. You can reduce or enlarge the amount of information displayed onscreen by changing the magnification from between 10 to 400 percent. You want to decrease the zoom percent to display more information in the window.

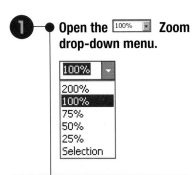

1 ● Open the `100%` Zoom drop-down menu.

100%	▼
200%	
100%	
75%	
50%	
25%	
Selection	

● Choose 75%.

Another Method
The menu equivalent is View/Zoom.

Your screen should be similar to Figure 3.35

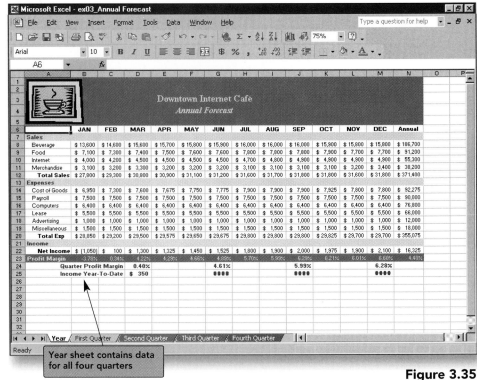

Figure 3.35

You can now see the entire worksheet.

2 ● Reduce the zoom percent to 50%.

Your screen should be similar to Figure 3.36

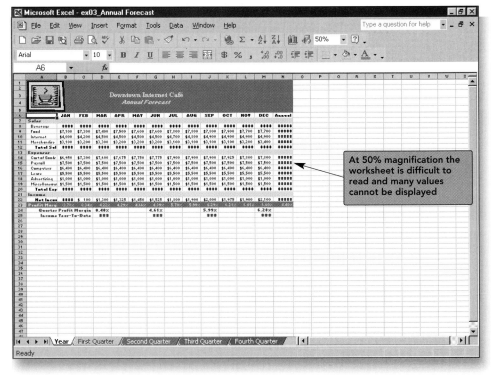

At 50% magnification the worksheet is difficult to read and many values cannot be displayed

Figure 3.36

As you reduce the percentage, more worksheet area is visible in the window. However, it gets more difficult to read and many cells display the error value ##### because the column width is not wide enough to fully display the result.

Going to a Specific cell

Most of the monthly values in the Year sheet, such as cell B8, contain linking formulas that reference the appropriate cells in the appropriate quarter sheets. Others, such as the total formulas and the formula to calculate the income, do not reference cells outside the Year worksheet.

To see several of the formulas in cells that reference the quarter sheets,

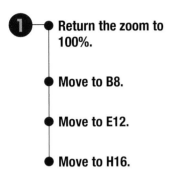

1 ● **Return the zoom to 100%.**

● **Move to B8.**

● **Move to E12.**

● **Move to H16.**

Your screen should be similar to Figure 3.37

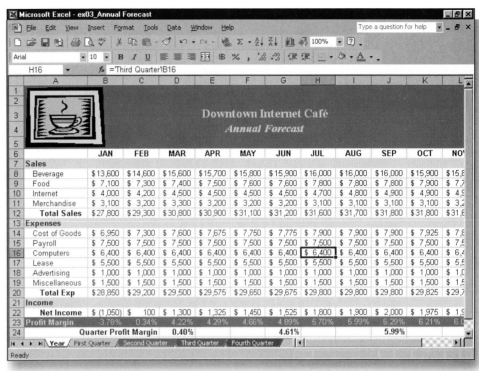

Figure 3.37

Each of these cells contained a formula that referenced a cell in the appropriate quarter sheet. To see the total formulas for the year in column N, you will move to cell N16 using the GoTo feature.

2 ● **Type N16 in the Name text box and press** ⏎Enter.

Another Method

The menu equivalent is Edit/GoTo and the keyboard shortcut is Ctrl + G or F5.

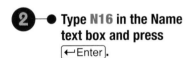

Your screen should be similar to Figure 3.38

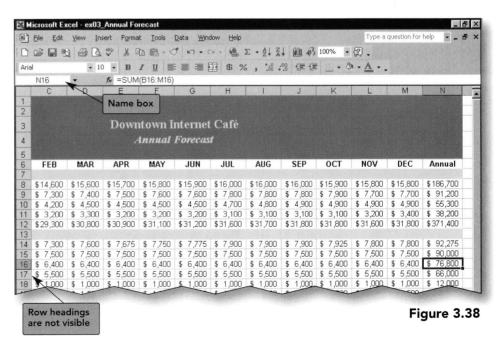

Figure 3.38

The cell selector jumps directly to cell N16 in the total column. The formula in this cell calculates the total of the values in row 16 and does not reference another sheet. However, it is difficult to know what the numbers represent in this row because the row headings are not visible. For example, is this number the total for the lease expenses, advertising expenses, or miscellaneous expenses? Without scrolling back to see the row headings, it is difficult to know.

Splitting Windows

Whenever you scroll a large worksheet, you will find that information you may need to view in one area scrolls out of view as you move to another area. Although you could reduce the zoom percent to view more of a worksheet in the window, you still may not be able to see the entire worksheet if it is very large. And as you saw, continuing to reduce the zoom makes the worksheet difficult to read and prevents some values from fully displaying. To view different areas of the same sheet at the same time, you can split the window.

concept 6

Split Windows

6 A sheet window can be split into sections called **panes** to make it easier to view different parts of the sheet at the same time. The panes can consist of any number of columns or rows along the top or left edge of the window. You can divide the sheet into two panes either horizontally or vertically, or into four panes if you split the window both vertically and horizontally.

Each pane can be scrolled independently to display different areas of the sheet. When split vertically, the panes scroll together when you scroll vertically, but scroll independently when you scroll horizontally. Horizontal panes scroll together when you scroll horizontally, but independently when you scroll vertically.

Panes are most useful for viewing a worksheet that consists of different areas or sections. Creating panes allows you to display the different sections of the worksheet in separate panes and then to quickly switch between panes to access the data in the different sections without having to repeatedly scroll to the areas.

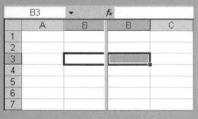

two vertical panes

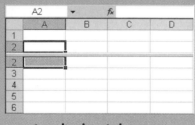

two horizontal panes

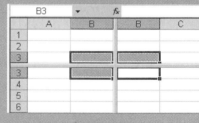

four panes

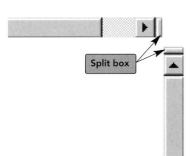

Split box

Dragging the split box at the top of the vertical scroll bar downward creates a horizontal split, and dragging the split box at the right end of the horizontal scroll bar leftward creates a vertical split.

You will split the window into two vertical panes. This will allow you to view the titles in column A at the same time as you are viewing data in column N.

1 ● **Point to the vertical split box in the horizontal scroll bar.**

Additional Information

The mouse pointer changes to a ╬ to show you can drag to create a split.

● **Drag to the left and position the bar between columns D and E.**

Your screen should be similar to Figure 3.39

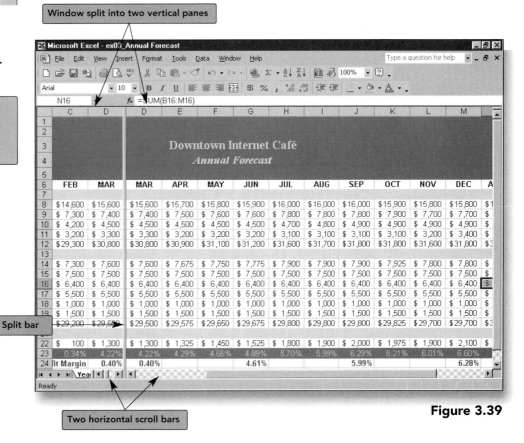

Window split into two vertical panes

Split bar

Two horizontal scroll bars

Figure 3.39

Additional Information

The <u>W</u>indow/<u>S</u>plit command can be used to quickly create a four-way split at the active cell.

There are now two vertical panes with two separate horizontal scroll bars. The highlighted cell selector is visible in the right pane. The left pane also has a cell selector in cell N16, but it is not visible because that area of the worksheet is not displayed in the pane. When the same area of a worksheet is visible in multiple panes, the cell selector in the panes that are not active is highlighted whereas the cell selector in the active pane is clear. The active pane will be affected by your movement horizontally. The cell selector moves in both panes, but only the active pane scrolls.

You will scroll the left pane horizontally to display the month headings in column A.

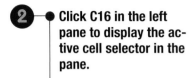

2 ● **Click C16 in the left pane to display the active cell selector in the pane.**

● **Press ← twice.**

Your screen should be similar to Figure 3.40

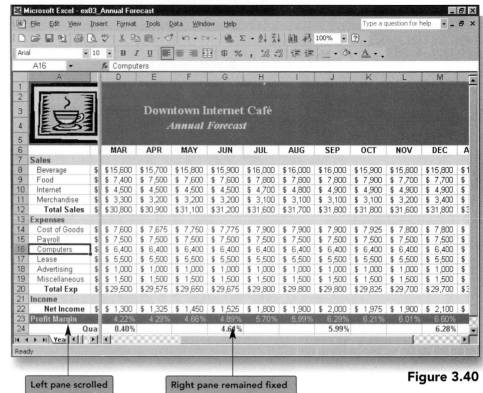

Left pane scrolled

Right pane remained fixed

Figure 3.40

The right pane did not scroll when you moved horizontally through the left pane to display the row headings. The cell selector in the right pane is in the same cell location as in the left pane (A16), although it is not visible. You want to change the location of the split so that you can view an entire quarter in the left pane in order to more easily compare quarters.

3 ● **Drag the split bar to the right three columns.**

● **Click cell E16 in the right pane.**

● **Press End →.**

● **Press → (three times).**

Your screen should be similar to Figure 3.41

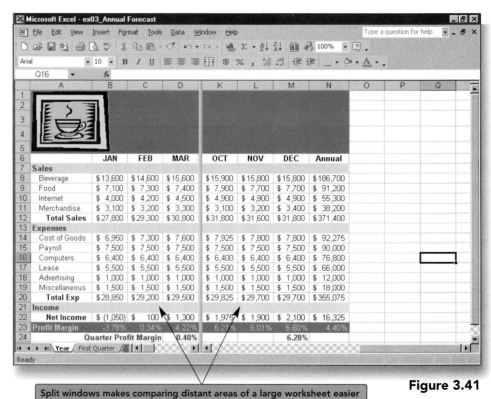

Split windows makes comparing distant areas of a large worksheet easier

Figure 3.41

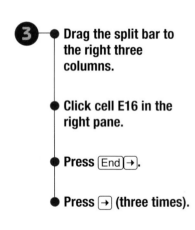

Now you can easily compare the first quarter data to the last quarter data. As you can see, creating panes is helpful when you want to display and access distant areas of a worksheet quickly. After scrolling the data in the panes to display the appropriate worksheet area, you can then quickly switch between panes to make changes to the data that is visible in the pane. This saves you the time of scrolling to the area each time you want to view it or make changes to it. You will clear the horizontal split from the window.

4 ● **Double-click anywhere on the split bar.**

Another Method

The menu equivalent is **W**indow/Remove **S**plit.

Your screen should be similar to Figure 3.42

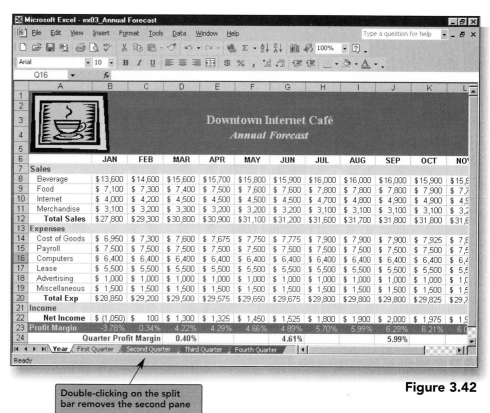

Double-clicking on the split bar removes the second pane

Figure 3.42

Freezing Panes

Another way to manage a large worksheet is to freeze panes.

concept 7

Freeze Panes

7 **Freezing panes** prevents the data in the pane from scrolling as you move to different areas in a worksheet. You can freeze the information in the top and left panes of a window only. This feature is most useful when your worksheet is organized using row and column headings. It allows you to keep the titles on the top and left edge of your worksheet in view as you scroll horizontally and vertically through the worksheet data.

You want to keep the month headings in row 6 and the row headings in column A visible in the window at all times while looking at the Income and Profit Margin data beginning in row 21. To do this, you will create four panes with the upper and left panes frozen.

When creating frozen panes, first position the worksheet in the window to display the information you want to appear in the top and left panes. This is because data in the frozen panes cannot be scrolled like data in regular panes. Then move to the location specified in the following table before using the Windows/Freeze Panes command to create and freeze panes.

To Create	Cell Selector Location	Example
Two horizontal panes with the top pane frozen	Move to the leftmost column in the window and to the row below where you want the split to appear.	Top Pane Frozen 9 Food $ 7,100 $ 7,300 10 Internet $ 4,000 $ 4,200 11 Merchandise $ 3,100 $ 3,200 12 Total Sales $27,800 $29,300 20 Total Exp $28,850 $29,200 21 Income
Two vertical panes with the left pane frozen	Move to the top row of the window and to the column to the right of where you want the split to appear.	Left Pane Frozen 9 Food $ 7,600 $ 7,600 10 Internet $ 4,500 $ 4,500 11 Merchandise $ 3,200 $ 3,200 12 Total Sales $31,100 $31,200 13 Expenses 14 Cost of Goods $ 7,750 $ 7,775
Four panes with the top and left panes frozen	Move to the cell below and to the right of where you want the split to appear.	Top and Left Pane Frozen 6 MAY JUN 7 Sales 8 Beverage $15,800 $15,900 9 Food $ 7,600 $ 7,600 10 Internet $ 4,500 $ 4,500 11 Merchandise $ 3,200 $ 3,200

You want to split the window into four panes with the month column headings at the top of the window and the row headings in column A at the left side of the window.

1 • **Scroll the window until row 6 is the top row in the window.**

• **Move to B7.**

• **Choose Window/Freeze Panes.**

Your screen should be similar to Figure 3.43

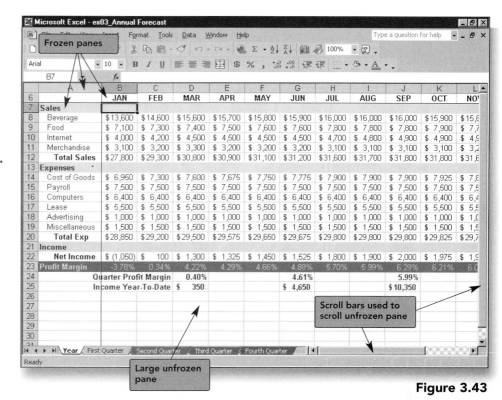

Figure 3.43

The window is divided into four panes at the cell selector location. Only one set of scroll bars is displayed because the only pane that can be scrolled is the larger lower-right pane. You can move the cell selector into a frozen pane, but the data in the frozen panes will not scroll. Also, there is only one cell selector that moves from one pane to another over the pane divider, making it unnecessary to click on the pane to make it active before moving the cell selector in it.

Because Evan has asked you to adjust the profit margin values, you want to view this area of the worksheet only.

2 • **Use the vertical scroll bar to scroll the window until row 21 is below row 6.**

• **Move to cell G24.**

Your screen should be similar to Figure 3.44

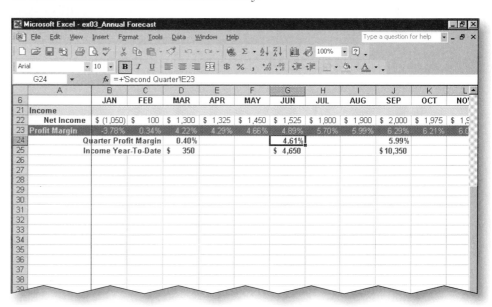

Figure 3.44

Now the Income and profit margin data is displayed immediately below the month headings in row six. The data in rows 7 through 20 is no longer visible, allowing you to concentrate on this area of the worksheet.

Watching Cells

While using a workbook with large worksheets and/or multiple sheets, you may want to keep an eye on how changes you make to values in one area effect cells in another. For example, if you change a value in one sheet that is referenced in a formula in another, you can view the effect on the calculated value using the Watch Window toolbar.

You will be changing values in the second quarter sheet next and want to be able to see the effect on the linked formulas in the Year sheet at the same time.

1 ● **Select cells G24 and N23.**

● **Choose <u>T</u>ools/Formula A<u>u</u>diting/Show <u>W</u>atch Window.**

● **Click  from the Watch window toolbar.**

Another Method

You can also open the Watch Window toolbar from the toolbar shortcut menu.

Your screen should be similar to Figure 3.45

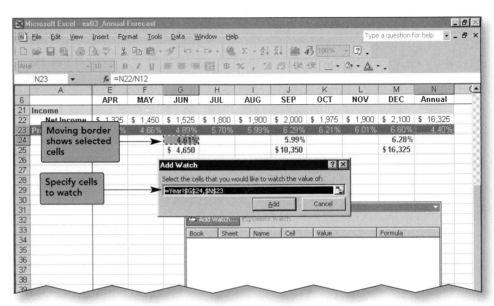

Figure 3.45

The Add Watch dialog box is used to specify the cells you want to see in the Watch Window toolbar. The currently selected cells are identified with a moving border. You will add these cells to the Watch Window.

2 ● **Click [Add].**

● **Size the Watch window toolbar just large enough to display the two cell values rows.**

● **Move the Watch window toolbar to the upper-right corner of the workbook window.**

Your screen should be similar to Figure 3.46

Additional Information

You can also watch linked cells in other open workbooks.

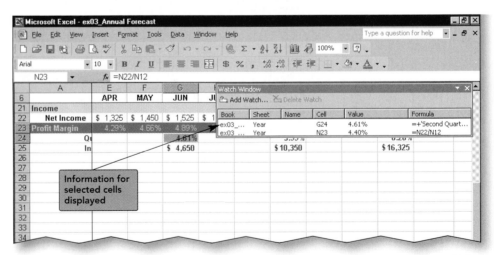

Figure 3.46

The values in the selected cells as well as the formula and location information are displayed in the Watch Window. The toolbar will remain open on top of the workbook as you move from one sheet to another.

Forecasting Values

Evan has asked you to adjust the forecast for the second quarter to show a profit margin of at least 5 percent for each month. After some consideration, you decide you can most easily reduce monthly payroll expenses by carefully scheduling employee work during these three months. Reducing the monthly expense will increase the profit margin for the quarter. You want to find out what the maximum payroll value you can spend during that period is for each month to accomplish this goal. The process of evaluating what effect changing the payroll expenses will have on the profit margin is called what-if analysis.

concept 8

What-If Analysis

8 **What-if analysis** is a technique used to evaluate the effects of changing selected factors in a worksheet. This technique is a common accounting function that has been made much easier with the introduction of spreadsheet programs. By substituting different values in cells that are referenced by formulas, you can quickly see the effect of the changes when the formulas are recalculated.

You can perform what-if analysis by manually substituting values or by using one of the what-if analysis tools included with Excel.

Performing What-If Analysis Manually

To do this, you will enter different payroll expense values for each month and see what the effect is on that month's profit margin. You will adjust the May payroll value first.

1 ● Make the Second Quarter sheet active.

● Enter 7300 in cell C15.

Your screen should be similar to Figure 3.47

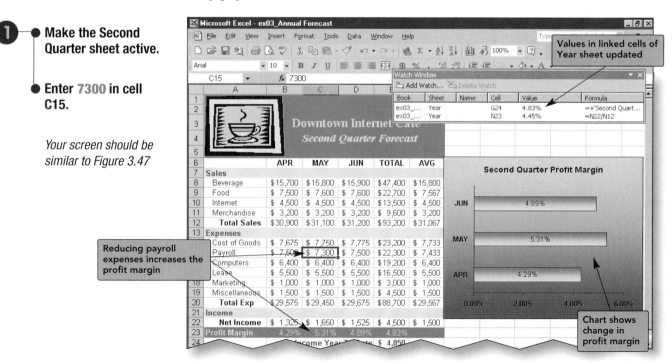

Figure 3.47

Now by looking in cell C23, you can see that decreasing the payroll expenses has increased the profit margin for the month to 5.31 percent. This is more than you need. Also notice the chart has changed to reflect the change in May's profit margin. The Watch Window shows that the values in the two linked cells in the Year sheet were updated accordingly.

You will continue to enter payroll values until the profit margin reaches the goal.

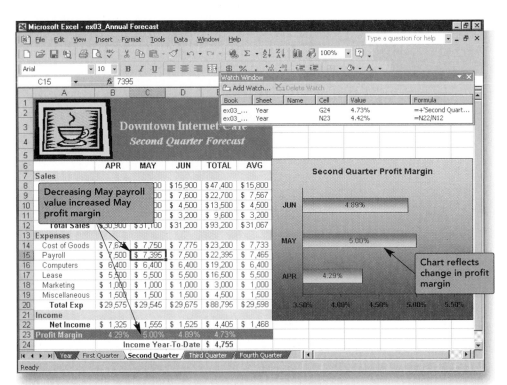

2 ● Enter **7400** in cell C15.

● Enter **7390** in cell C15.

● Enter **7395** in cell C15.

Your screen should be similar to Figure 3.48

Figure 3.48

That's it! Reducing the payroll value from 7500 to 7395 will achieve the 5% profit margin goal for the month.

Using Goal Seek

It usually takes several tries to find the appropriate value when manually performing what-if analysis. A quicker way is to use the what-if analysis Goal Seek tool provided with Excel.

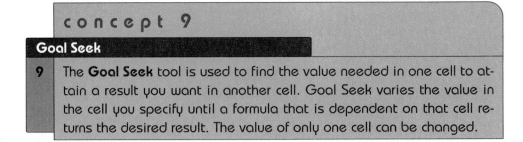

concept 9

Goal Seek

9 The **Goal Seek** tool is used to find the value needed in one cell to attain a result you want in another cell. Goal Seek varies the value in the cell you specify until a formula that is dependent on that cell returns the desired result. The value of only one cell can be changed.

You will use this method to find the payroll value for April that will produce a 5 percent profit margin for that month. The current profit margin value is 4.29 percent in cell B23.

Move to B23.

Choose Tools/Goal Seek.

Your screen should be similar to Figure 3.49

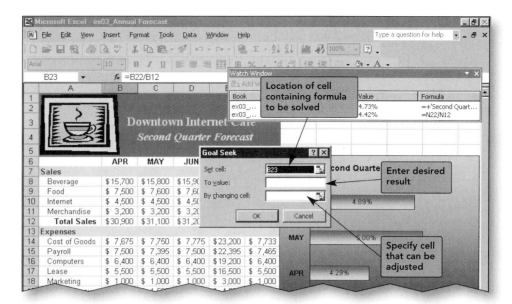

Figure 3.49

In the Goal Seek dialog box, you need to specify the location of the cell containing the formula to be solved, the desired calculated value, and the cell containing the number that can be adjusted to achieve the result. You want the formula in cell B23 to calculate a result of 5 percent by changing the payroll number in cell B15. The Set Cell text box correctly displays the current cell as the location of the formula to be solved. You will enter the information needed in the Goal Seek dialog box.

Click in the To Value text box and enter the value 5.00%.

Click in the By Changing Cell text box and then click on cell B15 in the worksheet to enter the cell reference.

Click OK.

Your screen should be similar to Figure 3.50

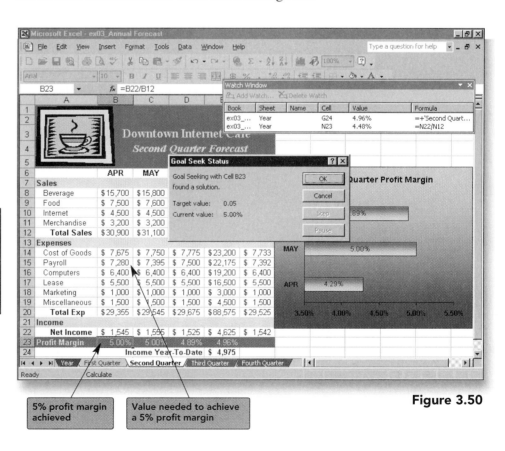

Figure 3.50

The Goal Seek Status dialog box tells you it found a solution that will achieve the 5 percent profit margin. The payroll value of 7280 that will achieve the desired result has been temporarily entered in the worksheet. You can reject the solution and restore the original value by choosing [Cancel]. In this case, however, you want to accept the solution.

3 ● Click [OK].

Your screen should be similar to Figure 3.51

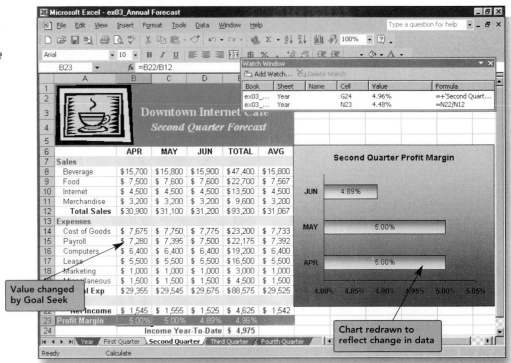

Figure 3.51

The payroll value is permanently updated and the chart redrawn to reflect the change in profit margin for April.

Changing Values Using a Chart

Finally, you need to adjust the June payroll value. This time you will find the value by dragging the June chart data marker to the 5% position on the chart. As you drag the data marker, a dotted bar line will show the new bar length and a ChartTip will display the new profit margin value. An indicator on the X axis also marks your location. Releasing the mouse button with the bar at the new position specifies the new value and opens the Goal Seek dialog box.

1 Click on the June data series bar twice (slowly) to select the individual bar.

- Drag the middle selection handle on the right end of the bar to increase the length of the bar. When the bar ChartTip value is 0.05 or as close as you can get, release the mouse button.

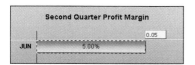

Your screen should be similar to Figure 3.52

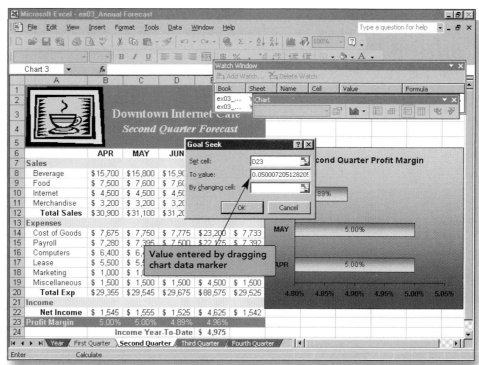

Figure 3.52

Dragging the data marker specifies the value you want to change to and the location of the cell containing the formula. The Goal Seek dialog box is displayed. The Set Cell location and value to attain are entered. Depending on the value you were able to attain by dragging the data marker, you may still need to adjust the value to the exact value of 0.05. You also need to specify the cell location of the value to change.

2
- If necessary, edit the To **V**alue contents to 0.05.

- Enter cell D15 in the By changing cell text box.

- Click ▢ OK ▢.

- Click ▢ OK ▢ to accept the solution.

Your screen should be similar to Figure 3.53

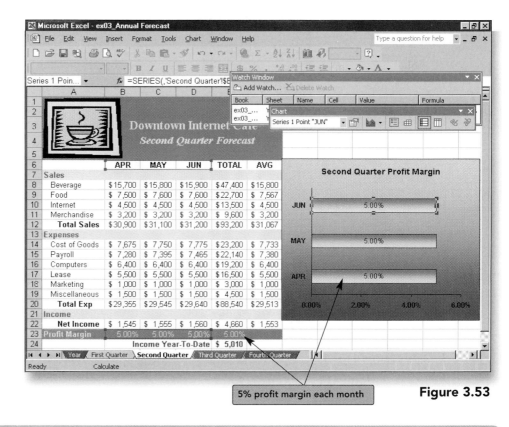

5% profit margin each month

Figure 3.53

The second quarter values are now at the 5 percent profit margin objective. The Watch Window also reflects te change in cell G24.

3 ● Click ⊠ Close to close the Watch Window toolbar.

● Make the Year sheet active to further verify that the profit margin values for the second quarter were updated.

● Choose **W**indow/Un**f**reeze Panes.

● Update the workbook properties by entering your name as author.

● Save the revised forecast as Annual Forecast Revised.

Customizing Print Settings

Now you are ready to print the workbook. Because your worksheet looks great on your screen, this does not mean it will look good when printed. Many times you will want to change the print and layout settings to improve the appearance of the output. Customizing the print settings by changing the orientation of the page, centering the worksheet on the page, hiding gridlines, and adding custom header and footer information are just a few of the ways you can make your printed output look more professional.

Changing Page Orientation

First you want to preview all the sheets in the workbook.

1 ● Right-click a sheet tab and choose Select All Sheets from the shortcut menu.

Additional Information

The tabs of all sheets appear white indicating they are selected; the active sheet tab name is bold.

● Click ⊡ Print Preview.

Your screen should be similar to Figure 3.54

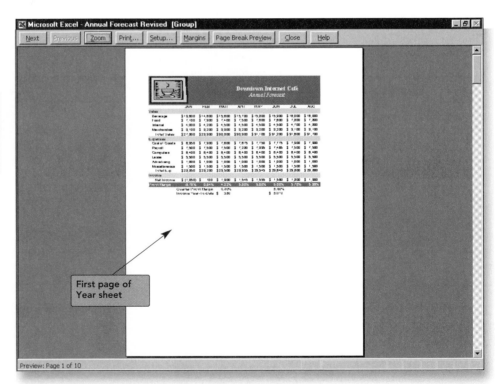

First page of Year sheet

Figure 3.54

The first page of the Year worksheet is displayed in the Preview window. Notice that the entire sheet does not fit across the width of the page. To see the second page,

2 ● Click .

Your screen should be similar to Figure 3.55

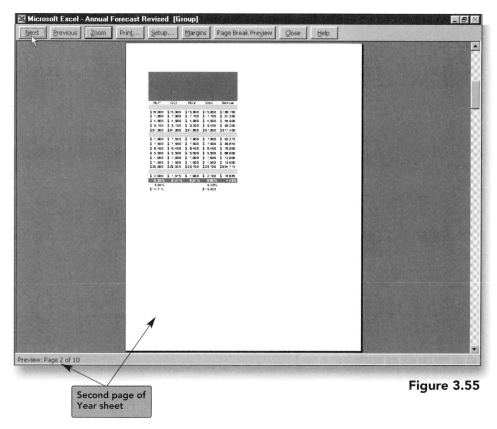

Second page of Year sheet

Figure 3.55

The last five columns of data appear on the second page. Although you could use the Fit To feature to compress the worksheet to a single page, this would make the data small and difficult to read. Instead you can change the orientation or the direction the output is printed on a page. The default orientation is **portrait**. This setting prints across the width of the page. You will change the orientation to **landscape** so that the worksheet prints across the length of the paper. Then you will use the Fit To feature to make sure it fits on one page with the new orientation.

In addition, notice that the total number of pages to be printed is 10. This is because each quarter sheet also requires two pages to print in portrait orientation. You will also change the orientation of these sheets to landscape.

3 ● Click Previous.

● Click Setup....

● If necessary, open the Page tab.

● Select **L**andscape.

● Select **F**it to.

● Click OK.

Your screen should be similar to Figure 3.56

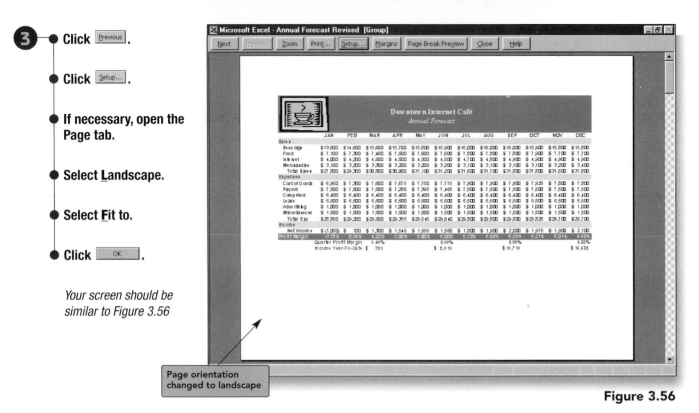

Page orientation changed to landscape

Figure 3.56

Displaying Gridlines and Centering on Page

The entire worksheet now easily fits across the length of the page. Because the worksheet is large, you also feel the worksheet may be easier to read if the row and column gridlines were printed. In addition, you want the worksheet to be centered horizontally on the page.

1 ● Click Setup....

● From the Sheet tab, select **G**ridlines.

● From the Margins tab, select Hori**z**ontally.

● Click OK.

Your screen should be similar to Figure 3.57

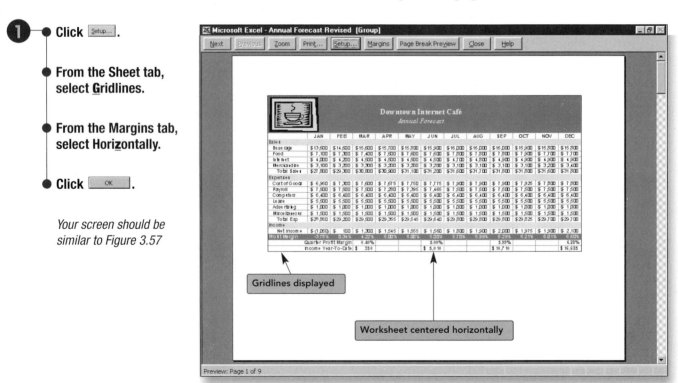

Gridlines displayed

Worksheet centered horizontally

Figure 3.57

The Preview screen is recreated showing how the sheet will appear centered horizontally and with gridlines.

Next, you want to change the orientation to landscape for the four quarterly sheets and to center them both horizontally and vertically on the page. Rather than change each sheet individually in the Preview window, you can make this change to the four sheets at the same time in the worksheet window.

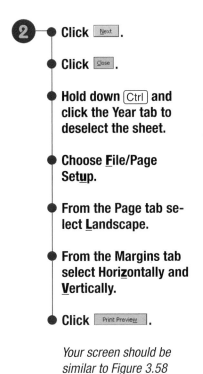

2 ● Click [Next].

● Click [Close].

● Hold down [Ctrl] and click the Year tab to deselect the sheet.

● Choose **F**ile/Page Set**u**p.

● From the Page tab select **L**andscape.

● From the Margins tab select Hori**z**ontally and **V**ertically.

● Click [Print Preview].

Your screen should be similar to Figure 3.58

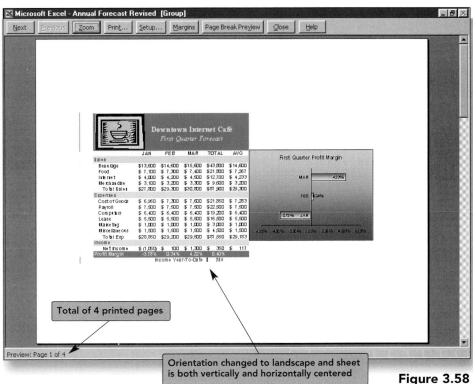

Total of 4 printed pages

Orientation changed to landscape and sheet is both vertically and horizontally centered

Figure 3.58

The worksheet is displayed in landscape orientation and centered both horizontally and vertically on the page. You can also see from the total number of pages to print (four) that the same changes have been made to the four selected sheets.

Adding Custom Headers and Footers

You would also like to add a custom footer to all the sheets. It is faster to add the footer to all sheets at the same time. If you make changes to the active sheet when multiple sheets are selected, the changes are made to all other selected sheets.

Additional Information

Be careful when making changes to multiple sheets as these changes may replace data on other sheets.

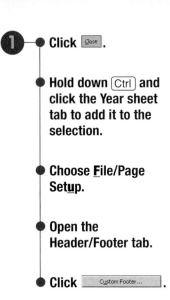

1 ● Click [Close].

● Hold down [Ctrl] and click the Year sheet tab to add it to the selection.

● Choose **F**ile/Page Set**u**p.

● Open the Header/Footer tab.

● Click [Custom Footer...].

Your screen should be similar to Figure 3.59

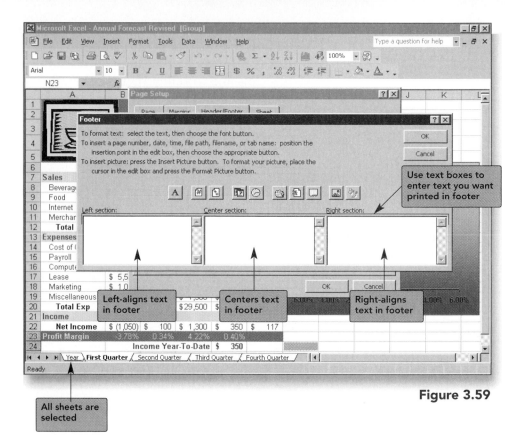

Figure 3.59

The Left Section text box will display the footer text you entered aligned with the left margin, the Center Section will center the text, and the Right Section will right-align the text. The insertion point is currently positioned in the Left Section text box. You want to enter your name, class, and the date in this box. You will enter your name and class by typing it directly in the box. Instead of typing the date, however, you will enter a code that will automatically insert the current date whenever the worksheet is printed.

The buttons above the section boxes (identified below) are used to enter the codes for common header and footer information.

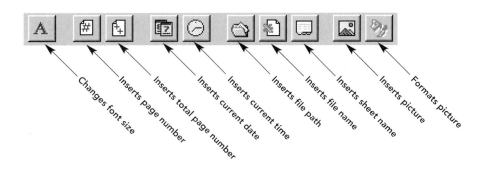

Changes font size

Inserts page number

Inserts total page number

Inserts current date

Inserts current time

Inserts file path

Inserts file name

Inserts sheet name

Inserts picture

Formats picture

2 • **Type Created by [your name].**

• **Press** Tab⇆.

• **Enter the name of your class and the section or time.**

• **Press** Tab⇆.

• **Click** 📅 **Date.**

Your screen should be similar to Figure 3.60

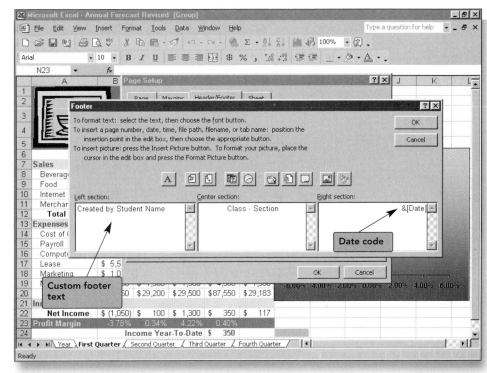

Figure 3.60

You want to make one final check to see how the footer will look before printing the workbook.

3 ● Click [OK].

● Click [Print Preview].

● Look at the other sheets to confirm that the footer was added to them as well.

● Display the Year sheet again.

Your screen should be similar to Figure 3.61

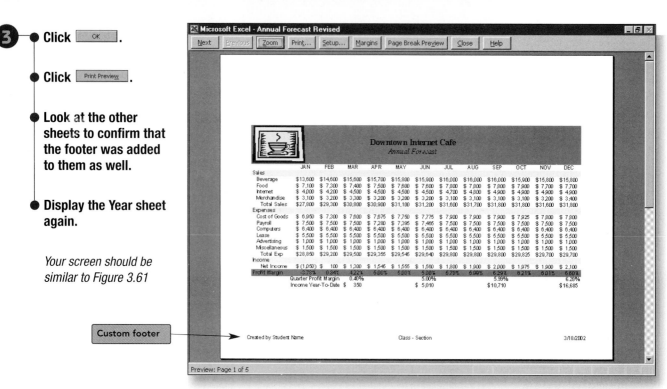

Custom footer

Figure 3.61

The footer as you entered it appears on all selected worksheets.

Printing Selected Sheets

You want to print the Year and Second Quarter worksheets only.

1 ● Best fit the Year sheet and display grid lines again.

● Close the Preview window.

● Right-click on a sheet tab and choose **Ungroup Sheets**.

● If necessary, make the Year sheet active.

● Save the file again.

● Hold down [Ctrl] and click the Second Quarter Sheet tab to add it to the selection of sheets to print.

● Click 🖨 Print.

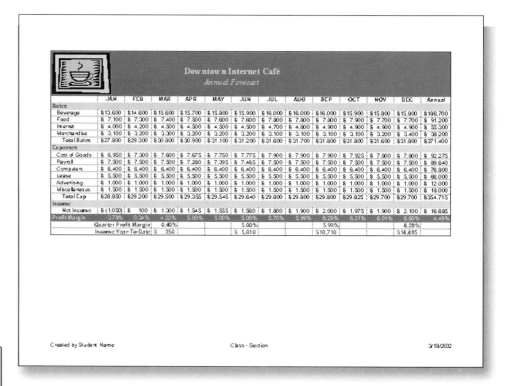

HAVING TROUBLE?

If you need to specify print settings that are different from the default settings on your system, use **File/Print** to print the worksheet.

Your printed output should look like that shown here and on the next page.

2 Close the workbook and exit Excel.

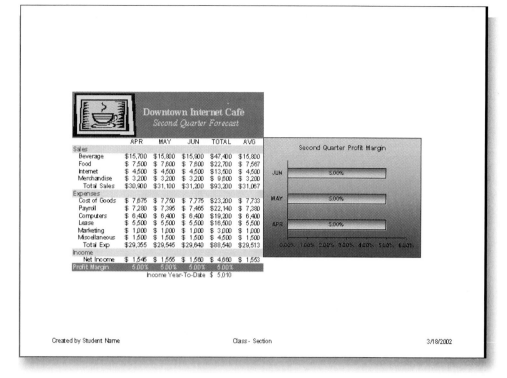

Managing and Analyzing a Workbook

Spell Checking   (EX3.5)

The spell-checking feature locates all misspelled words, duplicate words, and capitalization irregularities in the active worksheet and proposes the correct spelling.

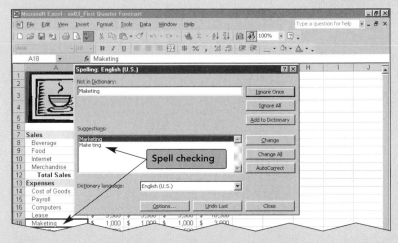

Absolute References   (EX3.16)

An absolute reference is a cell or range reference in a formula whose location does not change when the formula is copied.

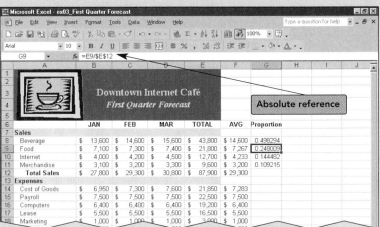

Sheet Names   (EX3.20)

Each sheet in a workbook can be assigned a descriptive name to identify the contents of the sheet.

AutoFill   (EX3.22)

The AutoFill feature makes entering long or complicated headings easier by logically repeating and extending the series.

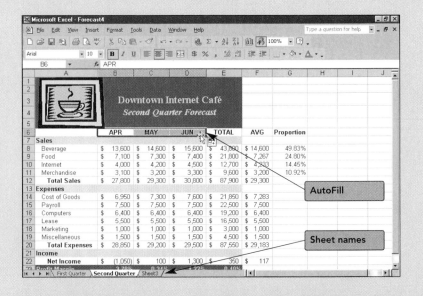

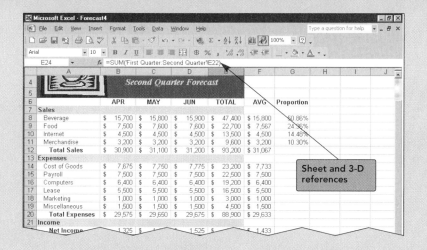

Sheet and 3-D References (EX3.24)

A formula containing sheet and 3-D references to cells in different worksheets in a workbook allows you to use data from other worksheets and to calculate new values based on this data.

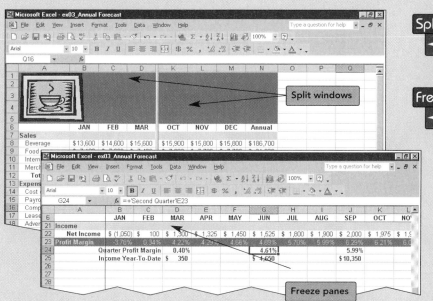

Split Windows (EX3.32)

A sheet window can be split into sections called panes to make it easier to view different parts of the sheet at the same time.

Freeze Panes (EX3.35)

Freezing panes prevents the data in the panes from scrolling as you move to different areas in the worksheet.

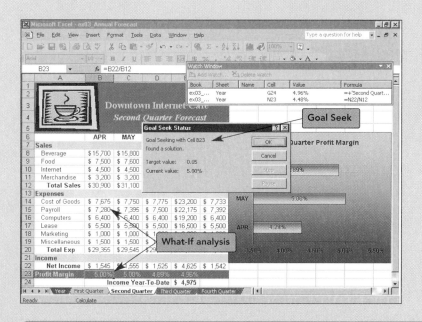

What-If Analysis (EX3.39)

What-if analysis is a technique used to evaluate the effects of changing selected factors in a worksheet.

Goal Seek (EX3.40)

Goal Seek is a tool that is used to find the value needed in one cell to attain a result you want in another cell.

key terms

3-D reference   EX3.24

absolute reference   EX3.16

AutoFill   EX3.22

custom dictionary   EX3.5

freeze panes   EX3.35

Goal Seek   EX3.40

landscape   EX3.45

main dictionary   EX3.5

mixed reference   EX3.16

pane   EX3.32

portrait   EX3.45

Sheet reference   EX3.24

Spelling Checker   EX3.5

what-if analysis   EX3.39

mous skills

After completing this lab, you have learned the following Microsoft Office User Specialist skills:

Skill	Description	Page
Working with Cells and Cell Data	Check spelling	EX3.4
Formatting and Printing Worksheets	Modify row and column settings	EX3.5
	Modify Page Setup options for worksheets	EX3.44
	Preview and print worksheets and workbooks	EX3.44
Modifying Workbooks	Insert and delete worksheets	EX3.27
	Modify worksheet names and positions	EX3.25
	Use 3-D references	EX3.24
Creating and Revising Formulas	Create and revise formulas	EX3.11
	Use statistcal, date and time, financial, and logical functions in formulas	EX3.11

command summary

Command	Shortcut Keys	Button	Action
Edit/**M**ove or Copy Sheet			Moves or copies selected sheet
File/Page Set**u**p/Page/**L**andscape			Changes orientation to landscape
Insert/**F**unction	⇧Shift + F3	f_x	Inserts a function
F**o**rmat/S**h**eet/**R**ename			Renames sheet
F**o**rmat/**S**tyle/**S**tyle name/Currency			Applies currency style to selection
F**o**rmat/**S**tyle/**S**tyle name/Percent		%	Changes cell style to display percentage
Tools/**S**pelling	F7	✓	Spell-checks worksheet
Tools/**G**oal Seek			Adjusts value in specified cell until a formula dependent on that cell reaches specified result
Tools/Formula Au**d**iting/Show **W**atch Window			Opens the Watch Window toolbar
View/**Z**oom		100% ▾	Changes magnification of window
Window/Un**f**reeze			Unfreezes window panes
Window/**F**reeze Panes			Freezes top and/or leftmost panes
Window/**S**plit			Divides window into four panes at active cell
Window/Remove **S**plit			Removes split bar from active worksheet

Terminology

screen identification

In the following worksheet and chart, several items are identified by letters. Enter the correct term for each item in the space provided.

A. _____
B. _____
C. _____
D. _____
E. _____
F. _____
G. _____

matching

Match the lettered item on the right with the numbered item on the left.

1. 'Second Quarter!'A13 _____ **a.** default page orientation
2. pane _____ **b.** spell-checks worksheet
3. portrait _____ **c.** pane that contains the cell selector
4. [F7] _____ **d.** the sections of a divided window
5. Sheet1:Sheet3!H3:K5 _____ **e.** sheet reference
6. #DIV/0! _____ **f.** mixed cell reference
7. landscape _____ **g.** 3-D reference
8. M34 _____ **h.** indicates division by zero error
9. active pane _____ **i.** prints across the length of the paper
10. $B12 _____ **j.** absolute cell reference

multiple choice

Circle the correct response to the questions below.

1. _____ styles display dollar signs, commas, and two or zero decimal places.
   a. currency
   b. comma
   c. normal
   d. percent

2. The cell reference to adjust row 4 without adjusting column C is:
   a. C4
   b. C4
   c. $C4
   d. C$4

3. The number 32534 displayed with the Currency[0] style would appear as _____ in a cell.
   a. 32,534
   b. $32534
   c. $32,534
   d. $32,534.00

4. Each sheet in a workbook can be assigned a descriptive name called a:
   a. sheet name
   b. reference name
   c. content name
   d. label name

5. A(n) _____ holds words you commonly use but that are not included in the dictionary supplied with the program.
   a. AutoFill
   b. custom dictionary
   c. spell checker
   d. main dictionary

6. A _____ reference is a reference to the same cell or range on multiple sheets in the same workbook.
   a. copied
   b. 3-D
   c. sheet
   d. workbook

7. A division of the worksheet window that allows different areas of the worksheet to be viewed at the same time is called a:
   a. window
   b. part
   c. pane
   d. section

8. The information in the worksheet can be _____ in the top and left panes of a window only.
   a. frozen
   b. fixed
   c. aligned
   d. adjusted

9. A common accounting function that helps evaluate data by allowing the user to adjust values to see the effect is called:
   a. auto calculate
   b. what-if analysis
   c. AutoFill
   d. value analysis

10. A cell address that is part absolute and part relative is called:
    a. absolute reference
    b. frozen
    c. adjusted
    d. mixed reference

true/false

Circle the correct answer to the following questions.

1.	=SUM(Sheet15:Sheet50!H6) sums the values in cell H6 of sheets 15 and 50.	True	False
2.	An absolute reference is a cell or range reference in a formula whose location does not change when the formula is copied.	True	False
3.	G8 is an absolute reference.	True	False
4.	If you hold down Ctrl while you drag the fill handle the entries will be incremented.	True	False
5.	You can freeze the information in the top and left panes of a window only.	True	False
6.	The sheet reference consists of the name of the sheet separated from the cell reference by an exclamation point.	True	False
7.	The Window/Split command can be used to quickly create a four-way split at the active cell.	True	False

8. To create two horizontal panes with the left pane frozen, move the cell selector in the top row of the window and select the column to the left of where you want the split to appear.

True   False

9. Dragging the fill handle activates the AutoFill feature and recognizes the cell entry as one that can be incremented.

True   False

10. Goal Seek varies the value in the cell you specify until a formula that is dependent on that cell returns the desired result.

True   False

Concepts

fill-in

Complete the following statements by filling in the blanks with the correct terms.

1. Excel checks spelling by comparing text entries to words in a(n) _____.

2. A(n) _____ is used to identify the contents of a sheet.

3. Changing the page orientation to _____ prints across the length of the page.

4. A(n) _____ reference is a cell or range reference in a formula whose location does not change when the formula is copied.

5. _____ is used to evaluate the effects of changing selected factors in a worksheet.

6. _____ panes prevents the data in the pane from scrolling as you move to different areas in a worksheet.

7. A(n) _____ allows you to use data from other worksheets and to calculate values based on this data.

8. When a window is _____, each pane can be scrolled independently.

9. Use _____ to make entering long or complicated headings easier by logically repeating and extending the series.

10. Use _____ to find the value in a single cell to achieve the result you want in another cell.

discussion questions

1. Define, compare, and contrast relative references, sheet references, and 3-D references. Provide a brief example of each.

2. Discuss how absolute and mixed cell references can be used in a worksheet. What is an advantage of using these types of references over a relative cell reference?

3. Discuss the differences between splitting a window and freezing a window. When would it be appropriate to split a window? When would it be appropriate to freeze a window?

4. Discuss the differences between what-if analysis and Goal Seek. Under what conditions would it be more appropriate to use what-if analysis. When would it be more appropriate to use Goal Seek?

Hands-On Exercises

step-by-step

Sandwich Shop Sales Forecast

★ **1.** Nick Walsh owns seven Sandwich Shop franchises. He has created a worksheet to record each store's first quarter sales. Nick would like you to extend this first quarter sales worksheet to another worksheet that provides a sales forecast for the second quarter. The completed worksheets are shown here.

a. Open the workbook ex03_Sandwich Shop. Spell-check the worksheet and correct any misspelled words. Insert a copy of Sheet1 before Sheet2. Rename the Sheet1 tab to **1st Quarter Sales** and then rename Sheet1(2) tab to **2nd Quarter Sales**. Add color to the tabs.

b. In the 2nd Quarter Sales sheet, change the monthly labels to **Apr, May**, and **June** using AutoFill.

c. Enter the following projected April sales figures:

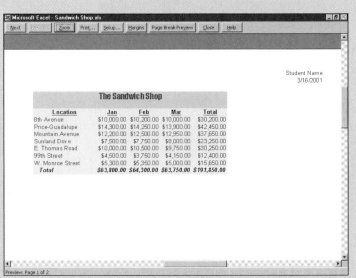

Type	Number
8th Avenue	19000
Price-Guadalupe	14250
Mountain Avenue	13000
Sunland Drive	7800
E. Thomas Road	9500
99th Street	3500
W. Monroe Street	5250

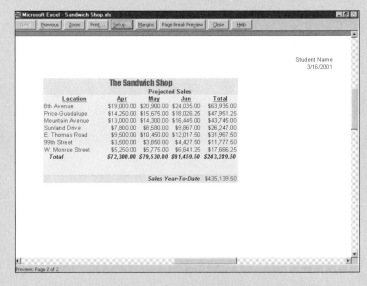

d. A new advertising campaign for May and June is expected to increase monthly sales. May sales for each location is expected to be 10 percent more than April sales and June sales are expected to be 15 percent more than May. Enter formulas to calculate May and June sales for the 8th Avenue location and then copy these formulas into the other appropriate cells.

e. Enter and bold the heading **Projected Sales** in cell C2. Center the heading over columns C and D.

f. Enter, bold, italicize, and right-align the heading **Sales Year-To-Date**: in cell D14. In cell E14, enter a formula to calculate the total sales for the first six months by summing cells E11 on both sheets. Format the value to currency with two decimal places.

g. Make the following changes in both sheets:
  - Format the numbers to currency with two decimal places.
  - Format the column headings to centered, bold, and underlined.
  - Format the worksheet title to 14 pt, center it across columns A through E, and add a color and font of your choice.
  - Indent, bold, and italicize the Total row heading.
  - Bold and italicize the Total row values.
  - Add a custom header that contains your name and the date right-aligned to both work sheets.

h. Preview the workbook. Save the workbook as Sandwich Shop2. Print the workbook.

Forecasting Sales

★ **2.** West's Bed and Bath is a small privately owned retail store. Their accountant, Jeremy, has just completed the budgeted income statement for the first quarter. You are going to use this statement to test the sensitivity of Sales to Net Income. The completed worksheet is shown here.

a. Open the workbook ex03_West Income Statement. Examine the contents of the cells under Jan. You will notice that Sales and Fixed Costs are values while the other entries are formulas. This is also the case for the cells for Feb through Jun.

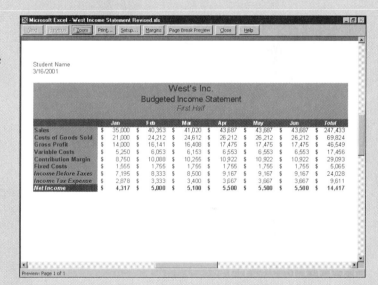

b. Jeremy has been told there may be a rent increase beginning in February that will increase fixed costs to 1755. Update the fixed expense values to see the effect of this increase.

c. Next Jeremy would like to know what level of sales would be necessary to generate a February Net Income of $5000, March of $5100, and $5500 for April through June. Use Goal Seek to answer these questions and update the sales figures.

d. Add a custom header that contains your name and the date left-aligned. Change the print orientation to landscape. Save the workbook as West Income Statement2. Print the workbook.

Tracking Hours Worked

★ ★ **3.** Parker Brent works for United Can Corp. He is paid $8.50 per hour plus time and a half for overtime. For example, this past Monday Parker worked 10 hours. He earned $68 (8 hours times $8.50 per hour) for regular time plus $25.50 (2 hours times $8.50 per hour times 1.5) for overtime for a total of $93.50. He has started to create a worksheet to keep track of weekly hours. You are going to complete this worksheet and create another that Parker will use to schedule next week's hours. The completed worksheets are shown here.

3/16/2001   Student Name

Week #1 Time Sheet

	Regular Hours	Overtime Hours	Total Hours	Pay
Monday	8	2	10	$ 93.50
Tuesday	7	0	7	$ 59.50
Wednesday	7	0	7	$ 59.50
Thursday	8	1	9	$ 80.75
Friday	8	4	12	$ 119.00
Total	38	7	45	$ 412.25

Preview: Page 1 of 2

3/16/2001   Student Name

Week #2 Time Sheet

	Regular Hours	Overtime Hours	Total Hours	Pay
Monday	8	0	8	$ 78.43
Tuesday	8	3	11	$ 122.55
Wednesday	7	0	7	$ 68.63
Thursday	8	4	12	$ 137.25
Friday	8	1	9	$ 93.14
Total	39	8	47	$ 500.00

Hourly Wage $9.80

Reg. Pay To-Date: $ 754.90
Overtime To-Date: $ 147.06
Total Pay To-Date: $ 901.96

Preview: Page 2 of 2

a. Open the workbook ex03_Time Sheets. Enter a formula in E8 that calculates Monday's total hours by adding Monday's regular and overtime hours. Enter formulas to calculate total hours for the other days by copying the formula in E8 down the column. Center the total hours in the cells.

b. Using an absolute reference to the Hourly Wage in cell C15, enter a formula in cell F8 to calculate Monday's pay. Be sure to include regular and overtime pay in the formula. Enter formulas to calculate pay for the other days by copying the formula in cell F8 down the column. Calculate the total Pay. Format the Pay column using the Accounting format with two decimal places.

c. Parker has received his work schedule for next week and would like to record those times by extending the current worksheet to a second week. Insert a copy of Sheet1 before Sheet2. Rename the Sheet1 tab to **First Week** and then rename Sheet1(2) tab to **Second Week**. Add color to the tabs.

d. In the Second Week sheet, change the title in cell B4 to **Week #2 Time Sheet** and enter the following work hours.

	Regular Hours	Overtime Hours
Monday	8	0
Tuesday	8	3
Wednesday	7	0
Thursday	8	4
Friday	8	1

e. Enter, bold, and right-align the following labels:

Reg. Pay To-Date: in cell D17

Overtime To-Date: in cell D18

Total Pay To-Date: in cell D19

f. Enter a formula in cell E17 to calculate the regular pay to date by summing cells C13 on both sheets and multiplying by the hourly wage. Enter a similar formula in cell E18 for overtime pay to date. Calculate the total pay to date in cell E19. Format these values using the Accounting format with two decimal places.

Parker is thinking about asking for a raise from $8.50 to $9.00 to be effective next week. To evaluate the impact of the raise, change the hourly rate in the Week 2 sheet.

g. Use Goal Seek to determine the hourly rate required to achieve a weekly total pay of $500 for Week 2.

h. Add a custom header to both sheets that contains the date centered and your name right-aligned. Preview the workbook. Save the workbook as Time Sheets2. Print the workbook.

Calculating Total Points and GPA

★ ★ **4.** Amy Marino is a college student who has just completed the first two years of her undergraduate program as a business major. In this exercise, you will calculate semester and cumulative totals and GPA for each semester. The completed worksheet for Spring 2002 is shown here.

a. Open the workbook ex03_Grade Report. Look at the four sheets. Rename the sheet tabs **Fall 2000**, **Spring 2001**, **Fall 2001**, and **Spring 2002**. Add color to the tabs.

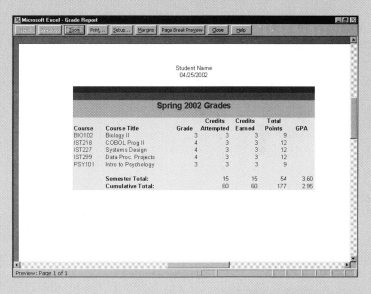

b. You need to enter the formulas to calculate the Total Points and GPA for the four semesters. You will do this for all four sheets at the same time. Select the four sheets. In the Fall 2000 sheet, multiply the Grade by the Credits Earned to calculate Total Points for Intro to Business. Copy that formula down the column. Sum the Credits Attempted, Credits Earned, and Total Points columns and display the results in the Semester Total row.

c. In cell G13, divide the Semester Total's Total Points by the Semester Total's Credits Earned to calculate the GPA for the semester. Use what-if analysis to see what Amy's GPA would be if she had earned a 3 instead of a 2 in Western Civ. Change the grade back to a 2.

d. Look at each sheet to see that the formulas were entered and the calculations performed.

e. Go to cell D14 in the Fall 2000 sheet. Enter the reference formula =D13 to copy the Semester Total Credits Attempted number to the Cumulative Total row. Copy the formula to cells E14 and F14 to calculate Credits Earned and Total Points.

lab exercises

f. Go to the Spring 2001 sheet and calculate a Cumulative Total for Credits Attempted by summing the Spring 2001 Semester Total and the Fall 2000 Cumulative Total. (*Hint:* You can use pointing to enter the Cumulative Totals formula.)

g. Copy that formula to the adjacent cells to calculate Cumulative Totals for Credits Earned and Total Points. Repeat this procedure on the Fall 2001 and Spring 2002 sheets.

h. Go to the Fall 2000 sheet. Select all four sheets. In cell G14, calculate the GPA for the Cumulative Total. Format the Semester Total GPA and the Cumulative Total GPA to display two decimals. Look at each sheet to see the cumulative GPA for each semester. (*Hint:* Amy's cumulative GPA at the end of the Spring 2002 semester is 2.95.) Display the Sheet tab shortcut menu and ungroup the sheets.

i. Go to the Fall 2000 sheet and preview the workbook. Add a custom header that contains your name and the date center-aligned to the sheets. Save the workbook file as Grade Report2. Print the Spring 2002 sheet centered horizontally on the page.

Preparing the Homeowners Association Budget

★★★ 5.
★

Stuart Philips is president of the Garden Springs Homeowners Association. He has nearly completed a six-month budget for the association. Stuart wants to complete the six-month budget, and extend it for the next six months; The completed second half budget is shown here.

a. Open the workbook ex03_Springs Forecast. Spell-check and correct any errors in the workbook.

b. Enter the function to calculate the Average in cell I6. Copy the function down the column. Clear any cells that contain division by zero errors.

c. Insert a copy of Sheet1 before Sheet2. Rename the Sheet1 tab to First Half and rename Sheet2 to Second Half. Add color to the tabs.

d. Use the AutoFill feature to replace the months JAN through JUN with JUL through DEC on the Second Half sheet. Update the title of the Second Half sheet to **Second Half Forecast.**

e. Stuart expects Receipts for July to increase by 2 percent over June and then to increase 1 percent per month beginning August until the end of the year. Create a formula to calculate the receipts for July by taking the receipts figure from June in the First Half sheet and multiplying it by 1.02. Create a formula to calculate August's receipts by taking the receipts in July and multiplying it by 1.01. Copy this formula down and across to calculate the remaining receipts.

f. The maintenance and miscellaneous expenses for July through December are difficult to determine. At this point Stuart would like to plug in values that average the expenses for the first half of the year. Enter **10200** for Maintenance expense and **270** for Miscellaneous expense for July. Copy the values to August through December.

g. Add a custom header that contains the file name left-aligned, the date centered, and your name right-aligned. Preview the workbook. Save the workbook as Springs Forecast2. Print the Second Half worksheet using landscape orientation.

African Safari Cost Analysis

★★★ **6.** Alice, a travel analyst for Adventure Travel Tours, is evaluating the profitability of a planned African Safari package. She has researched competing tours and has determined that a price of $4,900 is appropriate. Alice has determined the following costs for the package.

Item	Cost
Air transport	$1,800 per person
Ground transportation	$360 per person
Lodging	$775 per person
Food	$750 per person
Tour Guides	$3,000
Administrative	$1,200
Miscellaneous	$4,000

Alice has started a worksheet to evaluate the revenues and costs for the African Safari. She wants to know how many travelers are needed to break even (revenues equal costs), how many are needed to make $5,000, and how many are needed to make $10,000. The three worksheets of the completed analysis are shown here and on the next page.

a. Open the workbook ex03_African Safari. Notice that Alice has already entered the tour price and an estimated number of travelers.

b. Spell-check and correct any errors in the workbook.

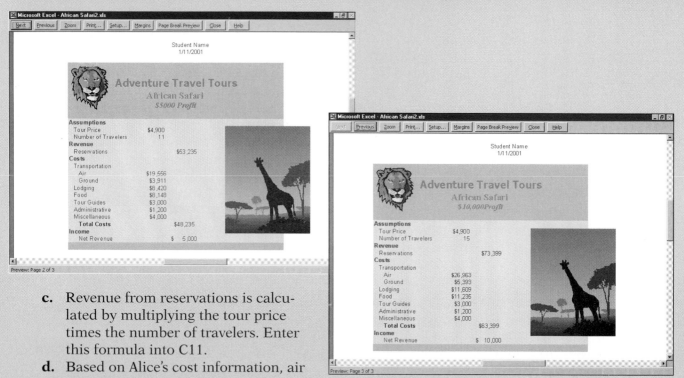

c. Revenue from reservations is calculated by multiplying the tour price times the number of travelers. Enter this formula into C11.

d. Based on Alice's cost information, air transportation is $1800 times the number of travelers. Enter this formula into B14. Enter formulas into B15, B16, and B17 for the other expenses (see table above) related to the number of travelers.

e. Enter the remaining expenses into cells B18, B19, and B20.

f. Calculate total costs in cell C21. Net revenue is the difference between revenue from reservations and total costs. Enter this formula into cell C23.

g. Format the currency values in the worksheet to Currency with no decimal places.

h. Use Goal Seek to determine the number of travelers required to just break even (net revenue equals zero).

i. Rename the sheet tab to **Break Even**. Insert a copy of the Break Even sheet before Sheet2 and rename the tab of the copy **$5000**. Add color to the tabs.

j. In the $5000 sheet, change the title in B5 to **$5,000 Profit**. Use Goal Seek to determine the number of travelers needed to produce a net revenue of $5,000.

k. Insert a copy of the $5000 sheet before Sheet2 and rename the tab of the copy to $10,000. Change the title in B5 to **$10,000 Profit**. Use Goal Seek to determine the number of travelers needed to produce a net revenue of $10,000.

l. Preview the workbook. Add a custom header that contains your name and the date center-aligned to the three sheets. Center the worksheet horizontally. Save the workbook file as African Safari2. Print the workbook.

lab exercises

Expanding Budget Projections

★1. In On Your Own exercise 2 of Lab 1, Personal Budget, you created a workbook for a three-month budget. Extend this workbook by adding two additional sheets. One sheet is to contain a budget for the next six months. The final sheet is to present a full year's summary using 3-D references to the values in the appropriate sheets.

Consider making a special purchase, such as a car, a new computer, or perhaps taking a trip. On a separate line below the total balance in the summary sheet, enter the amount you would need. Subtract this value from the total balance. If this value is negative, reevaluate your expenses and adjust them appropriately. Format the sheets using the features you have learned in the first three labs. Add a custom header on all sheets that includes your name. Preview, print, and save the workbook as Personal Budget2.

Program Expense Comparisons

★★2. Obtain yearly income and expense data for three major art programs at your college or university. In a workbook, record each program's data in a separate sheet. In a fourth sheet, calculate the total income, total expenses, and net income for each program. Also in this sheet, calculate the overall totals for income, expense, and net income. Format the sheets using the features you have learned in the first three labs. Add a custom header on all sheets that includes your name. Preview, print, and save the workbook as Art Expenses.

Stock Data Analysis

★★★3. Select three stocks listed on the New York Stock Exchange. Using the Internet or the library, determine each stock's month-ending price for the past year. In a workbook containing four sheets, record each stock's prices in separate worksheets. In a fourth sheet, calculate the average, standard deviation, and maximum and minimum for each of the three stocks. Also, in the final sheet, chart the average data for the three stocks. Format the sheets using the features you have learned in the first three labs. Add a custom header on all sheets that includes your name. Preview, print, and save the workbook as Stock Analysis.

★★★ Owning and managing a small business is a dream of many college students. Do some research on the Web and choose a business that interests you. Create a projected worksheet for four quarters in separate worksheets. In a fifth sheet, show the total for the year. Include a year-to-date value in each quarterly sheet. In the last quarter sheet, select one expense and determine what value the expense would have to have been so that the net income for that quarter would have been 10 percent higher than the current level. Format the sheets using the features you have learned in the first three labs. Add a custom header on all sheets that includes your name. Preview, print, and save the workbook as My Business.

Working Together: Linking, Embedding, and E-mailing

Evan, the Café owner, is particularly concerned about the first quarter forecast. Your analysis of the sales data for the first quarter shows a steady increase in total sales. However, as you suggested, if a strong sales promotion is mounted, Internet sales will increase sharply. Evan has asked you to send him a memo containing the worksheet data showing the expected sales without a strong sales promotion and the chart showing the projected Internet sales with a sales promotion.

Additionally, Evan wants a copy of the second quarter forecast showing the 5 percent profit margins for each month. He also wants a copy of the workbook

file so that he can play with the sales values to see how they would affect the profit margin.

You will learn how to share information between applications while you create these memos. Additionally, you will learn how to send the workbook via e-mail. Your completed document will look like that shown below.

Note: This lab assumes that you already know how to use Word and that you have completed Labs 2 and 3 of Excel. You will need the file Café Sales Charts you created in Lab 2 and Annual Forecast Revised from Lab 3.

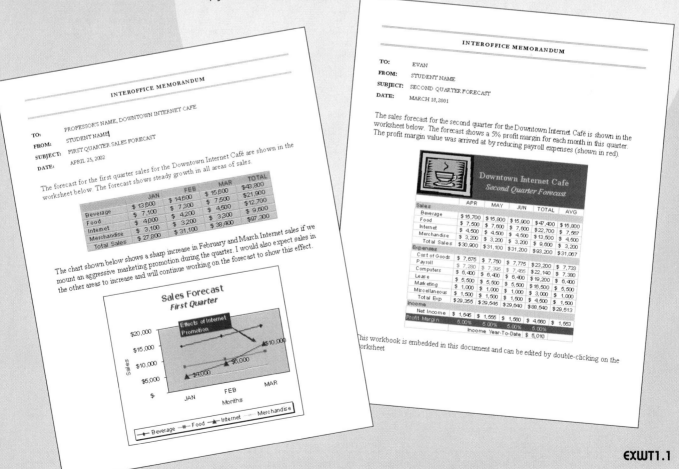

Copying between Applications

The memo to the manager about the analysis of the sales data has already been created using Word. However, you still need to add the Excel worksheet data and charts to the memo. All Microsoft Office applications have a common user interface such as similar commands and menu structures. In addition to these obvious features, they have been designed to work together, making it easy to share and exchange information between applications.

You will begin by copying the worksheet from Excel into a Word document. You can also use the same commands and procedure to copy information from Word or other Office XP applications into Excel.

Copying a Worksheet to a Word Document

1

● **Start Word and open the document** exwt1_Sales Forecast Memo.

● **In the memo header, replace Professor's Name with your instructor's name and Student Name with your name.**

Your screen should be similar to Figure 1

Figure 1

You will insert the worksheet data of the first quarter sales forecast below the first paragraph. Below the second paragraph, you will display the combination chart of sales by category. To insert the information from the Excel workbook file into the Word memo, you need to open the workbook.

2 **Start Excel and open the workbook** Cafe Sales Charts.

● **If necessary, move to cell A9 of Sheet1.**

Your screen should be similar to Figure 2

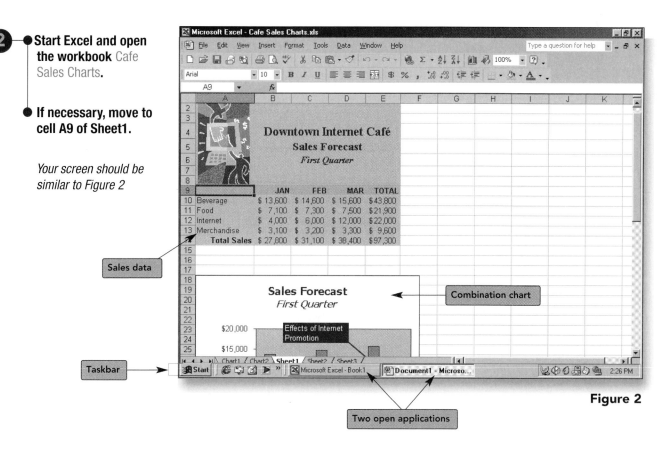

Sales data

Combination chart

Effects of Internet Promotion

Taskbar

Two open applications

Figure 2

There are now two open applications, Word and Excel. Word is open in a window behind the Excel application window. Both application buttons are displayed in the taskbar. There are also two open files, Cafe Sales Charts in Excel and exwt1_Sales Forecast Memo in Word. Excel is the active application and Cafe Sales Charts is the active file.

First you will copy the worksheet data into the Word memo. While using the Excel application, you have learned how to use cut, copy, and paste to move or copy information within the same document. You can also perform these operations between documents in the same application and between documents in different applications. For example, you can copy information from a Word document and paste it into an Excel worksheet. The information is pasted in a format that the application can edit, if possible.

You want to copy the worksheet data in cells A9 through E14 into the memo.

3 ● Select cells A9 through E14.

● Click 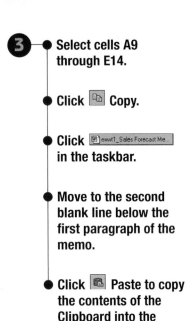 Copy.

● Click ⊞ exwt1_Sales Forecast Me... in the taskbar.

● Move to the second blank line below the first paragraph of the memo.

● Click 🗈 Paste to copy the contents of the Clipboard into the memo.

Your screen should be similar to Figure 3

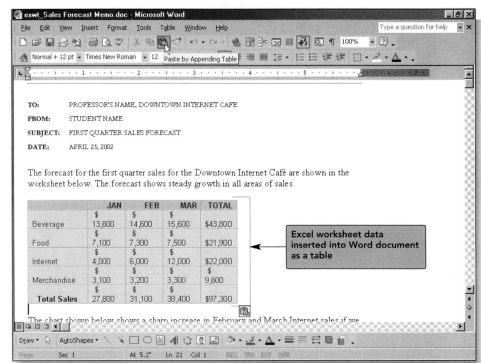

Figure 3

The worksheet data has been copied into the Word document as a table that can be edited and manipulated within Word. Much of the formatting associated with the copied information is also pasted into the document. You need to adjust the column widths of the table to display the data correctly. Then you will center the table between the margins.

4 ● Choose Table/Select/Table.

● Double-click on the column border of any column to fit the columns to the size of the data.

● Click ▤ Center.

● Deselect the table.

Your screen should be similar to Figure 4

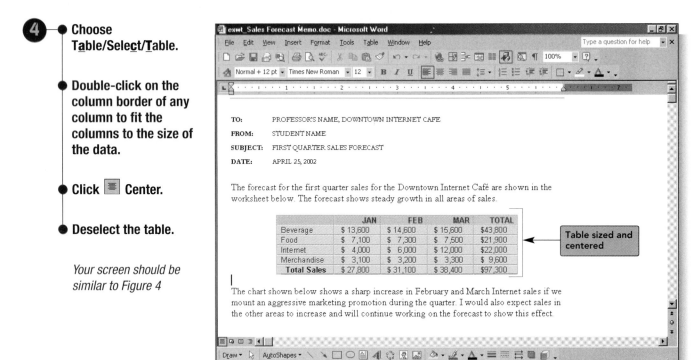

Figure 4

Next you want to return the Internet sales data in the table to the original forecasted values assuming an aggressive marketing campaign is not mounted.

5 ● **Change the value in C4 to 4,200, in D4 to 4,500 and E4 to 12,700.**

Your screen should be similar to Figure 5

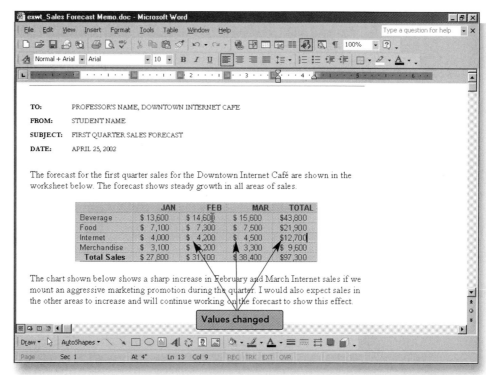

Figure 5

6 ● **Switch to Excel.**

Your screen should be similar to Figure 6

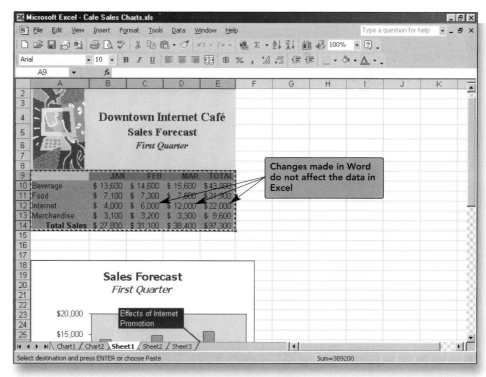

Figure 6

The change in data made in the Word table does not affect the data in the worksheet. This is because the Word table is simply a copy of the Excel worksheet.

Linking between Applications

Next you want to display the combination chart showing the sales trends for Internet sales if an aggressive marketing campaign is mounted below the second paragraph in the memo. You will insert the chart object into the memo as a **linked object**. Information created in one application can also be inserted as a linked object into a document created by another application. When an object is linked, the data is stored in the **source file** (the document it was created in). A graphic representation or picture of the data is displayed in the **destination file** (the document in which the object is inserted). A connection between the information in the destination file to the source file is established by the creation of a link. The link contains references to the location of the source file and the selection within the document that is linked to the destination file.

When changes are made in the source file that affect the linked object, the changes are automatically reflected in the destination file when it is opened. This is called a **live link**. When you create linked objects, the date and time on your machine should be accurate. This is because the program refers to the date of the source file to determine whether updates are needed when you open the destination file.

Linking a Chart Object to a Word Document

You will insert the chart as a linked object. By making the chart a linked object, it will be automatically updated if the source file is edited.

1. ● Select the combination chart.

● Click 🖺 Copy to copy the selected chart object to the Clipboard.

● Switch to the Word application and move to the second blank line below the second paragraph of the memo.

● Choose Edit/Paste Special.

● Select Paste link.

Your screen should be similar to Figure 7

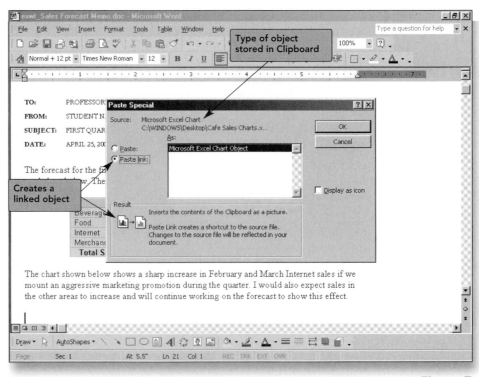

Figure 7

The Paste Special dialog box displays the type of object contained in the Clipboard and its location in the Source area. From the As list box you select the type of format in which you want the object inserted into the destination file. The only available option for this object is as a Microsoft Excel Chart Object. The Result area describes the effect of your selections. In this case, the object will be inserted as a picture and a link will be created to the chart in the source file. Selecting the Display as Icon option changes the display of the object from a picture to an icon. Double-clicking the icon displays the object picture. The default selections are appropriate.

2 • Click  .

• Set the Zoom to 75%.

• Position the window so you can see both the worksheet and the chart on the page.

• Center the chart object on the page.

Your screen should be similar to Figure 8

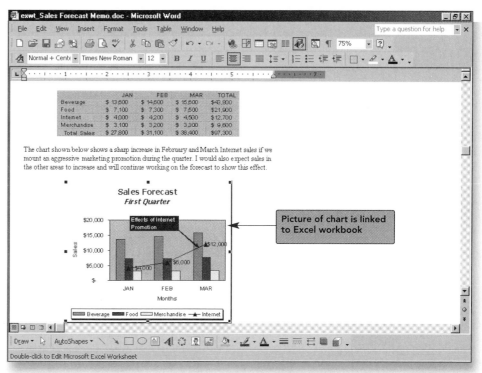

Figure 8

Updating a Linked Object

While reading the memo and looking at the chart, you decide to change the chart type from a combination chart to a line chart. You feel a line chart will show the sales trends for all sales items more clearly. You also decide to lower your sales expectation for Internet sales from 12,000 to 10,000 for March.

To make these changes, you need to switch back to Excel.

Additional Information

Double-clicking on a linked object quickly switches to the open source file. If the source file is not open, it opens the file for you. If the application is not open, it both starts the application and opens the source file.

1 Double-click the chart object.

Another Method
The menu equivalent is Edit/Linked Worksheet Object/Edit Link.

● If necessary, select the chart.

● Click 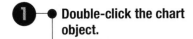 Chart Type.

● Click ⬈ Line chart.

● Change the value in cell D12 to **10000**.

● Scroll the window to see both the chart and worksheet data.

Your screen should be similar to Figure 9

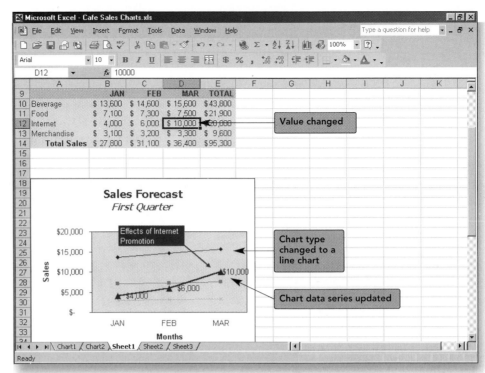

Figure 9

The chart type has changed to a line chart and the chart data series has been updated to reflect the change in data. Now you will look at the memo to see what changes were made to the worksheet and chart.

2 Switch to the Word document.

Your screen should be similar to Figure 10

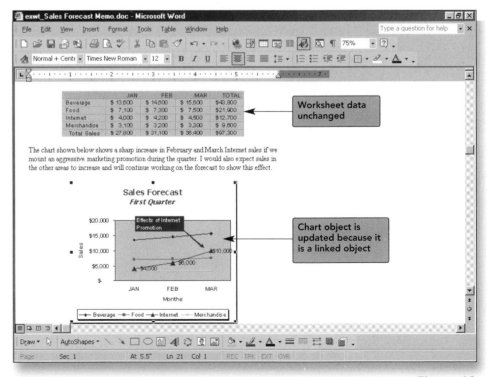

Figure 10

The chart in the memo reflects the change in both chart type and the change in data for the Internet sales. This is because any changes you make in the chart in Excel will be automatically reflected in the linked chart in the Word document. However, because the worksheet data is a word table and not a linked object, it does not reflect the change in data made in Excel.

Editing Links

Whenever a document is opened that contains links, the application looks for the source file and automatically updates the linked objects. If there are many links, updating can take a lot of time. Additionally, if you move the source file to another location or perform other operations that may interfere with the link, your link will not work. To help with situations like these, you can edit the settings associated with links. To see how you do this,

1 ● **If necessary, select the chart object.**

● **Choose Edit/Links.**

Your screen should be similar to Figure 11

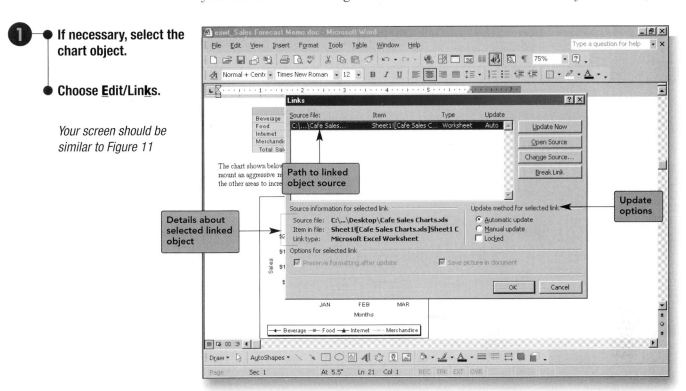

Figure 11

The Links dialog box displays the object path for all links in the document in the list box. The field code specifies the path and name of the source file, the range of linked cells or object name, the type of file, and the update status. Below the list box, the details for the selected link are displayed. The other options in this dialog box are described in the table below.

Option	Effect
Automatic	Updates the linked object whenever the destination document is opened or the source file changes. This is the default.
Manual	The destination document is not automatically updated and you must use the Update Now command button to update the link.
Locked	Prevents a linked object from being updated.
Open Source	Opens the source document for the selected link.
Change Source	Used to modify the path to the source document.
Break Link	Breaks the connection between the source document and the active document.

2 ● **Click**  .

● **Deselect the chart and save the Word document as** Sales Forecast Memo Linked.

● **Preview, print, then close the document.**

● **Save the Excel workbook as** Cafe Sales Charts Linked **and close the file.**

Embedding an Object in Another Application

The last thing you need to send Evan is a memo that describes and shows the second quarter forecast. To do this, you'll open the memo already created for you in Word and **embed** the sections from the Annual Forecast Revised workbook that Evan wants in the appropriate locations. An object that is embedded is stored in the destination file and becomes part of that document. The entire file, not just the selection that is displayed in the destination file, becomes part of the document. This means that you can modify it without affecting the source document where the original object resides.

Embedding a Worksheet in a Word Document

1 **Open the Word document** exwt1_Forecast Memo.

In the memo header, replace the Student Name with your name.

Move to the second blank line below the first paragraph of the memo.

Your screen should be similar to Figure 12

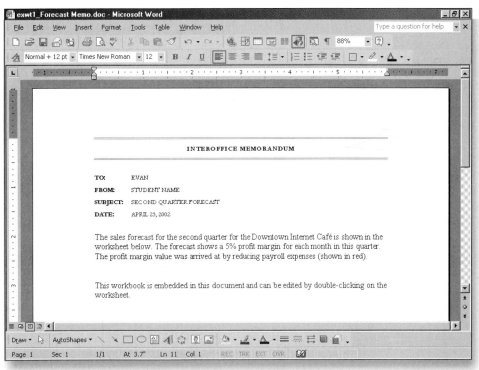

Figure 12

You will embed the first quarter 2002 forecast worksheet in the Word document.

2 **Switch to Excel and open the workbook file** Annual Forecast Revised.

Make the Second Quarter sheet active.

Copy the range A1 through F24.

Switch to Word.

Choose Edit/Paste Special.

Additional Information

To embed an entire file, use Insert/Object.

The dialog box on your screen should be similar to Figure 13

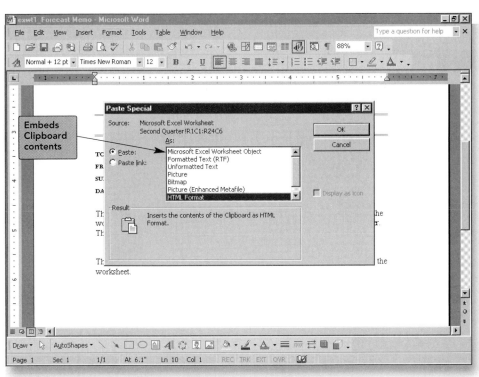

Figure 13

The Paste option inserts or embeds the Clipboard contents in the format you specify from the As list box. To embed the contents of the Clipboard into a document so it can be edited using the server application, select the option that displays the server name, in this case Excel.

3 ● **Select Microsoft Excel Worksheet Object.**

● **Click** OK .

Your screen should be similar to Figure 14

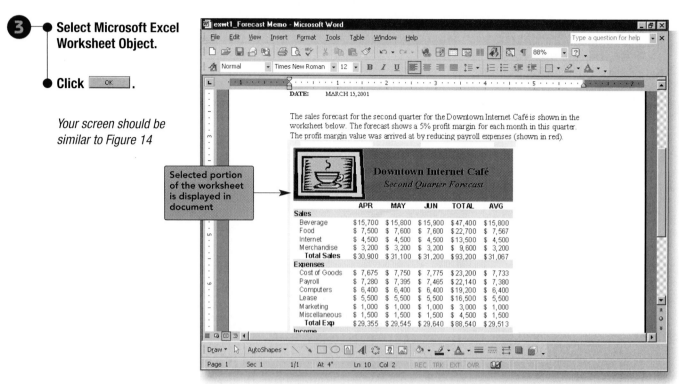

Selected portion of the worksheet is displayed in document

Figure 14

The selected portion of the worksheet is displayed in the memo at the location of the insertion point. As you can see, the object is a bit large.

4 ● **Decrease the size of the worksheet object slightly and center it between the margins.**

Your screen should be similar to Figure 15

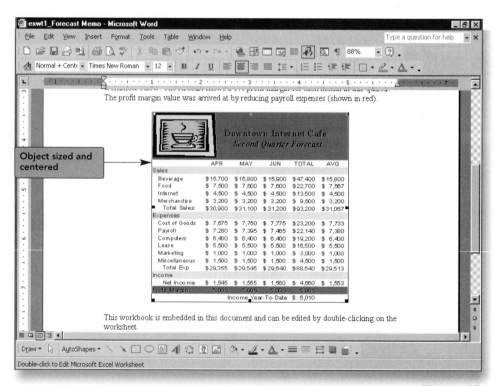

Object sized and centered

Figure 15

Updating an Embedded Object

You want to add color to the payroll range of cells you adjusted to arrive at the 5% profit margin. Because the worksheet is embedded, you can do this from within the Word document. To demonstrate how an embedded object works, you will close the Excel source file and application and edit the worksheet from within the Word document.

1 ● **Switch to Excel.**

● **Close the workbook without saving changes and exit Excel.**

The server application is used to edit data in an embedded object. To open the server application and edit the worksheet, you double-click the embedded object.

2 ● **Double-click the worksheet object.**

Your screen should be similar to Figure 16

Excel menus and toolbar

HAVING TROUBLE?
If the worksheet does not fully display the numbers, click outside the worksheet to return to the document, make the worksheet object larger, and then open the server application again.

Excel server application open

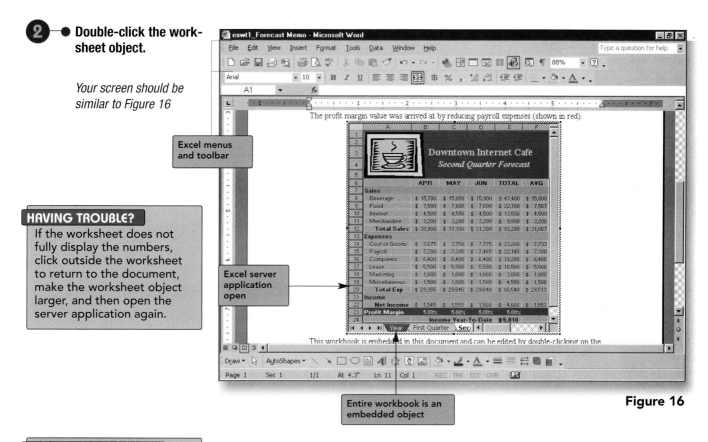

Entire workbook is an embedded object

Figure 16

Additional Information
The user must have the server application on his or her system to be able to open and edit the embedded object.

The server application, in this case Excel, is opened. The Excel menus and toolbars replace the menus and toolbars in the Word application window. The selected portion of the embedded object is displayed in an editing worksheet window. Now you can use the server commands to edit the object.

● Change the font color of cells B15 through D15 to red.

● Close the server application by clicking anywhere outside the object.

Your screen should be similar to Figure 17

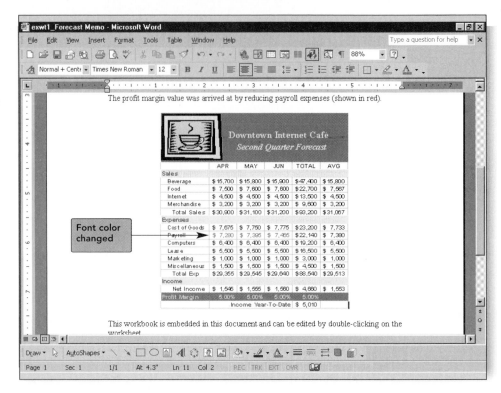

Figure 17

The embedded object in the memo is updated to reflect the changes you made.

E-Mailing the Memo

Finally, you want to e-mail the memo to Evan.

1 ● Click 🔘 E-mail.

If you do not have an e-mail program installed, the 🔘 button is not displayed and you will need to skip this section.

The menu equivalent is File/Send to/Mail Recipient.

The process to e-mail is the same in Excel.

Your screen should look similar to Figure 18

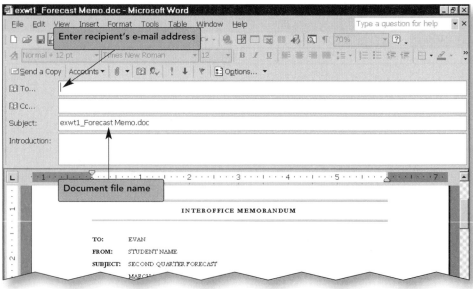

Figure 18

An e-mail message box is displayed at the top of the document. You use the message box to specify the recipient's e-mail address, the e-mail address of anyone you want to send a copy of this message to (cc:), and the subject of the message. You can also use the toolbar buttons to select recipient names from your e-mail address book, attach a file to the message, set the message priority (high, normal, or low priority), include a follow-up message flag, and set other e-mail options. The name of the document appears in the Subject box by default. And finally, you can use the Introduction box to include a brief note along with the copy of the memo.

2 ● Enter the e-mail address of the person you want to send the message to in the To: box.

HAVING TROUBLE?

Ask your instructor what e-mail address to use. For example, if you have a personal e-mail address, your instructor may want you to use it for this exercise.

● In place of the information displayed in the Subject box, enter **Second Quarter Forecast**.

Your screen should look similar to Figure 19

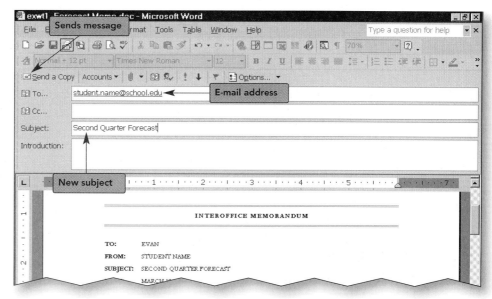

Figure 19

That is all the information that is required to send the e-mail message. You are now ready to send your e-mail message.

3 ● Click .

HAVING TROUBLE?

If you do not have an Internet connection established, you will not be able to send this message. Click Cancel to cancel the connection message.

Your message is sent and the e-mail message box is removed from the screen.

4 ● Save the memo as Second Quarter Forecast.

● Preview and print the memo.

● Exit Word.

Deciding When to Link or Embed Objects

Linking documents is a very handy feature, particularly in documents whose information is updated frequently. If you include a linked object in a document that you are giving to another person, make sure the user has access to the source file and application. Otherwise the links will not operate correctly.

Keep the following in mind when deciding whether to link or embed objects.

Use linking when:	Use embedding when:
File size is important	File size is not important
Users have access to the source file and application	Users have access to the application but not to the source file
The information is updated frequently	The data changes infrequently

Working Together: Linking, Embedding, and E-Mailing

key terms

destination file   EXWT1.6

embed   EXWT1.10

linked object   EXWT1.6

live link   EXWT1.6

source file   EXWT1.6

command summary

Command	Button	Action
File/Send to/Mail Recipient		Sends the active document to the e-mail recipient
Edit/Paste Special		Inserts the object as an embedded object
Edit/Paste Special/Paste Link		Creates a link to the source document
Edit/Links		Modifies selected link
Edit/Linked Object/Edit Link		Modifies selected linked object

Hands-On Exercises

step- by-step

Rescue Foundation Income Memo

★★ 1. The Animal Rescue Foundation's agency director has asked you to provide her with information about income for 2002. You want to create a memo to her and include a copy of the worksheet analysis of this data in the memo. The completed memo is shown below.

a. Start Word and open the document exwt1_Rescue Memo.

b. In the header, replace the From placeholder with your name.

c. Start Excel and open the workbook exwt1_Contributions.

d. Insert both worksheets as links below the first paragraph in the Word memo. Size and center the worksheets below the paragraph.

e. Enter the income of **$2,650** for May raffle ticket sales.

f. Save the Excel workbook as Contributions2. Exit Excel.

g. If necessary, adjust the size and placement of the worksheets in the memo. Save the Word document as Rescue Memo Linked. Preview and print the document.

h. E-mail the memo to your instructor and carbon copy yourself. Include appropriate information in the subject.

Memo

To: Barbara Wood

From: Student Name

CC: Mark Wilson

Date: 04/25/2001

Re: Income

Below is the completed analysis of income for 2002. As you can see, the income for both periods is very close, with Fall/Winter slightly higher.

Animal Rescue Foundation

	March	April	May	June	July	August	Total
Annual Memberships	$4,000	$4,583	$8,395	$2,834	$5,384	$5,481	$30,677
Phone Solicitation	1200			2000			3200
Corporate Donations			12000			8000	20000
Raffle Tickets			2650				2650
Pet Shows		7000					7000
Other	2000	2000	2000	2000	2000	2000	12000
Total	$7,200	$13,583	$25,045	$6,834	$7,384	$15,481	$75,527

Animal Rescue Foundation

	September	October	November	December	January	February	Total
Annual Memberships	$6,540	$4,523	$4,395	$1,834	$1,384	$5,481	$24,157
Phone Solicitation	1,200					2,000	3,200
Corporate Donations		15,000				10,000	25,000
Raffle Tickets			2,894				2,894
Pet Shows		9,000					9,000
Other	2,000	2,000	2,000	2,000	2,000	2,000	12,000
Total	$9,740	$30,523	$9,289	$3,834	$3,384	$19,481	$76,251

I would like to set up a meeting for next week to brainstorm about ways we can increase income for next year. Please let me know what your schedules are like so I can set a date and time.

1

Tour Status Memo

★★ **2.** Adventure Travel Tours travel agency sends a monthly status report to all subsidiary offices showing the bookings for the specialty tours offered by the company. Previously the worksheet data was printed separately from the memo. Now you want to include the worksheet in the same document as the memo.

a. Start Word and open the exwt1_Tour Status Report document. Replace Student Name with your name on the From line in the heading.

b. Start Excel and open the exwt1_Adventure Travel Monthly workbook.

c. Copy the worksheet as a linked object into the memo below the paragraph.

d. Enter the following data for the March bookings in the worksheet.

Tour	March Data
Tuolumne Clavey Falls	20
Costa Rica Rainforest	4
Kilimanjaro	4
Machu Picchu	3
Himalayas	6
Tanzania Safari	6

e. Save the workbook as Adventure Travel Monthly2. Exit Excel.

f. Center the worksheet object in the word document.

g. Save the Word document as March Status Report. Print the memo.

h. E-mail the memo to your instructor and carbon copy yourself. Include appropriate information in the subject.

INTEROFFICE MEMORANDUM

TO: ADVENTURE TRAVEL EMPLOYEES
FROM: STUDENT NAME
SUBJECT: TOUR STATUS REPORT
DATE: 3/20/01

The bookings to date for our upcoming specialty tours are displayed in the following table. As you can see the new white water rafting tour to below the Tuolumne Clavey Falls in California is almost full to capacity and we are considering offering a second week. Because several others are also close to capacity you may want to advise any clients who are considering one of these tours to make reservations as soon as possible.

Adventure Travel Tours
Speciality Tours Status Report

Tour	Jan	Feb	Mar	Total	Tour Capacity
Tuolumne Clavey Falls	8	14	20	42	46
Costa Rica Rainforests	5	9	4	18	36
Kilimanjaro	2	2	4	8	15
Machu Picchu	4	8	3	15	30
Himalayas	0	0	6	6	18
Tanzania Safari	4	3	6	13	21

Hotel Occupancy Memo

★★ **3.** Karen works for a large hotel chain in the marketing department. She has recently researched hotel occupancy rates for the Phoenix area and has created a worksheet and stacked-column chart of the data. Now Karen wants to send a memo containing the chart to her supervisor.

a. Start Word and open the document exwt1_Hotel Memo.

b. In the header, replace the placeholder information in brackets with the following:

TO:	Brad Wise
FROM:	Karen Howard
CC:	[your name]
RE:	Hotel Occupancy

c. Start Excel and open the workbook exwt1_Hotel Data. Embed the column chart below the paragraph in the Word memo. Center the chart in the memo. Exit Excel.

d. You decide you need to clarify that the data for 2003 and 2004 is projected. Add a second title line **(2003 - 2004 projected)** to the embedded chart in 12 point, italic, no bold.

e. Save the Word document as Hotel Memo2. Preview and print the document.

f. E-mail the memo to your instructor and carbon copy yourself. Include appropriate information in the subject.

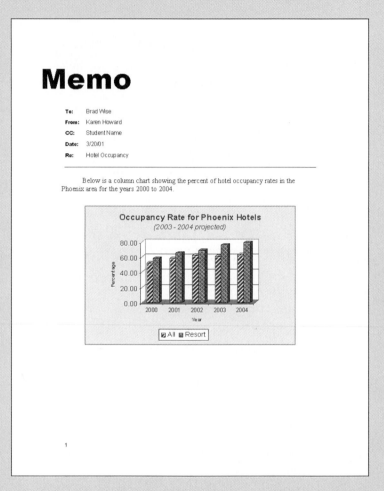

Command Summary

Command	Shortcut	Button	Action
File/Open <file name>	Ctrl + O		Opens an existing workbook file
File/Close		X	Closes open workbook file
File/Save <file name>	Ctrl + S		Saves current file on disk using same file name
File/Save As <file name>			Saves current file on disk using a new file name
File/Send to/Mail Recipient			Sends the active document to the e-mail recipient.
File/Page Setup/Page/Landscape			Changes orientation to landscape
File/Page Setup/Header/Footer			Adds header and/or footer
File/Print Preview			Displays worksheet as it will appear when printed
File/Print	Ctrl + P		Prints a worksheet
File/Print/Entire Workbook			Prints all the sheets in a workbook
File/Properties			Displays information about a file
File/Exit		X	Exits Excel 2000
Edit/Undo	Ctrl + Z		Undoes last editing or formatting change
Edit/Redo	Ctrl + Y		Restores changes after using Undo
Edit/Copy	Ctrl + C		Copies selected data to Clipboard
Edit/Paste	Ctrl + V		Pastes selections stored in Clipboard
Edit/Paste Special			Inserts the object as an embedded object
Edit/Paste Special/Paste Link			Creates a link to the source document
Edit/Links			Modifies selected link
Edit/Linked Object/Edit Link			Modifies selected linked object
Edit/Fill			Fills selected cells with contents of source cell
Edit/Clear/Contents	Delete		Clears cell contents
Edit/Delete/Entire row			Deletes selected rows
Edit/Delete/Entire column			Deletes selected columns
Edit/Move or Copy Sheet			Moves or copies selected sheet
View/Toolbars			Displays or hides selected toolbar
View/Zoom		100%	Changes magnification of window
Insert/Copied Cells			Inserts row and copies text from Clipboard

Command	Shortcut	Button	Action
Insert/**R**ows			Inserts a blank row
Insert/**C**olumns			Inserts a blank column
Insert/C**h**art		▥	Inserts chart into worksheet
Insert/**F**unction	⇧Shift + F3	*fx*	Inserts a function
Insert/**P**icture/**F**rom File			Inserts picture at insertion point from disk
F**o**rmat/C**e**lls/Number/Currency			Applies Currency format to selection
F**o**rmat/C**e**lls/Number/Accounting		$	Applies Accounting format to selection
F**o**rmat/C**e**lls/Number/Date			Applies Date format to selection
F**o**rmat/C**e**lls/Number/Percent		%	Applies Percent format to selection
F**o**rmat/C**e**lls/Number/Decimal places		⦀ ⦀	Increases or decreases the number of decimal places associated with a number value
F**o**rmat/C**e**lls/Alignment/ **H**orizontal/ Left (Indent)		▤	Left-aligns entry in cell space
F**o**rmat/C**e**lls/Alignment/ **H**orizontal/Center		▤	Center-aligns entry in cell space
F**o**rmat/C**e**lls/Alignment/ **H**orizontal/Right		▤	Right-aligns entry in cell space
F**o**rmat/C**e**lls/Alignment/**I**ndent/1		▤	Indents cell entry one space
F**o**rmat/C**e**lls/Alignment/ **H**orizontal/Center Across Selection		▦	Centers cell contents across selected cells
F**o**rmat/C**e**lls/Font			Changes font and attributes of cell contents
F**o**rmat/C**e**lls/Font/F**o**nt Style/Bold	Ctrl + B	**B**	Bolds selected text
F**o**rmat/C**e**lls/Font/F**o**nt Style/Italic	Ctrl + I	*I*	Italicizes selected text
F**o**rmat/C**e**lls/Font/**U**nderline/Single	Ctrl + U	U̲	Underlines selected text
F**o**rmat/C**e**lls/Font/**C**olor		A⋅	Adds color to text
F**o**rmat/C**e**lls/Patterns/**C**olor		⬧⋅	Adds color to cell background
F**o**rmat/**R**ow/He**i**ght			Changes height of selected row
F**o**rmat/**C**olumn/**W**idth			Changes width of columns
F**o**rmat/**C**olumn/**A**utoFit Selection			Changes column width to match widest cell entry
F**o**rmat/S**h**eet/**R**ename			Renames sheet
F**o**rmat/**S**tyle			Applies selected style to selection
F**o**rmat/**S**tyle/**S**tyle name/Currency			Applies currency style to selection
F**o**rmat/**S**tyle/**S**tyle name/Percent		%	Changes cell style to display percentage
F**o**rmat/S**e**lected Data Series/ Data Labels	Ctrl + 1		Inserts data labels into chart
F**o**rmat/S**e**lected Legend	Ctrl + 1	▣	Changes legend
F**o**rmat/S**e**lected Chart Title	Ctrl + 1	▣	Changes format of selected chart title

Command	Shortcut	Button	Action
F**o**rmat/**Se**lected Data Series	Ctrl + 1	▣	Changes format of selected data series
F**o**rmat/**Se**lected Object		▣	Changes format of embedded objects
Chart/Chart T**y**pe		▣ ▾	Changes type of chart
Chart/Chart Opt**i**ons			Adds options to chart
Chart/**L**ocation			Moves chart from worksheet to chart sheet
Tools/**S**pelling	F7	▣	Spell-checks worksheet
Tools/**G**oal Seek			Adjusts value in specified cell until a formula dependent on that cell reaches specified result
Tools/Formula A**u**diting/ Show **W**atch Window			Opens the Watch Window toolbar
Window/Un**f**reeze Panes			Unfreezes window panes
Window/**F**reeze Panes			Freezes top and/or leftmost panes
Window/**S**plit			Divides window into four panes at active cell
Window/Remove **S**plit			Removes split bar from active worksheet

Glossary of Key Terms

3-D reference A reference to the same cell or range on multiple sheets in the same workbook.

absolute reference A cell or range reference in a formula whose location remains the same (absolute) when copied. Indicated by a $ character entered before the column letter or row number or both.

active cell The cell displaying the cell selector that will be affected by the next entry or procedure.

active pane The pane that contains the cell selector.

active sheet A sheet that contains the cell selector and that will be affected by the next action.

adjacent range A rectangular block of adjoining cells.

alignment The vertical or horizontal placement and orientation of an entry in a cell.

area chart A chart that shows trends by emphasizing the area under the curve.

argument The data used in a function on which the calculation is performed.

AutoFill Feature that logically repeats and extends a series.

AutoFormat A built-in combination of formats that can be applied to a range.

automatic recalculation The recalculation of a formula within the worksheet whenever a value in a referenced cell in the formula changes.

category-axis Another name for the X-axis of a chart.

category-axis title A label that describes the X-axis.

category name Labels displayed along the X-axis in a chart to identify the data being plotted.

cell The space created by the intersection of a vertical column and a horizontal row.

cell selector The heavy border surrounding a cell in the worksheet that identifies the active cell.

chart A visual representation of data in a worksheet.

chart gridlines Lines extending from the axis lines across the plot area that make it easier to read and evaluate the chart data.

chart object One type of graphic object that is created using charting features included in Excel 2002. A chart object can be inserted into a worksheet or into a special chart sheet.

chart title Appears at the top of a chart and is used to describe the contents of the chart.

ClipArt A collection of graphics that is usually bundled with a software application.

column A vertical block of cells one cell wide in the worksheet.

column letters The border of letters across the top of the worksheet that identifies the columns in the worksheet.

combination chart A chart type that includes mixed data markers, such as both columns and lines.

constant A value that does not change unless you change it directly by typing in another entry.

copy area The cell or cells containing the data to be copied.

custom dictionary An additional dictionary you create to supplement the main dictionary.

data labels Labels for data points or bars that show the values being plotted on a chart.

data marker Represents a data series on a chart. It can be a symbol, color, or pattern, depending upon the type of chart.

data series The numbers to be charted.

date numbers The integers assigned to the days from January 1, 1900, through December 31, 2099, that allow dates to be used in calculations.

default Initial program settings.

destination The cell or range of cells that receives the data from the copy area or source.

destination file A document in which a linked object is inserted.

drawing object Object consisting of shapes such as lines and boxes that can be created using features on the Drawing toolbar.

embedded chart A chart that is inserted into another file.

embedded object Information inserted into a destination file of another application that becomes part of this file but can be edited within the destination file using the server application.

explode To separate a wedge of a pie chart slightly from the other wedges in the pie.

fill handle A small black square located in the lower-right corner of the selection that is used to create a series or copy to adjacent cells with a mouse.

font The typeface, type size, and style associated with a worksheet entry that can be selected to improve the appearance of the worksheet.

footer A line (or several lines) of text that appears at the bottom of each page just above the bottom margin.

format Formats are settings that affect the display of entries in a worksheet.

Formatting toolbar A toolbar that contains buttons used to change the format of a worksheet.

formula An entry that performs a calculation.

Formula bar The bar near the top of the Excel window that displays the cell contents.

freeze To fix in place on the screen specified rows or columns or both when scrolling.

function A prewritten formula that performs certain types of calculations automatically.

Goal Seek Tool used to find the value needed in one cell to attain a result you want in another cell.

graphic A non-text element or object, such as a drawing or picture that can be added to a document.

group An object that contains other objects.

header A line (or several lines) of text that appears at the top of each page just below the top margin.

heading Row and column entries that are used to create the structure of the worksheet and describe other worksheet entries.

landscape The orientation of the printed document so that it prints sideways across the length of the page.

legend A brief description of the symbols used in a chart that represent the data ranges.

line chart A chart that represents data as a set of points along a line.

linked object Information created in a source file from one application and inserted into a destination file of another application while maintaining a link between files.

live link A linked object that automatically reflects in the destination document any changes made in the source document when the destination document is opened.

main dictionary The dictionary included with Office XP.

margins The blank space around the edge of the paper.

merged cell A cell made up of several selected cells combined into one.

minimal recalculation The recalculation of only the formulas in a worksheet that are affected by a change of data.

mixed reference A cell address that is part absolute and part relative.

name box The area located on the left side of the formula bar that provides information about the selected item such as the reference of the active cell.

nonadjacent range Cells or ranges that are not adjacent but are included in the same selection.

number A cell entry that contains any of the digits 0 to 9 and any of the special characters + = ( ) , . / $ % Σ =.

number formats Affect how numbers look onscreen and when printed.

object An element such as a text box that can be added to a workbook and that can be selected, sized, and moved.

operand A value on which a numeric formula performs a calculation.

operator Specify the type of calculation to be performed.

order of precedence Order in which calculations are performed and can be overridden by the use of parentheses.

pane A division of the worksheet window, either horizontal or vertical, through which different areas of the worksheet can be viewed at the same time.

paste area   The cells or range of cells that receive the data from the copy area or source.

picture   An illustration such as a scanned photograph.

pie chart   A chart that compares parts to the whole. Each value in the data range is a wedge of the pie (circle).

plot area   The area of the chart bounded by the axes.

point   Measure used for height of type; one point equals 1/72 inch.

portrait   The orientation of the printed document so that it prints across the width of the page.

range   A selection consisting of two or more cells in a worksheet.

reference   The column letter and row number of a cell.

relative reference   A cell or range reference that automatically adjusts to the new location in the worksheet when the formula is copied.

row   A horizontal block of cells one cell high in the worksheet.

row numbers   The border of numbers along the left side of the worksheet that identifies the rows in the worksheet.

sans serif font   A font, such as Arial or Helvetica, that does not have a flair at the base of each letter.

selection handles   Small boxes surrounding a selected object that are used to size the object.

selection rectangle   Border around selected object indicating it can be sized or moved.

series formula   A formula that links a chart object to the source worksheet.

serif font   A font, such as Times New Roman, that has a flair at the base of each letter.

sheet reference   Used in references to other worksheets and consists of the name of the sheet enclosed in quotes and is separated from the cell reference by an exclamation point.

sheet tab   On the bottom of the workbook window, the tabs where the sheet names appear.

sizing handle   Box used to size a selected object.

source   The cell or range of cells containing the data you want to copy.

source file   The document that stores the data for the linked object.

Spelling Checker   Feature that locates misspelled words and proposes corrections.

spreadsheet   A rectangular grid of rows and columns used to enter data.

stack   The order in which objects are added in layers to the worksheet.

stacked-column chart   A chart that displays the data values as columns stacked upon each other.

Standard toolbar   A toolbar that contains buttons used to complete the most frequently used menu commands.

style   A named combination of formats that can be applied to a selection.

syntax   Rules of structure for entering all functions.

tab scroll buttons   Located to the left of the sheet tabs, they are used to scroll sheet tabs right or left.

task pane   A pane that provides quick access to features as you are using them.

text   A cell entry that contains text, numbers, or any other special characters.

text box   A rectangular object in which you type text.

thumbnail   Miniature images displayed in the Clip Organizer.

title   In a chart, descriptive text that explains the contents of the chart.

typeface   The appearance and shape of characters. Some common typefaces are Roman and Courier.

value axis   Y axis of a chart that usually contains numerical values.

value axis title   A label that describes the values on the Y axis.

variable   The resulting value of a formula that changes if the data it depends on changes.

what-if analysis   A technique used to evaluate what effect changing one or more values in formulas has on other values in the worksheet.

word wrap   Feature that automatically determines when to begin the next line of text.

workbook   The file in which you work and store sheets created in Excel 2002.

workbook window   A window that displays an open workbook file.

worksheet   Similar to a financial spreadsheet in that it is a rectangular grid of rows and columns used to enter data.

X-axis   The bottom boundary line of a chart.

Y-axis   The left boundary line of a chart.

Z-axis   The left boundary line of a 3-D chart.

Supplied/Used file	Created/Saved As
Lab 1	
	Forecast
ex01_Forecast2	Forecast3
ex01_Internet (graphic)	
Step-by-Step	
1. ex01_Improvements	Park Improvements
2. ex01_New Positions	Jobs
3. ex01_Poverty Level	Poverty Level
ex01_Family (graphic)	
4. ex01_IT Salaries	IT Salaries
ex01_Disks (graphic)	
5. ex01_Springs Budget	Springs Projected Budget
On Your Own	
1.	Class Grades
2.	Personal Budget
3.	Weekly Sales
4.	Job Analysis
5.	Membership
On the Web	
1.	Spreadsheet Design
Lab 2	
ex02_Cafe Sales	Cafe Sales Charts
Step-by-Step	
1. ex02_Real Estate Prices	Real Estate Charts
2. ex02_Tiger Data	Tiger Charts
3. ex02_Birds	Bird Observations
4.	Youth Sport Charts
5. ex02_Higher Education	Higher Education Charts

Supplied/Used file	Created/Saved As
On Your Own	
1. ex02_Job Market	Seminar
2.	Grades
3.	Stocks
4.	Statistics
5.	Insurance
Lab 3	
ex03_First Quarter Forecast	Forecast4
ex03_Annual Forecast	Annual Forecast Revised
Step-by-Step	
1. ex03_Sandwich Shop	Sandwich Shop2
2. ex03_West Income Statement	West Income Statement2
3. ex03_Time Sheets	Time Sheets2
4. ex03_Grade Report	Grade Report2
5. ex03_Springs Forecast	Springs Forecast2
6. ex03_African Safari	African Safari2
On Your Own	
1. Personal Budget (from Lab 1)	Personal Budget2
2.	Art Expenses
3.	Stock Analysis
On the Web	
1.	My Business
Working Together	
exwt1_Sales Forecast Memo	Sales Forecast Memo Linked
Cafe Sales Charts (from Lab 2)	Cafe Sales Charts Linked
exwt1_Forecast Memo	Second Quarter Forecast
Annual Forecast Revised (from Lab 3)	
Practice Exercises	
1. exwt1_Rescue Memo	Rescue Memo Linked
exwt1_Contributions	Contributions2
2. exwt1_Tour Status Report	March Status Report
exwt1_Adventure Travel Monthly	Adventure Travel Monthly2
3. exwt1_Hotel Memo	Hotel Memo2
exwt1_Hotel Data	

Excel Core Certification

Standardized Coding Number	Activity	Lab Exercises			
		Lab	Page	Step-By-Step	On Your Own
Ex2002-1	**Working with Cells and Cell Data**				
Ex2002-1-1	Insert, delete, and move cells	1 3	1.36,1.37,1.53 3.14	1,2,3,4,5 1,2,3,4,5	1,2,3,4,5 1,2,3,4,5
Ex2002-1-2	Enter and edit cell data including text, numbers,and formulas	1	1.15–1.23,1.39, 1.42,1.59	1,2,3,4,5	1,2,3,4,5
Ex2002-1-3	Check spelling	3	3.4	1,5,6	
Ex2002-1-4	Find and replace cell data and formats	3	3.31		
Ex2002-1-5	Use automated tools to filter lists				
Ex2002-2	**Managing Workbooks**				
Ex2002-2-1	Manage workbook files and folders	1	1.28	1,2,3,4,5	1,2,3,4,5
Ex2002-2-2	Create workbooks using templates	1	1.5		
Ex2002-2-3	Save workbooks using different names and file formats	1	1.26	1,2,3,4,5	1,2,3,4,5
Ex2002-3	**Formatting and Printing Worksheets**				
Ex2002-3-1	Apply and modify cell formats	1	1.54–1.60	1,2,3,4,5	1,2,3,4,5
Ex2002-3-2	Modify row and column settings	1 3	1.48 3.5	1,2,3,4,5 1,2,3,4,5	
Ex2002-3-3	Modify row and column formats	1	1.24–1.26,1.49	1,2,3,4,5	
Ex2002-3-4	Apply styles	1	1.61	1,2,3,4,5	
Ex2002-3-5	Use automated tools to format worksheets				
Ex2002-3-6	Modify Page Setup options for worksheets	2 3	2.51 3.44,3.47	1,2,3,4,5 1,2,3,4,5,6	
Ex2002-3-7	Preview and print worksheets and workbooks	1	1.69	1,2,3,4,5	1,2,3,4
Ex2002-4	**Modifying Workbooks**				
Ex2002-4-1	Insert and delete worksheets	3	3.27	1,3,4,5,6	2,3,4
Ex2002-4-2	Modify worksheet names and positions	3	3.25,3.27	1,3,4,5,6	2,3,4
Ex2002-4-3	Use 3-D references	3	3.24	1	

Standardized Coding Number	Activity	Lab Exercises			
		Lab	Page	Step-By-Step	On Your Own
Ex2002-5	**Creating and Revising Formulas**				
Ex2002-5-1	Create and revise formulas	1	1.39,1.41,1.46		
		3	3.11	1,2,3,4,5,6	1,2,3,4
Ex2002-5-2	Use statistical, date and time, financial, and logical functions in formulas	1	1.42	1,2,3,4,5	1,2,3,4
		3	3.11	1,2,3,4,5,6	1,2,3,4
Ex2002-6	**Creating and Modifying Graphics**				
Ex2002-6-1	Create, modify, position, and print charts	2	2.7–2.22,2.49	1,2,3,4,5	1,2,3,4,5
Ex2002-6-2	Create, modify, and position graphics	1	1.65–1.68	1,2,3,4,5	
Ex2002-7	**Workgroup Collaboration**				
Ex2002-7-1	Convert worksheets into Web pages				
Ex2002-7-2	Create hyperlinks				
Ex2002-7-3	View and edit comments				

Index